Worlds Apart

Worlds Apart

Civil Society
and
The Battle for Ethical Globalization

John D. Clark

Kumarian
Press, Inc.

Worlds Apart: Civil Society and the Battle for Ethical Globalization

Published 2003 in the United States of America by Kumarian Press, Inc. 1294 Blue Hills Avenue, Bloomfield, CT 06002 USA

Copy editing, design, and production by Joan Weber Laflamme, jml ediset, Vienna, Va.
Index by Barbara DeGennaro.
Proofread by Beth Richards.
The text of this book is set in 10/12 Sabon.

Printed in the United States of America by Thomson-Shore. Text printed with vegetable oil-based ink.
∞: acid free.

Library of Congress Cataloging-in-Publication Data

Clark, John, 1950–
 Worlds apart : civil society and the battle for ethical globalization
/ John Clark.
   p. cm.
Includes bibliographical references and index.
 ISBN 1-56549-167-X (pbk. : alk. paper) — ISBN 1–56549–168–8 (cloth :
alk. paper)
 1. Civil society. 2. Globalization—Moral and ethical aspects. 3.
Social justice. I. Title.
 JC337.C583 2003
 300—dc21
                                    2003001637

---

12 11 10 09 08 07 06   10 9 8 7 6 5 4 3 2   First Printing 2003

To Mary, my wife,
who gave me more help, encouragement, and inspiration
than words can tell.
I am eternally indebted.

Contents

PART THREE
THE PATH TO ETHICAL GLOBALIZATION

Figures, Tables, and Boxes

FIGURES

TABLES

BOXES

Preface

Politicians, economists, business leaders, and right-of-center journalists angrily berate those who protest against globalization for peddling ridiculous notions that are anti-progress, anti-poor, and simply not realistic. I tend to agree. But I wonder how many of them there are. Most of those I have spoken to, the leaders of the main groups opposed to the current order, are not arguing against globalization, but against a way of managing world affairs that puts business before people, trade before development, that is blind to widening gaps in wealth and power, and that ignores today's buildup of environmental and sectarian problems. They are not latter-day Luddites, but people who seek social justice—leaving aside for the present whether or not their ideas would work.

Similarly, those who criticize the status quo often construct a grotesque parody of the policies advanced by international organizations and governments in order to make the task of condemning them easier. Most of these agencies *try* to promote policies that are for the common good, not just for the few—though it isn't always easy to ensure that opportunities are equally taken up, and governments of large countries often have difficulty seeing beyond their frontiers.

Both sides in this debate either don't understand, or won't listen to, what the other is saying. *Worlds Apart* tries to bridge this divide and seeks to be fair to each. It gets behind the polemics to look at the issues through the lens of poor people and poor countries. It is not a search for a middle ground—I am closer to the critics of the present order than its defenders—but a search for an ethical management of world affairs that promotes enterprise and growth, that reduces barriers between peoples and countries, and that ensures everyone shares in these opportunities.

Worlds Apart assesses how citizens' pressure—through a myriad of civil society channels—has shaped the debate about globalization and indeed fundamentally changed the political landscape. But it also looks at how the same forces and opportunities that have changed the worlds of business and economics are also transforming civil society. Organizations that once worked just at the national level are now global in scope, and transnational citizens networks are transforming debate on international issues.

Civil society stands at the cusp of great opportunity, but this could be a brief window. It enjoys unparalleled public trust, global interconnectedness, strong communications skills, and great influence. But its advocacy skills lie largely in pillorying the deficiencies of the "system" rather than promoting viable alternatives. It proves quite easy to reach broad consensus among an array of civil society actors on what is wrong today, but each has his or her own lists of what should be done differently tomorrow. *Worlds Apart* looks at the system's faults—including the deficiencies in civil society itself—but with a view to suggesting a framework with broad civil society appeal that could transform global relations and redress today's injustices.

Worlds Apart at times praises civil society pressure yet finds fault with some of its messages; at times it criticizes the big institutions, such as the World Bank and World Trade Organization, and other times defends them. It may, therefore, appear rather schizophrenic—but this speaks to the diverse perspectives my career has given me. I have worked in radical pressure groups and experienced libel writs from transnational corporations. I have managed campaigning and policy-advocacy for Oxfam GB. I have worked alongside Southern NGOs fighting issues of international injustice, but I have also worked nine years in the World Bank (mostly running its NGO and Civil Society Unit), and I have advised governments from both North and South.

Perhaps it is the Gemini in me—but everywhere I have worked I have had colleagues whose perspectives I share or respect (I'm not saying *all* colleagues). I am convinced that these people are all equally committed to fighting poverty and injustice, even if they have radically different ideas about how best to do so. As with looking at a landscape, what you see depends on where you sit. Some vantage points are better to see the far horizon, others to obtain a closeup of the immediate surroundings. One is not necessarily better than the other. In fact, if you truly want to know the terrain, you need to see it from many angles. It is a great shame, therefore, that there are often walls of distrust compartmentalizing people into different disciplines and different institutions. The main thrust of my career over the last twenty years has been to try to break through these divides, and I hope this book proves a contribution to this endeavor. Nothing would please me more than to learn it has encouraged people of good faith from different institutions to understand one another better—to get together, drop the customary defensiveness and aggression, and seek areas of agreement rather than disagreement.

What else did I hope for in writing this book? First, I hope it is of practical help to people who work in civil society organizations; that it gives them a convincing picture of how global changes affect their sector, of the challenges posed and how best to handle them, and of future opportunities. Second, I hope it is useful for those who are studying or are interested in civil society as a sector and why it has suddenly become so forceful in power and impact. And finally, I hope it is useful for everyone who is horrified by the extent of poverty and inequality in our world and wants to know what ordinary citizens can do about it.

Though much of it is about global processes, this book started for me in a small village I visited many years ago, when working for Oxfam, in the poor tribal belt of Gujarat State, India. Some people worked for forest contractors, and others made incomes gathering spices and other produce from the forest. Although the government set fair prices for the goods they bought *and* sold, the villagers knew that the local trader was cheating them by using two sets of rigged scales—one for sales and one for purchases. The solution was to buy the villagers their own set of scales. A lad would sit near the merchant's shop so that everyone could check the weight of whatever they bought or sold, and when there was an error, the whole community went to demand recompense. The merchant had to give up his trickery. Overnight their real income went up 20 percent. More important was the confidence this ability to seize justice through collective action instilled in the community. Its members went on to join other tribal villages in forming a new trade union of forest workers, and after a long struggle they forced through an increase in their pay.

This is a reference point for me—the scales of justice. It is a parody of the global economic system. On the surface, the rules are fair, but in reality the terms are stacked against the poor. To break through this requires access to critical information, an effective campaign strategy (drawn up with the help of a trustworthy civil society organization) and—most important—the newfound collective action of the poor. Combined, these generate a force that can be turned toward ever-greater challenges. What was true in Gujarat then is true in the wider world today.

STRUCTURE OF THIS BOOK

Part One describes the processes of globalization—how they generate huge new opportunities and why they are controversial (because the benefits are so unequally shared). Chapter 1 is an overview of these themes and how they relate to the rest of the book. Chapter 2 examines the economic issues the sources of inequities—this is the macro-view. Chapter 3 takes a more micro-view, looking at globalization from the perspective of poor people and how it generates widening disparity from the local to the global level. Chapter 4 then looks at global changes in the political realm, the causes of the increasingly apparent "democracy deficit," and the important roles that civil society can play in tackling these problems.

Part Two looks at the challenges *to* civil society in the globalizing world. Chapter 5 describes how the forces that are reshaping the economic and corporate worlds are also changing the citizen's sector, fostering a new "global civil society." Chapter 6 then examines the various challenges this brings, why very different organizations are facing remarkably similar problems, and how they are addressing them. The following chapter looks specifically at the international development NGOs, and, in contrast, Chapter 8 examines the vigorous "anti-globalization" protest movement and its related Internet-based mobilizing groups (or "dot-causes"). There is a rapid dynamic in civil society, but what are its prospects? As it becomes more influential, it is experiencing increasingly sharp challenges, both from the establishment outside and from internal conflict. Chapter 9 describes these and discusses how it might stand up to the backlash.

Part Three addresses morals, voice, and responsibility; that is, how governments, international organizations, and corporations could be reformed to assume responsibility for the "global footprint" of their decisions. In particular, it looks at the role of civil society in these reforms. Chapter 10 looks at *processes*—how globalization could be "civilized" by reforms in the governance of the institutions that steer it. The final chapter looks more at *content*—what would the reformed institutions *do;* how could they contribute to a style of development that is fully inclusive and equitable. It sketches a new international moral order—a shift from narrow *economic* to *ethical* globalization.

Acknowledgments

I wrote this book while a visiting fellow at the Centre for Civil Society at London School of Economics. My first debt, therefore, is to Helmut Anheier, director of the Centre, and the other staff and students there, for providing both the stimulating environment that fueled many of the ideas in this book and the space to write it. I am also grateful to Guy Bentham and Jonathan Sinclair-Wilson for being helpful publishers—giving me both encouragement and discipline, and providing insightful comments on earlier drafts. Some of the case study material in Part Two draws on a research project I directed at LSE that was made possible by a generous grant by the Ford Foundation.

I thank everyone who agreed to meet with me in the course of writing this book. Though there are too many for me to name everyone, I would like to acknowledge the following individuals: Nancy Birdsall, Phil Boyer, Dave Brown, Dave Bull, Manuel Chiriboga, Jane Covey, Gurcharan Das, Biswajit Dhar, Mike Edwards, Joyti Ghose, Adam Habib, Bob Harris, Tony Hill, Virginia Hodgkinson, Richard Holloway, Prem Shankar Jha, Lisa Jordan, Tony Juniper, Sanjeev Khagram, Alan Leather, David Lewis, Marc Lindenberg, Ernst Litteringen, Carmen Malena, Tim Marchant, Madhusudan Mistry, Kumi Naidoo, Adil Najam, Paul Nelson, Ann Pettifor, Frances Pinter, Amara Pongsapich, Florian Rochat, Andrew Rogerson, Khun Rozana, "Men" Santa Ana, Jan Aart Scholte, Charles Secrett, Devendra Sharma, Salil Shetty, Ramesh Singh, Andrew Steer, Dr. Sulak, Rajesh Tandon, Sidney Tarrow, Nuno Themudo, Giles Ungpahorn, Aurelio Vianna, Robert Wade, Patti Whalley, Kevin Watkins, and Dennis Young.

Part One

The Impact of Globalization

1.

Globalization—Agony or Ecstasy?
Setting the Scene

Today's real borders are not between nations, but between powerful and powerless, free and fettered, privileged and humiliated. Today, no walls can separate humanitarian or human rights crises in one part of the world from national security crises in another. . . . We have entered the Third Millennium through a gate of fire.
—KOFI ANNAN, NOBEL PRIZE SPEECH,
DECEMBER 10, 2001

This book tells the story of globalization. Like others already published, it sees the crumbling of national boundaries today as one of the most powerful geo-political forces of our times. Like others, it finds that these forces have brought new opportunities as well as heightened risks—but that the distribution of these increases inequalities in terms of income, wealth, security, and power. Hence, like other books, it argues that what is needed is not a Canute-like bid to turn back the tide of globalization but a Herculean effort to harness its power for the common good.

From this point, however, it takes a different route. It argues that civil society is emerging as the new critical player. Democracy, as we are familiar with it, has been thrown into turmoil—because globalization affects politics as profoundly as it does economics. This book explores the diverse issues of global change through the lens of poor people and the groups they associate with, and it explains why globalization is so controversial. It describes how civil society organizations from North and South[1] could hold the key to changing its course—insisting that it is managed so as to empower the weak and enrich the poor.

Civil society—the collective activities of citizens for purposes of social change rather than individual gain—is far from homogenous, and not always civil. But paradoxically, the same processes of globalization

3

that have made many rich and marginalized others, and that are so fiercely resisted by a growing protest movement, also afford civil society opportunities to grow immeasurably in strength.

New technology and communications enable a *global* civil society to emerge. The failure of national governments to wrestle effectively with global challenges has exposed the deficiencies of democracy and created a vacancy for new policy actors. The shabby scandals of corporate greed have dented faith in untrammeled markets and opened opportunities for market curbs, independent watchdogs, and codes of corporate ethics. And the proven ability of civil society to "get it right" so often, both in providing services and in advocating change, has inspired public confidence. Civil society, therefore, stands at the cusp of unprecedented opportunity—but this may be just a brief window. Already a major challenge to civil society has been leveled, questioning the legitimacy of the prominent voices in the policy debate.

Maximizing this opportunity calls for a strong vision and concerted strategy. Civil society will never be unified—its strength lies partly in its diversity—but a critical mass of respected activists, working together and with the confidence of a growing support base, could trigger a chain reaction of reform that defenders of the status quo would find difficult to stop. We are now starting to see such a broad coalition emerge.

Our bipolar world is on a diverging course in two senses. First, the gap between weak and powerful is growing shamefully. And second, the faith binding each school to its opposing philosophy and world view is strengthening such that the space for intelligent dialogue is shrinking. The cheerleaders of globalization and their critics might just as well live on different planets; the rich and poor virtually do so. We are *worlds apart*.

A global civil society coalition—spanning radicals, reformers, academics, activists, faiths, feminists, pressure groups, unions, charities, consumer groups, and others—such a grand coalition could bridge these gaps. It could construct a common ground, combining realism and idealism, that would be compelling to all but entrenched vested interests and the politically comatose; it could generate the political will for a coordinated management of globalization that brings benefits to all; it could create a popular demand for *ethical* globalization.

CONFLICTING WORLD VIEWS

The protagonists of the globalization conflict do not fall neatly into the left-right spectrum. Indeed the political fissure between internationalism and parochialism is to a large extent displacing old left-right divides (Kaldor 2000). Both the New Left and modernizing marketeers believe in international capitalism, embrace technological change, and think market integration will bring democratic values and human rights on its coattails (see, for example, DFID 2000a). Conversely, the old left and nationalistic conservatives distrust these trends; they think the growing power of global institutions is eroding national sovereignty. Though they see some gains, they are more mindful of the losses and hence want to minimize them through protection (Held 2000). The growth of nationalistic parties, from Netherlands to Thailand, and the clamor for increased import protection are reactions against globalization every bit as forceful as the anticapitalist protests (Hoffmann 2002). Two main schools of thought predominate.

The "agony school" thinks globalization breeds exclusion. It believes passionately that globalization causes misery for the poor in both industrialized and developing countries, widens inequalities between and within countries, heightens risks—particularly vulnerability to job loss and financial crises—weakens the voice and power of ordinary people, leads to a cultural takeover by the United States and the West as local choices are stifled, and threatens the planet through short-term policymaking (Hurrell and Woods 1999).

With less passion but equal certainty the "ecstasy school" holds that globalization is good for everyone—that, through integrating, the prosperity of the whole will become much more than the sum of isolated national economies. It thinks countless opportunities for enterprise and employment are lost due to border regulations and so all would gain from market openness—particularly the poor. It recognizes that there are bumps in this road—for example, risks of currency crises—but these are small compared with the potential benefits. This school sees third-world poverty and dangerous schisms between people not as detracting from their case but as illustrations of the danger of countries being left behind in the globalizing world (DFID 2000a).

There are good arguments and spurious claims on both sides of this debate. Part One of *Worlds Apart* analyses both cases to seek clarification as well as conclusions. It looks at the issues particularly through the lens of poor people and poor countries.

WHAT DOES GLOBALIZATION MEAN?

The misunderstanding between the two schools begins with the imprecision about what globalization actually means. Most who criticize the current order are angry to be labeled anti-globalization and point out that their movement is as global as capitalism itself. They mostly accept—even welcome—increasing transactions across national boundaries but resent the way this process is managed to serve largely the interests of multinational capital. It is the so-called neoliberal agenda to which they object;[2] they comprise an "anti-global capitalism" movement.

The kernel of the conflict is that there is not one globalization but many. Hoffmann (2002) describes three dimensions: economic globalization and the growth of capitalism, whose central dilemma is between efficiency and fairness; cultural globalization, whose dilemma is between uniformity (or Americanization) and diversity; and political globalization, characterized by the power of industrialized countries and US hegemony. The impact of these world changes is not just to expand markets but also to transform politics and to give birth to a new type of social and political movement (Woods 2000).

A consistent civil society message is that powerful governments and the international institutions they control should tolerate more diverse approaches to integration. There is a popular view that all developing countries are being pressed to fall into line with a "cookie-cutter style" neoliberal economic management that may not fit the countries' contexts. The tools to force this conformity are structural adjustment programs; these are commonly portrayed by civil society as hurting the poor and undermining Southern governments' efforts to protect their vulnerable industries. They are viewed as a hideous intrusion—a sort of "economic cleansing"—that is unconscionable, increases dependence on the global economy, and heightens vulnerability to crises.

There is a parallel in the natural world. The bio-systems that are most resilient to shocks and survive longest are those brimming with diversity. If this is supplanted by a high-yielding mono-crop, the total output may be higher but the risk of calamity is vastly increased. Many in civil society see globalization as courting homogenization: replacing rich diversity with conformity. The world approaching, they say, will have one set of enterprises (the transnational corporations, or TNCs), one set of political principles (liberal democratic capitalism), one dominant culture, and one set of genetically modified crops (Rifkin 2001). It may run faster, but it will often crash; when it does so, the poor will be hurt most.

Is this an overly Orwellian portrait? Globalization needn't be like this. At its broadest, globalization is simply the elimination or reduction of barriers to human interaction across national boundaries. Barriers can be dismantled through either policy or technological change. Stated thus, all but the most xenophobic would welcome it. Because there are so many forms of human interaction, there are different manifestations of globalization—each with its own set of controversies:

Box 1.1 The technology drivers of globalization

The cost of transmitting a million megabytes of information from Boston to Los Angeles has fallen from $150,000 in 1970 to 12 cents today.

The cost of a three-minute phone call from New York to London was $300 in 1930 and 20 cents in 2000 (1996 prices).

In 2001, more information could be sent over a single cable in a second than was sent over the entire Internet in a month in 1997.

From 1930 to 1990 the cost per mile of air travel fell from 68 to 11 cents (1990 prices).

The number of international air passengers rose from 75 million in 1970 to 409 million in 1996.

From 1960 to 1990 the cost of a unit of computing power fell by 99 percent in real terms.

Six megabytes of computer memory in 1999 cost about $1; in 1970 it cost about $31,000.

In January 1993 there were 50 sites on the World Wide Web; 8 years later there were 350 million.

Sources: UNDP Human Development Reports; World Bank; The Economist; Financial Times.

- *New technology:* the shrinking of the world due to cheaper and less restricted travel, cheaper and more widespread telecommunications, and the penetration of cheap information technology (Castells 2001); most welcome this.
- *Political conformity:* the convergence around increasing numbers of policy norms where divergence becomes impracticable in an "interconnected global political order" (Woods 2000); some describe this as harmonization, others as the erosion of sovereignty or "forced harmonization"—the loss of ability to pursue national political alternatives (Rodrik 1999).
- *Cultural exchange:* increased social and cultural interaction is to some an enrichment but is resented by others as unidirectional—the spread of Western (particularly American) culture and the dominance of English as a universal language (Huntington 1993; Barber 1995).
- *Global problems:* the need to cooperate to tackle global problems, such as climate change, HIV/AIDS, narcotics trade, and terrorism (Hutton and Giddens 2001).

- *Economic relations:* the removal of government-imposed barriers to foreigners as customers, investors, owners, or suppliers (Hirst and Thompson 1999). There is not *one* marketplace but many, each liberalizing at its own pace. This is the most controversial and most dominant aspect of globalization.

It is vital that the two sets of protagonists listen to each other's views about the direction of globalization, as the current debate is characterized by misrepresentation. Few in the agony school deny that trade is important, but there are different notions of what trade means. The dictionary defines it simply as "buying and selling." Modern economists tend to assume the words "between nations" follow; they focus only on trade that uses hard currency and is conducted in free markets. We need to dissect such assumptions.

Since all money in an economy ultimately derives from commerce, trade is self-evidently important. But what is often overlooked is that commerce can be internal or external. Western economists often overemphasize foreign trade—arguing that countries who opened their markets fastest also grew fastest and reduced poverty. They imply that trade must be external if it is to add to national prosperity (yet the world has enjoyed economic growth for most of the last fifty years without trading with a single other planet). In reality, the evidence that foreign trade is better for the economy or for poverty reduction than domestic trade is pretty flimsy. The only clear case is that external trade is much more important for small countries than large ones (see Chapter 3). This is an intuitive result. Trade is simply about matching producers and consumers; you may be able to find all the customers you need in a large economy but have to look outside the borders in the case of a small one. Advice given about opening markets should be more tailored to the country's situation; perhaps small countries could achieve the benefit of a large internal market by cooperating with one another (Chapter 11).

Globalization is not a new phenomenon. In many respects the world was more integrated one hundred years ago than it is today (Crafts and Venables 2001). There were fewer barriers to trade; the mobility of *people* was much easier (most countries didn't even require passports); and there was pretty free trade in currencies, with much of the world using the currencies of their colonial powers. Then two world wars and a severe economic depression evinced protectionist instincts. It took until the 1970s to reduce tariffs to their levels at the century's start. In the same decade a global communication system arrived that allowed twenty-four-hour global money markets to take off, and today's era of globalization was born (Giddens 1997).

What is new is that today's globalization is more selectively and selfishly managed, primarily by Western governments—and principally by the United States. It is not market openness that causes resentment in poor countries or riots at international meetings, but the self-serving way in which some markets are liberalized while barriers remain in others.

WHY IS GLOBALIZATION SO PAINFUL?

Basic economic textbooks talk about the different factors of production—such as raw inputs, labor, and capital—each of which has its own factor market. When any of these is liberalized, it increases the returns to its owners of that factor. The current order emphasizes liberalizing markets for capital, high-tech manufactured goods, modern services, and highly skilled labor but resists liberalizing markets in labor-intensive manufacturing, agricultural products, and unskilled labor, and strictly controls the market in "intellectual property rights" (patents and copyrights) where previously there was a virtual global free-for-all (Chapter 2).

It would be difficult to conceive an approach to globalization more biased toward the rich (who own capital, high-tech manufacturing, and the service giants, or who are Fortune 500 managers) and more loaded against the poor (the laborers and farmers in developing countries). Today's management skews the relative prices in all these markets in favor of the rich so that the wealth gap between rich nations and poor has grown; within rich and poor countries alike, rich people outstrip the poor (Hurrell and Woods 1999; Wade 2001a). This does little for the popularity of globalization.

A caveat is called for. I don't believe there is any deliberate conspiracy to hammer the poor. Pro-globalizers strongly believe in the win-win of free trade, and they would be right if trade were truly free. The theory of comparative advantage is one of the most elegant tenets of economics. (Any reader who isn't sure why this is so central to the free-trade argument is urged to read Appendix 1.) It explains how all different countries have different advantages, and that through producing what they are best at, and trading surpluses efficiently, *each* country's output—and therefore prosperity—will be much higher than without trade. It is *this* benefit the globalizers seek, not to wring the poor for their puny assets. The problem is that the governments of the richest countries (particularly the United States) dominate global trade negotiations, and they find it difficult to resist powerful domestic lobbies (especially those who contribute to party coffers). Their farmers, textile and clothing manufactures, steel industry, owners of patents, trade unions in ailing industries, and anti-immigrant nationalists all demand protection. Governments who espouse integration, therefore, approach trade negotiations with a string of exclusions in their brief and are blinkered by domestic, short-term perspectives. True globalizers should more vehemently oppose this; they will lose their case unless they can show it is good for everyone.

The current management of market integration is grotesquely unfair, then, but this is not because markets are inherently biased, but because politics is. As George Soros (1998) argues, markets are neither moral nor immoral—but *a*moral. They are powerful forces in societal change, but, when injustice results, this is not because of inherent bias but political manipulation. This is compounded by small players not having the same access to information or alternative options that large players do (Stiglitz 2002).

The major economic powers use international forums selfishly, loading the dice against those who could truly benefit from a more integrated world. That they use the language of free markets adds hypocrisy to injustice. Nowhere is this clearer than in world trade negotiations, in which political intervention appears bent on eroding every advantage nature bestows on poor countries (Chapter 2). This further widens the dangerous gaps in wealth and power that rend the world. Although social indicators worldwide are improving, this masks a deepening sense of loss—loss of culture, dignity, voice, opportunity, and security. We are moving into a bipolar world, not a geographic East-West divide or even a North-South split, but a divide between haves and have-nots, between the included and the excluded (Chapter 3). This is not just morally wrong; it is dangerous.

WHAT DO PEOPLE THINK OF GLOBALIZATION?

When political issues are fiercely contested, passionately held moral or religious convictions are usually at the core of the ethical schism. The vehement battles over abortion rights, the death penalty, and animal testing are obvious examples. The cleavage over globalization, however, has attracted even fiercer battles, literally, but the debate is about means rather than ends. Both protagonists agree that what is important—and what ordinary people want—is growth, opportunity, security, choice, and voice; both believe with equal passion that their route best offers this.

The debate has exposed the fault lines between groups that have the skills and mobility to prosper in the global marketplace and those that don't, as Harvard economist Dani Rodrik argues (1997). First, it widens inequalities because the opportunities offered vary vastly; less skilled workers face uncertainty and lose bargaining power because production has become more mobile. Second, it creates policy conflict within and between nations over labor practices, laws, and environmental standards. And third, governments find it increasingly difficult to protect their citizens from economic risks; the usual fiscal policy instruments are much weaker tools. People have good reason to feel less secure and to be worried about the erosion of sovereignty.

Though most world leaders are in favor of further market integration, it is clear that they haven't managed to persuade their populations of this. Surveys show that while many feel passionately about the issue, there are two roughly equal camps. Probably the most comprehensive (and repeated) survey indicated that, across twenty-two countries, 42 percent of the population think that free trade best serves the interests of their country and 47 percent favor protectionism to safeguard local industries (Angus Reid poll 1998). The free traders are stronger in Korea, Taiwan, Thailand, Japan, Hong Kong, and Germany; the protectionists are stronger in the United States, the UK, India, Chile, Brazil, and Australia, and very much stronger in Russia, the Philippines, Malaysia, and Indonesia. Paradoxically, the most positive and most negative opinions are found in East Asia. In the United States a different survey shows public opinion to be almost equally split, with a narrow majority supporting globalization *if* there are support policies to help the losers. Those with college degrees tend to support liberalization; those with the fewest skills tend to be most opposed (Scheve and Slaughter 2001).

Among the G7,[3] French citizens are most resistant; 68 percent of those in one survey were hostile or anxious about globalization (*Wall Street Journal*, January 29, 2002). An independent multi-country survey (half Northern, half Southern) conducted in different years indicated somewhat more positive attitudes toward globalization generally, and increasing, rather than diminishing, support (Environics 2001 and 2002). In the 2002 survey, 62 percent of those polled felt that globalization was in their interests (14 percent strongly so) while only 22 percent saw it as bad for them (the comparable figures in 2000 were 55, 10, and 26 percent respectively). However the same polls revealed a great deal of anxiety. The majority thought that globalization threatened their national culture and that the anti-globalization protestors were more to be trusted to reflect their views than governments (Environics 2001), and more than half thought that globalization will worsen problems of the environment, poverty, and unemployment (Environics 2002). The most negative views were found in the economic-crisis countries of Argentina and Turkey; elsewhere in Latin America and Africa there were stronger reservations, though most Asian countries were favorable.

Another multi-country Angus Reid poll (2000) showed that most people consider the World Trade Organization to have a positive impact (especially in Netherlands, Mexico, Canada, Germany, and New Zealand), while Thais, Malaysians, and the French were most critical—as were most Americans. A note of caution needs to be sounded about all such opinion polls. The sampling and interviewing techniques tend to be weighted toward urban, better-off, and educated populations and hence may not accurately reflect concerns of the poorer segments in developing countries.

Public opinion is anything but predictable, however. In Nicaragua a popular picket of the US Embassy demanded an end to the US campaign *against* sweatshop conditions because it entailed boycotting the goods they produced, so hitting their livelihood. Picketers argued that though conditions weren't good, at least it was a job (*The Guardian,* February 2, 2001). Likewise, in Bangladesh in 1996 there was a strong public counter-reaction to a US trade boycott in 1996 concerning child labor. An estimated fifty-five thousand children lost jobs in garment industries as a result, and few of these went back to school instead. Campaigns of Northern pressure groups may be well intended but misplaced if they don't heed the wishes of those in the South they aim to support (see Chapter 9; Edwards 1999).

THE PROBLEM WITH POLITICS

Underlying the globalization controversy are fundamental weaknesses in today's political systems. They have failed to keep up with the pace of economic and technical change. The "democratic deficit" is due, in part, to decisions affecting the lives of ordinary citizens being made increasingly in political forums or corporations where their voices are not heard (Chapter 4). Balancing a general preference of the majority with the fervent wish of a minority has always been a test for democratic systems. A country may want energy without pollution, for example, but hydroelectric schemes are vehemently resisted by those who would be displaced or who don't like dams. If a scheme goes ahead, the political skill is in negotiating fair compensation. But when those most hit by a *trade* decision live in another country, as increasingly is the case, there is no such search for balance.

When rich countries erect barriers to keep out textiles, steel, or food produced in poor countries, millions suffer in developing countries without any hint of compensation. This does not infer that those who make the decisions are malicious or that their electorates are mean; it simply signifies that they are doing the job of national politics—looking after national interests. The concerns of importers, consumers, and the national economy are all relevant, as well as those of workers who crave for their jobs to be protected, but there is no imperative to think about those affected overseas. It would be unthinkable for a country to dam a river close to a border with another country, flooding valleys where people live in that country, without negotiating fair compensation—but that displacement is in effect what happens every day in the world of trade.

Critical contemporary problems—concerning the environment, HIV/ AIDS, economic crisis, debt, world poverty, grand corruption, terrorism, and other issues—are global in nature and call for global solutions. But political inertia in industrialized nations makes it unlikely that significant new global institutions will be constructed to address them (and if they are, little real power will be vested in them). Politics continues to be played out in national arenas, bound by national rules, addressing parochial issues, in the time frame of electoral cycles. Even the management and use of international bodies—from the World Bank, International Monetary Fund, and World Trade Organization to the United Nations Security Council, Panel on Climate Change, and global summits—are often driven by short-term, domestic priorities.

There are signs of change, however, as these global priorities achieve growing constituencies of citizen concern. They want direct involvement in the deliberative process, and they want to be represented not just according to their physical locality but by their community of interests (Held 1998 and 2002). Organized in transnational civil society networks, such constituencies are providing the political glue that welds policy debate and policy action on their priority issues internationally. They create a common language of concern and a concerted framework of demands. In the absence of global government, they are the prime movers of global policies and ethical norms. Collectively, these currents of citizen pressure are bent on a civilizing mission: to inject new ethical norms into political discourse; to press world leaders to face up to these critical problems; and to correct official myopia.

AGE OF CIVIL SOCIETY

Civil society offers a partial solution to the democracy deficit and to politically induced market injustices. This is not an entirely new phenomenon. The Peasant Revolt following the passage of the English

Statute of Labourers in 1351 was a prototypical example of modern protest. The statute came shortly after the Great Plague, when labor was in short supply and workers were pressing for higher wages. It put a ceiling on wages and compelled workers to stay with their employers—cruelly blocking the one occasion in which market forces worked in their favor. The revolt forced major concessions until it was brutally put down and its leaders executed.

The Anti-Corn Law League was a more successful civil society campaign. It was founded in 1839 to protest the extortionate price of staple foods due to high import duties and market restrictions designed to protect British landowners. After six years of struggle and bread riots the government gave way and repealed the Corn Law. It was an early example of a pressure group, and it was established to campaign *for* globalization.

Modern campaigns, supported by modern media and working globally, can achieve more power in less time (Chapters 5 and 6). But civil society is no alternative to elected government; instead, it serves to make democracy more effective by constructing bridges linking decision-makers with the people most affected by their decisions. Some complain that the growing power of civil society is unproved by the ballot box. This misses the point. The exciting transition in politics today is from *delegative* democracy, where all hinges on citizens' occasional chance to pick delegates they prefer from a narrow slate, to *deliberative* democracy, in which citizens are more actively engaged in decisions that particularly concern them (Held 1998). This is only feasible if they have conduits—civil society organizations (CSOs)[4]—through which to channel their voice, to become a *civicus*, not just an electorate. But for this to be realized without losing what is good in electoral systems calls for greater self-discipline in the use of these channels. Civil society is coming of age, but with this comes responsibility.

Numerous campaigns have molded public opinion, put the most powerful governments on the defensive, and transformed debate on major issues ranging from climate change to gender and from human rights to debt (Chapter 8). Ironically, the same forces and opportunities that propel change in the economic and corporate spheres have made this ascendancy of civil society possible, catapulting it into the global power league. But to date its campaigns have focused on specific concerns. The acid test now is whether the disparate groups can coalesce to present a more holistic political philosophy and can maneuver themselves into a more formal negotiating role in global governance. If they do, they will truly be a global force with a higher-order game plan. They stand at the gate of this opportunity, but it is a valid debate about what right they have to be there (Chapter 9) and what use they might make of the opportunity. The final part of *Worlds Apart* suggests a reform agenda that could be charted to "civilize" the institutions that direct and manage globalization (Chapter 10) and to present an agenda for managing globalization so that poor countries and people get a fair reward (Chapter 11). None of this will be possible without a critical mass of civil society, supported by a wide cross-section of publics, all pushing in the same direction.

A CIVIL SOCIETY AGENDA FOR ETHICAL GLOBALIZATION

There is clearly a growing head of steam for a new departure. As the Nobel Prize–winning economist Amartya Sen says: "The real debate on globalization is, ultimately, not about the efficiency of markets, nor about the importance of modern technology. The debate, rather, is about the inequality of power, for which there is much less tolerance now than in the world that emerged at the end of the Second World War" (Sen 2000). Equity of power, opportunity, and resources is the cornerstone of what could be a different course—that of ethical globalization. Civil society is the driving force—and has growing opportunity. Summits rarely happen these days without some roles for CSOs, and these are no longer just optional extras after the important delegates leave. Heads of governments are keen to reach out to hear their citizens' voices. The prime minister of Belgium, Guy Verhofstadt, for example, convened a special conference in October 2001 to ensure that civil society concerns about globalization were heard.

Civil society covers a wide spectrum and embraces motives fair and foul. Collectively, however, a current has emerged that forcefully challenges the management of global affairs by the powerful players. It is making a mark—but is not always fair itself. This movement finds easy scapegoats in intergovernmental institutions, as if these bodies act independently of the governments who own them, and uses stories about their forcing cuts in basic services or insisting on privatization that are outdated, distorted, or concocted (Chapter 5). And it is often more energetic in attacking global agreements than the much more pernicious and prevalent alternative—a patchwork of bilateral deals forged between major powers and their trading partners in which those powers act as prosecution, judge, and jury. The alternative to globalization isn't a free-for-all but a free-for-*some*.

It is particularly important for US CSOs to reflect on these issues. People in the South are concerned, as we have heard, about market integration, but they also see clear benefits and have some trust in global negotiations, including those of the WTO. It is equally clear that there is increasingly vocal concern about US hegemony and the undiluted self-interest driving the Bush administration. People of the South may have misgivings about the WTO but have much less faith in US-led processes being good for them. US CSOs need to listen to these views and strive to be a constructive conduit for this global angst at home. The current wave of anger is largely anti-Bush but is widely couched as anti-Americanism. As a defensive backlash, more and more Americans are tending to return hostility and advocate unilateralism. This could spiral into a dangerous rift between Americans and the rest of the world. US CSOs urgently need to prevent this. Opinion polls show that 75 percent of Americans want their government to be more involved internationally, especially in tackling poverty (UN Foundation 2002)—but to the rest of the world they don't seem to be doing much about it. CSOs need to ensure that the US media see evidence of this, that the US government is aware of it, and that people throughout the world see that they have allies. Joining in with a global citizen effort for responsible US government is much more important today than mounting campaigns against international organizations such as the WTO. CSOs should see themselves as genuine partners, not leaders, in this effort.

European CSOs, likewise, need to counter US-centric foreign policy and trade policy and fight for true internationalism. The 2002 steel spat makes this clear. When President Bush slapped 30 percent tariffs on imported steel, the EU—like South Africa, Russia, Malaysia, and others—complained to the WTO, but it also started bilateral pressure. This was largely successful. As of August 2002, half of EU exports had been exempted and a US-EU trade war was probably averted (*The Economist*, August 31, 2002). But other exporters, with much less economic or political power, stand little chance of winning similar concessions. European civil society should urge governments to use the WTO and global processes, rather than cut bilateral deals, so that their victories can be gains for all.

There are two sources of unfairness in globalization today: bureaucracy and policy. Some problems stem from the Northern- or elite-bias of the institutions driving change—governments, intergovernmental organizations (IGOs), and corporations. Civil society can tackle these by vigorously promoting governance and mandate reform, frameworks of ethics, and public accountability that lead to the "civilizing" of these institutions (Chapter 10). Another, broader, set of problems stems from the policies that are either unfair or progressive but not implemented. Civil society needs to construct and promote a different slate, designed to redress inequities and to share power more fairly (Chapter 11).

No blueprint for action is offered—civil society is far too heterogeneous to make this realistic—but some high priorities are suggested. *Worlds Apart* includes an appeal. Most successful civil society campaigns have been to *stop* things from happening or to *oppose* policies.

It is time to start pressing for what *should* be done, if we want to foster a new consensus about managing globalization differently and putting the needs of poor people first. It is time for a civil society coalition uniting behind what it stands *for*—a compelling vision of ethical globalization—not just what it is *against*.

CONCLUSIONS

The main messages of this chapter form a foundation of key premises that underpin the rest of this book. Briefly summarized, these are the following:

- *The problem is not with globalization but with how the processes are managed:* There is not one but many globalizations afoot; different markets, different aspects of society are integrating at different rates. These change processes are currently being managed in ways that expand inequities, but this could be made to change.
- *We inhabit a bipolar world:* The fault line in global society is no longer East-West or North-South, but between the included and the excluded; gaps in wealth, power, opportunities, and security are widening in ways that are both immoral and dangerous.
- *There is a shift from delegative to deliberative democracy:* World changes influence politics as well as markets. Citizens are increasingly dissatisfied with a democracy that permits them only a proxy voice on national issues; they want a direct say in issues that concern them, from local to global levels. CSOs make this possible.
- *Our global leaders have a dangerous lack of global vision:* The leaders of powerful nations (and companies) make decisions that have long-term and global impacts based on parochial, short-term considerations of self-interest; US isolationism is particularly grave; there is neither the courage nor the vision for the big solutions that are needed.
- *Civil society can blaze a different path and pull our politicians with it:* CSOs offer the only hope for addressing this lacuna; there is a growing voice of concern, and if from this a common call for change emerges, its force could be irresistible.

The next three chapters expand, in turn, the first three premises. Later chapters will return to the others. First, how is it that globalization has affected markets so strongly, how do changes in world trade affect poor countries, and why are civil society organizations right to claim that "the dice are loaded"?

2.

How Globalization Affects Markets— Distortion and Extortion

Though threats to national culture and the erosion of sovereignty are common concerns about globalization found throughout the world, it is the sense of economic injustice that fuels greatest public anger. Just when the ideological debate between capitalism and communism seemed to have been resolved once and for all, just when governments—for the most part—have recognized that markets are better at producing what people want than state bureaucracies, suddenly a great misgiving about capitalism has erupted. Though the media has played a part, the concern—and the protests, campaigns, and ethical alternatives that have been blazed in response—has largely been driven by civil society.

Previous CSO campaigns in recent decades have focused on specific injustices of TNCs—irresponsible baby-milk marketing, profiting from apartheid, banks who fueled the debt crisis, using child labor, sweatshops, and so on. And they attacked specific actions of the World Bank and other international organizations. Today's campaigns about globalization have become bolder and attack the system itself. This is partly because new information and communications technology (ICT) makes bolder strategies possible. It is partly because earlier campaigns have enabled CSO leaders to appreciate how global institutions work, how they are best influenced, and where their Achilles' heels lie. But it is also, most critically, because an alternative analysis of markets, business, ethics, and global governance has been evolved by a myriad of civil society groups, substantiated by field-level research involving Southern civil society, and shared through the World Wide Web so as to construct a common language of political analysis and grievance. This is the foundation for the social movement against neoliberal globalization that has emerged (we return to this in Chapter 8).

This chapter analyses the movement's basic argument—that economic globalization hurts poor countries, that "free trade" is promoted by big business and Northern government cheerleaders as a panacea but is really a poison for poor countries. We start with some theory: why doesn't free trade deliver all it promises? How have rich countries been able to consolidate their power over poorer ones? Then we examine the World Trade Organization (WTO) to understand why it has failed to ensure that all countries gain from free trade. The next section estimates the cost to the South of Northern distortions. Then we unpack economics into its component markets and ask what the last twenty years of globalization have done for each. This enables us to construct a balance sheet of winners and losers—showing how poor people and poor countries have fared so badly. The chapter concludes with some civil society priorities for redressing these biases.

COMPARATIVE ADVANTAGE FOR SOME; ABSOLUTE DISADVANTAGE FOR OTHERS

Governments and their economic advisors the world over love trade. However unjust the terms, they want to stay in the game rather than retreat behind a protectionist shell. Behind this faith lies a cornerstone of classical economics—the law of comparative advantage (see Appendix 1; Ricardo 1973). Mostly, however, the North-South gap continues to widen because of powerful governments' hypocrisy—preaching free markets yet practicing market distortion that systematically undermines poor countries' opportunities. Three powerful forces tear into the South's comparative advantage.

First, industrialists seek to protect their domestic market by lobbying for tariffs, quotas, and other restrictions on imports. Since the United States, the European Union, and Japan account for over 60 percent of world imports, these governments and their industrialists are in a commanding position. Second, workers the world over fear unemployment and so reinforce the protectionist demands of their bosses. Mechanization actually kills far more jobs in rich countries than imports do, but the train of technology can't be halted. Every Northern job saved (probably temporarily) is at the cost of several in the labor-intensive South, so the net effect of Northern protection is to replace Southern workers by Northern machines. Third, the theory assumes that investors lead the production shift toward the advantage of that country. In reality, investment flows globally—usually to profitable havens in the North or Asia. Investors, in practice, are more inclined to back uncompetitive production in a protected market than comparative advantage in a fragile economy. This is why an estimated 40 percent of African private wealth resides outside Africa (World Bank 2002b).

As Pascal Lamy, EU trade commissioner said: "We have proved . . . our ability to create fabulous wealth on this planet for the few. But we have not yet shown that we have the slightest idea how to get to a fairer, a wise distribution of that wealth" (Lamy 2000). Not quite so. The powerful players know full well how wealth could be more equitably shared—simply by permitting a genuinely level playing field for products where the South has advantages. What they do, however, is the precise opposite; they fight for the interests of strong lobbies in their countries, thus tilting the playing field against the South. Agriculture, textiles, and garments are the sectors that developing countries are most interested in, accounting for 70 percent of their exports (*The Economist*, March 30, 2002); these are the very sectors in which Northern protectionism is strongest. How is such tilting accomplished?

HOW FREE IS FREE TRADE?

Whether fair or unfair, world trade is undoubtedly growing rapidly. Over the 1990s, global GDP rose on average 2 percent a year while export volumes rose 12 percent a year. Export volumes are sixteen times their 1950 level, and the growth rate is accelerating (see Figure 2.1).

Figure 2.1 Increase in world trade since 1950

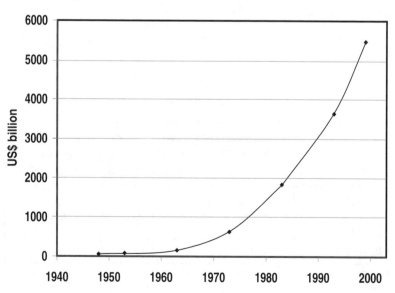

Source: WTO.

Much of this trade growth stems not from free global markets but from regional and bilateral trade agreements. Over one-fifth of all world trade (22.5 percent) is intra-EU trade. The United States is expanding regional agreements in Central and South America and elsewhere. It is vital to distinguish between Free Trade *Areas* and free trade. If there are two routes to expanding trade— one, the gradual elimination of trade barriers through global agreements; the other, a gradual thickening of bilateral agreements—it is clear which would be best for poor countries. They don't feature high on any country's list of pre-ferred trade partners. Free Trade Areas are the *opposite* of free trade to those left out. Hence, Africa has seen its share of world trade dwindle from the low level of 3.1 percent in 1951 to just 1.2 percent in 1999.

All categories of export have increased over the past twenty years, but a quick look at the statistics makes it appear that manufactures have grown strongly, while agriculture and minerals are sluggish (see the first column in Table 2.1). Using real prices reinforces this. But actually, the export *volumes* of commodities have grown quite strongly. The apparent sluggishness is because prices of primary commodities have fallen in real terms, while manufactures have held up.

From 1996 to 1999 the volume of developing country exports in-creased an impressive 27 percent, but earnings rose just 8.3 percent (UNCTAD 2001a). This was a bargain for the rich countries, which imported most of these cut-price goods, but bad news for the South. Africa was worst hit; its exports increased 8.8 percent in volume but *fell* 6.8 percent in earnings. NGOs, such as Oxfam International, Cen-ter of Concern (US), and World Development Movement (UK) have decried the futility of mobilizing more aid and debt relief for the Third World when so much more is lost through unfair trade. They have mounted campaigns to inform the public about such injustice and

Table 2.1 World trade 1977–1999:
changes in value and volume

	Ratio of exports 1999:1977 $ (current)	Ratio of exports 1999:1977 $ (constant-1990)	Ratio of export volume 1999:1977
Agriculture	2.9	1.5	2.0
Minerals	2.1	1.1	1.7
Manufactures	6.5	3.4	3.7
TOTAL	4.9	2.6	2.9

Sources: UNCTAD 2001a; World Bank 2001.

promoted debate about more ethical trade policies. So far, Northern governments have been deaf to such arguments.

US negotiators are particularly blatant about their unilateral interests. Former US trade negotiator Carla Hills spoke of "using a crowbar" to open markets "so that our private sector can take advantage of them." And George W. Bush, in his election campaign, pledged to "work aggressively to open markets for US products and producers. . . . With 96 percent of the world's population outside the US . . . the future prosperity of America's farmers depends on expanding markets overseas" (Curtis 2001).

Perversely, "protection" by Northern governments sounds virtuous to domestic constituencies—honoring their duty to protect the weak, to protect the rural way of life, to protect workers or depressed industrial zones, to protect consumers from products that might be substandard, and to protect communities from untrammeled immigration. But Northern governments decry protectionism abroad and extol the virtues of free trade.

The British government has consistently advocated integration. "We remain an unabashed champion of free trade today," said Tony Blair in 1998. "Protectionism does *not* bring prosperity." Yet neither the British government nor other champions of trade have been able to level the playing field. To understand why, and to build a credible civil society platform for reform, it is necessary to delve into the workings of global trade negotiations and the WTO, which coordinates them.

WTO—FRIEND OR FOE

In world trade the odds are loaded against developing countries, but this doesn't mean they should opt out. Especially for small countries, external trade is the surest route out of poverty. Hence the paramount development challenge is to secure the fairest possible trade terms for poor countries. This ought to make the World Trade Organization their best ally. Its founding principles include "raising standards of living . . . [ensuring] that developing countries, and especially the least developed amongst them, secure a share in the growth in international trade commensurate with the needs of their economic development . . . [and] the elimination of discriminatory treatment in international trade relations" (WTO 1995). These sentiments were reinforced by the declaration of the WTO's ministerial meeting in Doha: "International trade can play a major role in the promotion of economic development and the alleviation of poverty. . . . We seek to place [developing countries'] needs and interests at the heart of the Work Programme adopted in this

Declaration. . . . We are committed to addressing the marginalization of least-developed countries in international trade" (WTO 2001).

Sadly, however, the WTO has so far failed to make world trade work for the poor. Many campaigners claim that it is too powerful and evil, but this is simplistic. Its failings do not stem from its staff or structure, or indeed from its strength. The problem is politics. Arguably, the main problem is that it is not powerful enough. The power in world trade resides, as ever, with rich countries, particularly the United States. The WTO has not been able to avoid being used by these powers to advance a distorted interpretation of free trade.

The net effect is that the WTO acts not to help raise living standards of the *poor* but to retain the trade advantages of the richest countries. The source of this is *sequencing*. US and EU negotiators agree that their textile and agriculture markets should be liberalized, that their farm subsidies should go, and that the least developed countries should have special preferences—*but not quite yet.* They protest that they first have to overcome some powerful political lobbies back home. Meanwhile, they suggest, let's start with some liberalization that is easier to do. Let's reduce tariffs on manufactured goods globally (except, of course, textiles and garments), let's free up financial markets, let's liberalize the whole service sector, and let's have a global commitment to respect patents.

This list comprises the priorities rich countries want, while postponing till tomorrow everything developing countries want. The latter go along with it, however, because there is always a possibility that tomorrow will come. Developing countries, says the World Bank (2002b), agreed to a "grand bargain" in which they lowered tariffs and agreed to respect patents in exchange for the abolition of rich-country quotas on textiles and clothing, reduced agricultural protection, and abolition of "voluntary export restraints." Developing countries have done their bit, but rich countries have reneged.

Polarizing the imbalance, the most powerful countries usually agree on their world-trade negotiating positions in advance. The United States, the European Union, Japan, and Canada (collectively known as the Quad) first decide their joint position, then invite other OECD countries to join them, and only then present it to a handful of the larger developing countries. Many of the most important WTO negotiations have been in so-called Green Room discussions, which are restricted to twenty to thirty key negotiators. And aid is often used as a lever to win over key Southern governments. Hence, the WTO has often been a divisive instrument, not well serving the interests of the South. There is a general recognition of this, and the 2001 ministerial meeting in Doha narrowly avoided a walkout by developing countries by agreeing to use more inclusive procedures and more transparency.

This power imbalance is not denied; Northern representatives often stress how much WTO benefits their country. Christian Aid, the UK campaigning NGO, quotes Charlene Barshefsky (then US trade representative) after the Seattle WTO meeting: "The trade gains that the US has won through the WTO agreement and other trade policies have been a major contributing factor to our thriving economy. Studies estimate that the effects of full implementation of the WTO agreement will be to boost US GDP by $125–250bn per year. We have a great stake in expanding opportunities for US companies and workers in manufacturing, agriculture and service industries through the WTO" (Curtis 2001). More information about the WTO and trade inequity is given in Appendix 2.

EXTORTION: THE COST OF DISTORTION

Most countries practice some degree of trade protection, which hurts would-be exporters whose products are subject to the barriers. The cruelest aspect of world trade is that those worst hit are poorer countries—especially exporters of agricultural products, textiles, and garments. The regime of tariffs and other trade barriers, largely determined by richer countries, greatly reduces opportunity in these sectors while progressively liberalizing other manufacturing sectors, which account for 82 percent of OECD countries' exports (World Bank 2002c).

Collectively, developing countries represent 85 percent of world population yet just 25 percent of world exports. While some regions, notably East Asia, have been able to increase their market share, the poorest countries are being left behind. The forty-nine least developed countries (comprising over one-tenth of the world's population) accounted for just 0.8 percent of world trade in 1980, and this fell to 0.4 percent in 1999.

An informal (unpublished) World Bank estimate breaks down the costs of protectionist barriers to developing countries as follows:

- *Tariff protection on goods*: costs developing countries $12 billion in agricultural exports and $31 billion in manufactures;
- *Non-tariff barriers*: including quota restrictions, the use of anti-dumping restrictions, and excessively rigid trade standards cost approximately $50 billion;
- *Protection of developed country service sector*: costs about $50 billion;
- *Trade-related intellectual property rights*: generate South-to-North transfers of about $20 billion a year.

Combined, these costs are $163 billion a year, or four times the amount of aid developing countries received in 1999. UNCTAD (2001a) gives a higher estimate, suggesting that developing countries could earn $700 billion more by 2005 from expanded exports were it not for Northern protectionism. UNDP says that the provisions agreed upon during the Uruguay trade round loaded the dice further against poor countries and estimates that this costs the least developed countries $600 million a year and Africa $1.2 billion a year.

Even senior WTO officials recognize that its processes are loaded and very slow in matters of special concern to the South. Mike Moore (the head of the WTO) once said: "Sometimes I feel like joining the kids outside. When they say the system's unfair, they're not always wrong" (*The Economist*, November 11, 2000).

SLICING THE MARKET

Just how unfair is "the system"? To assess this it is necessary to get behind the aggregates to look at how globalization influences the many markets composing the world economy. These include the various financial markets; markets in shares and other investments; markets in raw commodities, services, labor-intensive and high-tech manufactured goods; the market in skilled and unskilled labor; and the market in patents and copyright. Let us look briefly at how each of these markets has fared, starting with various financial markets since these have been most transformed by globalization. After that, we can bring it all together to see the balance sheet of gains and losses.

Foreign direct investment

Firms based in one country have always made investments in subsidiaries or related businesses in other countries. As the regulations restricting capital movement have been stripped away, and as governments increasingly follow business-friendly policies, global flows of foreign direct investment (FDI) have soared, quadrupling from 1988 to 2001, from US$192 billion to $760 billion (UNCTAD 2001b). The share of FDI going to developing countries fluctuates but has risen to about one quarter. It is now their largest external source of finance ($225 billion in 2001)—about six times total aid. This undoubtedly helps their growth by fostering new manufacturing capacity and employment and by bringing modern industrial techniques and technology. It has spearheaded the dramatic shift from commodity dependence to the production of manufactured goods.

It also brings controversy, however: concerns about "sweat-shop conditions" in factories supplying TNCs and about "exporting" to the South lax environment, labor-rights, and social standards; resentment about the special privileges foreign investors extract from host governments, notably tax holidays; claims of foul play by domestic industrialists who think such privileges perversely disadvantage them; and the growing practice of attracting foreign investors by establishing export processing zones (EPZs), where rights, tax, and other laws are relaxed (there are now about two thousand EPZs throughout the South).

FDI to developing countries is highly polarized. In 1998 over half went to just three countries (China, Brazil, and Mexico), and little goes to low-income countries. Only one-fortieth of it went to Africa. For those countries receiving FDI, little goes to their poorer regions or to employing very poor people. Many would argue, therefore, that FDI does not relieve poverty directly, though it spurs growth and hence relieves poverty indirectly.

Foreign exchange and short-term capital flows

This market has seen the most explosive growth, thanks to the liberalization of capital markets over the last twenty years. The lifting of exchange controls, the floating and convertibility of more and more currencies, powerful computers, and telecommunications have heralded global, instant, twenty-four-hour financial markets. While world trade tripled from 1980 to 1999, currency exchange increased fifty fold. Fifty years ago the main reason to exchange currency was to buy goods for importing, but now only about 1.3 cents of each dollar exchanged relates to trade, compared with 19 cents in 1983. The rest is for short-term investment, speculation, and other purposes (Castells 2001). In 2001, $1.2 trillion ($1,200 billion) of foreign exchange transactions took place every business day, compared with $10–20 billion a day in 1973 and $60 billion in 1983 (*The Economist*, October 23, 1999, and May 18, 2002). This is equivalent to the World Bank's total lending in its fifty-seven-year history being exchanged every eight hours, twenty-four hours a day.

While third-world debt has become widely recognized, the world's most indebted country is the United States because of its growing trade deficit and the willingness of savers worldwide to finance this gap between what the country wants to consume and what it produces. As a proportion of its economy, its external debt is quite small, but at $2.2 trillion it is similar to all third-world debt combined (Greenhill and Pettifor 2002), and it soaks up capital that otherwise might go to more needy countries. This illustrates that there are two reasons for debt: (1) not being able to live within one's means, and (2) not being *willing* to do so.

Deregulation means that money can flow frictionlessly from one country to another, whether it stays ten years or ten hours. This makes it easy for investors not to take a long-term view. Instead, they play the markets, seeking arbitrage opportunities when there are price differences in different markets (whether commodities, real estate, equities or derivatives). When big investors have privileged access to information, such as satellite information about crop yields or tip-offs about US policy changes, or when the intensity of speculation exacerbates price trends, such speculation becomes unfair. And whereas domestic investors are more naturally disposed to stand firm at the onset of a downturn, foreign investors tend to cut and run, precipitating financial crises.

The litany of ninety banking crises over the past twenty years (each resulting in bank losses that, in proportion to GDP, exceeded the costs of the US banking collapse of the Great Depression) is testimony to this. The East Asian crisis, starting in 1997, was a particularly savage example (see Box 2.1). "As in every financial crash since the 17th century tulip crisis [in Holland] greed suddenly turned to fear. The difference this time [in the East Asian and Russian crises] was that the effect was global, not just local," said *The Economist* (January 30, 1999).

Paul Volker, former chairman of the US Federal Reserve, is clear that the problem was global malaise, not policy errors by the East Asian governments (Volker 2001). Yet when the crisis broke, the spotlight was put on "structural defects" in these countries—weaknesses in banking supervision, government subsidies, crony capitalism, and so on. These are valid concerns but had persisted for decades with neither apparent ill effect nor international opprobrium. The problem was not regional but lay in the herd-like characteristics of the markets.

This crisis could have hit anywhere. When the mood is positive, investors pile in, outstripping need and creating a bubble (in East Asia this was a real-estate boom). The currency appreciates—thus undercutting trade competitiveness—and a trade deficit grows. While the economy is booming everyone is relaxed. But when the first big investor has doubts and starts pulling out, there is a rush for the exit; the exchange rate comes under pressure (magnified by currency speculators); capital flight starts; reserves are depleted and interest rates soar as the central bank tries unsuccessfully to protect the currency; inflationary forces rise; and a crisis is born. The IMF then comes in with a standard prescription—a financial bailout on condition of cutting government spending, hiking interest rates further, and honoring external debts.

Box 2.1 The East Asian crisis and the price to the poor

This crisis started in July 1997 with a sudden devaluation of the Thai bhat. Within days the currency and stock markets throughout the region were nose-diving, banks and industries were closing their doors, and the world's confidence in the "East Asian economic miracle" was dashed. These countries had all deregulated their financial markets in keeping with the modern economic advice; however, their banks had opaque practices and banking regulation was weak. Previously, investors hadn't asked questions; $500 billion of international investment came into the region between 1993 and 1997 (*The Economist,* January 30, 1999). Industrialists or property developers could borrow what they wanted. But some investors grew suspicious that there might not be tenants for all the new office blocks or factories and decided to pull out, triggering the collapse.

The governments sought IMF emergency loans, but many believe that the terms demanded compounded the problems. Governments were told to cut spending, even though they didn't have large deficits; not to bail out their companies and banks but instead to streamline bankruptcy procedures; to hike interest rates massively to shore up their currencies; and not to restrict currency mobility. Such prescriptions make sense when crises arise from profligate governments, but in East Asia this wasn't the case; they stemmed from the private, not public, sector (Stiglitz 2002). The prescription created sharp deflation at a time when just the opposite was needed; hence, what started as a financial crisis quickly turned into a *social* crisis. Countless firms with hard currency loans found that their debts multiplied overnight simply because of the devaluation. They were viable one week but technically bankrupt the next.

The social sectors of the World Bank conducted some rapid social assessments that revealed that the poor were the real losers. First, huge numbers were laid off, particularly urban formal-sector workers. Though not the very poorest, most supported worse-off family members or sent remittances to relatives, so the indirect effect was serious. Second, the prices for basic necessities went up steeply, especially for imported goods. Third, the cost of credit also went up steeply, hitting informal-sector workers particularly. Fourth, there was a sharp return of migrant workers from neighboring countries, where they had been the first casualties of recession. Fifth, health and education services were hit due to budget cuts coupled with escalating prices of imported drugs and equipment. And sixth, there was severe damage to the social fabric as families were split up; traditional support mechanisms failed; drugs, violence, crime, and other antisocial activities grew; and longer working hours eroded time devoted to community activities.

Though the financial crisis has eased, the social scars remain. Employment may have picked up again, but the jobs are not the same—they lack the security, and the terms are worse.

Behind each crisis there are policy errors of banks and governments, but no economy can be perfect, hence strategists are increasingly asking whether it isn't time to change financial regulations to lessen risks of such systemic collapses. I remember organizing a meeting in 1998 between NGOs and the World Bank chief economist, Joe Stiglitz, in which the Nobel economist drew a parallel: If one or two cars crash on a bend in the road, you blame the drivers, he said, but if there are scores of accidents in the same spot it may be time to change the road. In Chapter 11 we look at proposed ways of doing this.

Markets in bonds, equities, and derivatives

Investors, particularly institutional investors, like to diversify their portfolios to spread risks. Whereas twenty years ago there was very little cross-border trade in bonds or shares, it now accounts for about $600 billion in bonds every day (*The Economist*, October 23, 1999) and $30 billion in equities. In 1980 foreigners held less than 1 percent of French government bonds, but by 1992 they held 43 percent (*The Economist*, October 7, 1995). While the vast majority of this is trade between industrialized countries, close to $100 billion of developing country equities and bonds were sold to foreign investors in 1996, about twenty times the 1990 level.

Derivatives constitute a particularly modern form of investment; they constitute a confusing array of options to buy or sell future equities, currencies, or commodities, or contracts to share future gains or losses as a given market rises or falls. They are very old instruments, originally designed to allow traders to hedge against the risk of market swings between purchasing goods and getting them to markets. However, their use for speculation is relatively new and has grown explosively. Derivative trading amounted to about $30 trillion a year in 1994 and $120 trillion in 2001—or four times global GDP (*The Economist*, October 7, 1995, and May 18, 2002). Currency speculation became notorious after George Soros's Quantum Fund made a $1 billion profit by speculating on Sterling in a single day in 1992—Black Wednesday— and by so doing drove the pound out of the European Exchange Rate Mechanism.

As the celebrated economist John Maynard Keynes said in 1936: "Speculators may do no harm as bubbles on a steady stream of enterprise. But the position is serious when enterprise becomes the bubble on a whirlpool of speculation. When the capital development of a country becomes a by-product of the activities of a casino, the job is likely to be ill-done." The French president, Jacques Chirac, famously described speculators as "the AIDS of the world economy" (*The Economist*, October 7, 1995).

Market for manufactured goods

The triumph of postwar trade negotiation has been the tumbling of tariffs, particularly in OECD markets, where average tariffs on manufactured imports have fallen from 40 percent in 1947 to 4 percent in 1999 (*The Economist*, October 3, 1998). There remain, however, many "spikes"—uncharacteristically high tariffs protecting specific markets, often reflecting powerful industrial lobbies rather than strategic interests. Peanut butter, for example, commands a 135 percent tariff in the United States yet is hardly pivotal to national security.

Other protectionist measures (non-tariff barriers, or NTBs) have strengthened, however, such as textile quotas, "anti-dumping" measures to bar products deemed to be sold below a "normal" price, and excessive health and safety standards. Unfortunately for developing countries, most of these barriers apply to the very products they wish to export. Their strong advantage is cheaper labor, hence they are best suited to produce labor-intensive goods such as textiles, clothing, and footwear. But powerful lobbies of domestic producers have succeeded in maintaining protectionist barriers (see Appendix 2).

Considerable progress has been made in other areas, however, and developing countries have been able to break into new markets, particularly for the assembly of manufactured goods. This has transformed the structure of developing countries' exports. Whereas manufactured products represented just 25 percent of their merchandise exports in 1980, and commodities (agricultural and mineral) accounted for 75 percent, by 1998 this had reversed and the share of manufactured products had risen to 80 percent (World Bank 2002b). Opportunities are very polarized, however. Over 60 percent of Southern manufactured exports are from China, Korea, Taiwan, Mexico, and Singapore (Oxfam 2002). Developing countries have also reduced their import tariffs (though not as steeply, from an average of 30 percent in 1982 to 11.3 percent in 1999), and most also reduced NTB use throughout the 1990s. As a consequence, there is now somewhat more trade among developing countries.

Trade in services

Trade in services has been a high-growth sector in recent decades, and now accounts for one-fifth of world trade (four-fifths of which is OECD-controlled). Many state services have been privatized (ranging from water and power utilities, road building, and railways to health, education, and rubbish collection), and new service specialist TNCs have emerged. Increased free time and disposable income in richer countries have also led to a growth in leisure, entertainment, restaurants, hotels, shopping malls, and other services. And increased prosperity, combined with increased concern for security, has fueled the growth of banking, insurance, pensions, mutual funds, and other finance-related services.

This diverse array of activities—not to mention transportation and ICT—has been greatly strengthened by globalization. While some services are perforce local, many are offered across borders. Call centers can be located around the world from the customers they handle (and operatives may even be briefed on the latest sports highlights and weather of the customers' country in order to appear local). Franchises for fast food or retail outlets allow companies to guarantee global standards. Hence, the export of services is a big growth market, now worth $1,350 billion per year. Of this, the South accounts for just 21 percent and the least developed countries for a puny 0.4 percent.

The TNC service giants, particularly in finance and ICT, are anxious to expand world trade and so have ensured that the liberalization of services (the General Agreement on Trade in Services—GATS) is prioritized in WTO negotiations. This wouldn't actually cost developing countries much, since their service sectors are relatively small and not greatly threatened by competition with TNCs. However, they resist it strongly for four reasons. First, they see it as a rich world priority for which little is offered to them in exchange (such as opening agricultural markets); second, their main domestic service companies are often politically powerful; third, they fear it would scupper the chance of domestic service companies growing in the future; and fourth—most powerfully—their citizens see it as threatening national identity and culture (Castells 1996).

Many fear that too much foreign control of the financial sector may add to insecurity. Western economists, the World Bank, and IMF say the opposite. To quote *The Economist* (January 30, 1999): "One of the best ways to increase domestic financial stability quickly is to encourage foreign banks to come in. Their presence reduces the risk of a banking panic, . . . Argentina now has only one bank of any size that is not owned or controlled by a large international bank." No Latin American country had so much foreign involvement—but two years later the economy was in ruin. According to Joe Stiglitz (2002), the foreign banks had invested in US Treasury bills and had been reluctant to lend to small domestic firms, who therefore couldn't grow. This was bad for the economy and added to unemployment. When the financial crisis struck, the citizens felt badly let down; the banks compounded this by closing their doors to customers in an attempt to stem the run. There were reports that they used armored vehicles to transport hard currency from their vaults to the airport and thence to Uruguay to protect their assets. Little surprise, then, that the riots on the streets targeted banks in particular.

Box 2.2 Tescos and Thailand

The year 2001 saw a mounting popular campaign against the surge of giant international retailers in urban Thailand. Led by domestic supermarket owners, but supported by an unlikely alliance of old-school nationalists and young leftist anti-globalizers, it protested against the growing numbers of Tescos, Carrefour, Walmart, Safeways, and other hypermarkets that hurt their livelihoods.

But the case is not that clear. Does Tescos damage the Thai culture or exploit its people any more than the Thai-owned supermarkets? The latter sell the same range of products; they don't have "buy locally" policies. Their prices are generally higher. Their salaries are somewhat lower than the multinationals, and they are much less likely to allow unionization. For locally purchased products they don't pay more—in fact, foreign companies are likely to commit to longer order books. So the consumers, shop workers, and local producers may all be relatively well served by the global giants. The local indignation is largely due to a sense of national takeover. The shopping precincts in metropolitan cities are coming to resemble those in the United States or Europe. These stores with their glitzy signboards are icons of this invasion.

Primary commodity markets

Though middle-income countries have shifted into labor-intensive manufacturing industries, poor ones remain dependent on exporting commodities for foreign exchange. But the global demand for their commodities is stagnant. As more countries seek to boost exports, and their options are severely limited, they all chase the same markets, leading to a relentless decline in commodity prices throughout the entire twentieth century—a decline that has accelerated during the last two decades. The average real price of non-oil commodities is now only one-third of its 1900 level, and it has more than halved in the last twenty years (World Bank 2002a)—hence developing countries have to sell very much more than they did twenty years ago to import the same manufactured goods. Commodity prices fell 30 percent from 1997 to 1998 alone, to hit their lowest level in 150 years (Castells 2001).

This is devastating, particularly for the poorest countries, and the harm is compounded by the relatively high tariffs the North imposes on processed commodities. While average tariffs on unprocessed commodities are 4 percent, they rise to 12 percent for processed agricultural products, so curbing the South's chance to enhance national incomes. Cocoa, for example, is imported into the European Union duty free (after all, it is not grown in Europe), but chocolate has up to 27 percent tariffs (Curtis 2001). Producing countries also get a declining share of the proceeds from trade. Mike Moore, former head of the WTO, wrote in *The Guardian* (August 5, 2002) that ten years ago the world "coffee economy" was $30 billion, of which farmers saw one-third. Now it is a $60 billion industry, but producers get just 9 percent.

Countries seeking to grow and perhaps export *temperate agricultural commodities* face even more grave problems, since they find themselves up against OECD farmers. These comprise a very powerful lobby, even though they account for a small proportion of the population. They have steadfastly resisted all WTO attempts to liberalize agricultural trade (see Appendix 2). The Uruguay Round agreed to phase out quotas and replace them by tariffs—hailed by many as a breakthrough. But in practice many of the new tariffs are so high that they act as import bans. Japan, for example, levies a 550 percent tariff on imported rice; the United States a 179 percent tariff on milk powder; Canada a 300 percent tariff on butter; and the European Union a 215 percent duty on frozen beef (*The Economist*, October 3, 1998).

OECD farmers—especially the largest—also get huge production and other subsidies. Half of the European Union's Common Agricultural Policy support goes to the richest 17 percent of farmers, and in the UK 80 percent of the subsidies go to the richest 20 percent (Curtis 2001). These OECD subsidies total $360 billion per year—six times all development assistance, and more than the entire GDP of Sub-Saharan Africa. It is difficult for developing countries to compete against this. To make matters worse, technical restrictions are often applied, perhaps on health or hygiene grounds.

Developing countries with considerable iron and coal deposits have also sought to develop steel industries. Here too they have been thwarted by Northern protectionism. America, the world's biggest steel consumer, has used anti-dumping laws to protect its producers. The legality of this has been strongly challenged through the WTO, but a group of sixty US Congressmen representing steel constituencies pressed the president not to make concessions. Developing nations, the European Union, other OECD countries, the WTO, and others all urged Mr. Bush not to give in to protectionist pressure to no avail. In March 2002 he announced 30 percent tariffs on steel imports. The opinion of the rest of the world counted little compared with the concerns of domestic politicians in an election year. Many governments are now challenging the tariffs through the WTO, but some of the most influential—such as the UK and the European Union—are putting more effort into securing bilateral concessions. But what chance do countries like South Africa have to win concessions? And where does this leave *global* trade negotiations?

Labor markets

The international movement of people has seen the opposite of liberalization. A century ago there was much more freedom to move from country to country; there was a huge migration of about 5 percent of the world's population (seventy million people) in just a few years, notably migrants from Europe moving to North America and Australia. Now, industrialized countries have tightened their immigration laws. The days when "huddled masses" were warmly invited to the North are over. Most migration of unskilled workers today is either illegal migration or asylum seeking, and even refugees from abusive regimes find it ever harder to gain asylum. Many of those lucky enough to reach their chosen destination live in a shadow world, facing constant insecurity, danger, and threat of deportation, perhaps turning to prostitution or street crime or accepting menial jobs for which they are grossly overqualified.

At the other end of the social spectrum, a truly global breed of workers has emerged—especially the high-flying executives of major corporations. TNCs are keen to have Western-educated managers running their foreign subsidiaries—preferably, since English is fast becoming the lingua franca of big business, from the English-speaking world. A lesser, but still highly paid, global class consists of highly trained ICT specialists. Until education output allows supply to catch up with demand, these will continue to enjoy greater mobility.

The market in intellectual property

While rich countries have long had reciprocal agreements recognizing each other's patents and copyrights, developing countries have either not had intellectual property rights (IPR) laws or have ignored them. So in developing countries, intellectual property was something of a free-for-all. Now, however, all countries joining the WTO must put IPR laws in place in a given period.

The Agreement in Trade-Related Intellectual Property Rights (TRIPs) will result in a major drain from South to North. India, for example, stands to transfer about $800 million a year to TNCs (Curtis 2001). Companies in rich countries hold 97 percent of patents worldwide, and 80 percent of patents registered in developing countries. In 1995, half of all the world's royalties and license fees went to US companies alone (UNDP 1999). As UNDP describes: "Poor people and poor countries risk being pushed to the margin in this proprietary regime controlling the world's knowledge. . . . From new drugs to better seeds, the best of the new technologies are priced for those who can pay. For poor people, they remain out of reach. Tighter property rights raise the price of technology transfer, blocking developing countries from the dynamic knowledge sectors. The TRIPs agreement will enable multinationals to dominate the global market even more easily." The imbalance is most acute in Africa. There were 51,781 patents filed by nonresidents with either the African Intellectual Property Organization or the African Regional Industrial Property Organization in 1997 compared with just 38 by residents (World Bank 2000c).

The South understandably resents the implication that all knowledge resides in rich countries and that only knowledge invented and patented in recent years has value. Adding injury to insult, a number of Western companies seek to patent extracts or genes from medicinal plants and high-value crops that have been used for centuries in the South. While TRIPs safeguard the patents of Western companies, they do nothing to protect traditional knowledge. A 1994 study commissioned by UNDP estimated that companies in industrialized countries make $4.5 billion profit each year from patents on natural resources that are found in and whose utility was discovered in developing countries. Those countries get no royalties and no patent rights (Curtis 2001). Firms often learn about the healing properties of plants from locals and then patent the active ingredient. Two cancer drugs, for example, were developed using a rose periwinkle plant found in Madagascar, but the country received no benefit (*The Economist*, November 10, 2001).

COMPILING THE BALANCE SHEET

Having looked at how all the individual markets are affected, we can now compile an overall balance sheet of gains and losses of global-

---

Box 2.3 Jasmine rice

Jasmine rice, or hommali, is the most sought after rice in Thailand. It is highly aromatic, dazzlingly white and highly nutritious. In recent years Thailand has established a flourishing export trade, selling it to the West. Much of the rice is grown in smallholdings. But fears are now mounting that this export potential may be lost just as it gets going because of bio-piracy. A US professor stands charged of stealing genetic data from jasmine rice germ and filing a patent for it in the United States. His plan is to mutate the distinctive genes so that it can be successfully grown in Florida (where the autumn temperatures are otherwise too low) and can be harvested by machine. If this is successful, Thai authorities fear, the country could lose its export market and millions of poor farmers would lose their income.

Sources: The Observer, *October 28, 2001; Hutanuwatr 1998*

ization. Different countries have different strengths. Some are labor rich, some have long banking traditions, others have plentiful natural resources. How do the relative advantages of different *markets* compare with the relative advantages of different *countries*?

The foundation of classical economics is the theory of supply and demand—firms produce more of a given product as its price rises (the supply curve) but the quantity consumers buy goes down (the demand curve). Where the two curves cross is the point of optimum satisfaction for both suppliers and consumers, and hence most trade. This is the market's equilibrium point at which supply equals demand. If anything happens to change the price (such as changes in taxes, subsidies, or input prices), then the curves shift to reach a new equilibrium point. This is the "invisible hand" of market forces.

In the real world, markets rarely reach such an equilibrium point because of asymmetries of power and knowledge. There are not, as elementary textbooks suppose, infinite numbers of producers and suppliers but imbalances—often monopolies and cartels, in which the market leaders dominate and set prices. If suppliers can take their products to a different country, they can hold out for a higher price in any one market; conversely, if laws prevent the mobility of the product, but customers are free to buy abroad, the suppliers will find themselves competing with one another, so driving down prices. And if one set of players has access to information that is denied the other set, this again biases the market—for example, big commodity dealers will have better intelligence than small producers on factors influencing production and demand. All these asymmetries lead to distortions away from market equilibrium that favor the more powerful players.

Globalization makes two key changes in the markets we have been discussing: It changes the *mobility* of what is sold and the degree of *competition*. Increased mobility is good news for sellers—they have more freedom to go to different markets. And, increased competition is good for customers—or alternatively where there is a strong imbalance between producers and consumers, the monopolist is favored.

How were the odds stacked twenty years ago, as today's round of globalization started, and how have they changed since? There is as yet no rigorous method for comparing the different impacts. For example, there is no single indicator of trade barriers that combines tariffs, quotas, licenses, and other non-tariff barriers. Hence, what is presented here is illustrative and schematic rather than quantitative and precise.

Capital Markets: As ever, there are few owners of capital and many borrowers. The big change is that financial market deregulation has made capital much more mobile. The use of derivatives also allows the strength of capital to be magnified, because contract options can be brought and sold for a fraction of their face value. Capital has always given a good return to its owners, but globalization has worked wonders for it.

High-technology manufactures: Tariffs have dropped steeply, easing trade; the increased ease of moving production overseas and the advent of ICT have all helped producers increase their mobility and plan global production for global markets. Globalization has helped manufacturers, but not as dramatically as owners of capital.

Labor-intensive manufactures: These require less capital, and so there has always been more competition and highest concentration in developing countries. The failure to remove barriers on the third-world's major manufactures—textiles, clothing, and footwear—means that globalization has brought few benefits. At the same time, the widespread encouragement to developing countries to integrate into the world economy has led to many more countries (such as China and Vietnam) chasing limited markets. They have never been lucrative; now they are more disappointing.

Services: Globalization has greatly helped transnational service providers. WTO rules have opened new doors for them, and the Washington Consensus has encouraged governments to privatize state services, particularly favoring the Northern giants who have considerable experience in this field.

Temperate agriculture: Producers of temperate crops or competing products face severe restrictions (excepting big Western farmers who enjoy huge subsidies). Globalization has not yet helped them, but reforms are promised. It has, however, increased the number of suppliers, depressing prices further. The outlook has always been bad; now it is bleaker.

Other primary commodities: Producers of other primary commodities are not as squeezed or penalized by OECD subsidies, but globalization has done little to increase demand—and today's high technology emphasizes substitutes for commodities of all kinds. Again, the number of competing suppliers continues to rise, hence the future prospects are difficult.

Unskilled labor: Employment is increasingly squeezed due to labor-replacing technology. The mobility of laborers is very restricted (more so than a century ago). Globalization has offered few new opportunities to Southern workers (excepting EPZs, call centers, and other TNC subsidiaries). Trade unions have weakened, job security has lessened, and wages have fallen in real terms, as industrial wage differentials have widened enormously (averaging $18 an hour in OECD and 25 cents an hour in India and China).

Highly skilled labor: In stark contrast, top managers and some highly specialized workers have become a truly global work force, and their compensation packages are legendary. Even the "golden handshakes" for managers who fail are incredibly lucrative.

Intellectual property rights: Twenty years ago patents were respected in OECD countries, but largely ignored elsewhere. WTO rules now compel members to fall into line and pay royalties for IPR, usually to Western companies. They have not, however, protected the South from bio-piracy—the patenting by TNCs of the rights to genes or extracts of natural resources found exclusively in developing countries. On both scores the owners of IPR do extremely well, while poor countries lose out.

BRINGING IT ALL TOGETHER

Table 2.2 illustrates the balance sheet for the nine different markets. It first shows whether the principle "sellers" in the market are Northern or Southern. The next column provides an illustrative "meter" showing how favorable the market was for sellers before the recent globalization era. The final column illustrates whether the globalization

*Table 2.2 The balance sheet of globalization
(for sellers in different markets)*

MARKET	Principal sellers	Situation before globalization (unfavorable — favorable)	Impact of globalization
Capital	N	favorable	extremely positive
High-tech manufactures	N	mid-favorable	positive
Labor-intensive manufactures	S	mid-unfavorable	negative
Services	N	mid-favorable	positive
Temperate agricultural commodities	S	unfavorable	negative
Other primary commodities	S	unfavorable	negative
Unskilled labor	S	most unfavorable	negative
Highly skilled labor	N	mid-favorable	positive
Intellectual property	N	mid-favorable	extremely positive

process has been positive or negative for the sellers in these markets. For example, owners of capital were highly favored in 1980, but the subsequent liberalization of capital markets has enormously benefited the financial sector. Conversely, unskilled labor faced a difficult situation in 1980, and globalization has widened competition (as capital and technology have become more mobile) rather than offered new opportunities. The table shows how globalization has improved the already rosy situation of capital owners, high-tech manufacturers, the modern service sector, highly skilled workers, and owners of patents, all of whom are typically wealthy and living in rich countries. It has, conversely, worsened the prospects for producers of labor-intensive manufactures, primary commodity producers (especially those not protected by OECD subsidies), and unskilled or semi-skilled labor—overwhelmingly poor people in developing countries. Only the largest developing countries have significant growth opportunities based on their domestic markets.

Globalization may bring other benefits to developing countries, but is clearly managed in a most biased way. It does not offer a rising tide that lifts all boats; it is selective—the large ships rise, while the rickety boats of the poor remain stuck in the mud. The G7 representatives who dominate the WTO negotiations have been preoccupied with narrow domestic considerations and are overly influenced by greedy business lobbies.

It is likely that these inequities will be increased as a result of 9/11, especially for small developing countries. A recent OECD paper predicts that the burden exporters face in dealing with all the additional security measures amount to 1–3 percent of the costs of the goods being transported—equivalent to all the concessions developing countries managed to win at the Uruguay trade round (*The Guardian,* June 10, 2002).

CONCLUSIONS

Our analysis explains why CSOs have good grounds to depict globalization as bad for poor countries. Northern government and corporate leaders often criticize their campaigns as exaggerated, inaccurate, politically opportunistic or unfair, but collectively they have done the South an invaluable service by elevating issues of trade and economic justice on the world stage and by challenging parochialism with internationalism. Just as environmentalists have argued points of governance on behalf of future generations, this new global economic justice lobby seeks to persuade politicians that poverty ten thousand miles away is now a domestic concern that they cannot afford to ignore.

The issues raised by these campaigns cover the need for reformed and more generous aid, for rapid resolution of the debt problem, for global priorities such as climate change and HIV/AIDS to be fought globally (financed by global taxes), for universal agreement on minimum standards for the environment and labor rights, and—above all—for justice in world trade, especially WTO reforms.

Many who join street protests about globalization will never see WTO trade negotiations as anything but conspiracies to favor the rich at the expense of the poor, but there are many (including development NGOs, unions, and church groups) who have become increasingly confident about their political influence and see their mission as "civilizing global capitalism." They don't argue for the South to turn anti-trade—since this would harm, not help, the poor—but want the enormous power of globalization to be harnessed for the good of all, making markets the world over poor-friendly.

Under such growing public pressure, some governments—such as the British—now see the future of the WTO as hinging on it offering more to the South; they urge that the next trade round be a "development round." Whether this is just a slogan remains to be seen. All players must be careful and honest in describing what they regard are the key features of a true development round. Leading CSO campaigns would say it needs to include:

- Increasing access by developing countries (especially least developed and African countries) to OECD markets;
- Sequencing trade negotiations so that Northern markets are significantly opened (particularly for textiles, garments, and agriculture) and progress is made in phasing out farm subsidies before further concessions are expected from the South;
- Establishing a social assessment process to gauge the impact of proposed trade reforms on potential losers;
- Curbing back-door protectionism (see Appendix 2), perhaps by setting up a quick dispute review process to assess the potential damage;
- Providing support for strengthened regional and South-South trade links, including cooperative trade agreements and the use of barter trade;
- Instituting measures that increase the South's bargaining power in international negotiations, including free "legal aid" for using the WTO's disputes settlement process;

- Ensuring coordination between the WTO and aid agencies to assure that opportunities of integration are realized and that the poor are protected from whatever risks; and
- Supporting programs that strengthen labor rights and environmental standards in developing countries (through aid rather than trade sanctions).

This growing economic-justice movement is global but far from uniform. In many developing countries it is linked to mainstream social movements—such as peasants' associations, women's movements, the urban poor, or the landless. Via Campesina is a global network of rural social movements that has become prominent in this context, and the World Social Forum has become a "trade fair" for such groups (Schönleitner 2003). In the UK, most development NGOs, environment groups, and church-based pressure groups are campaigning for fair trade, often working together. And in Northern Europe (especially Netherlands, Belgium, and Scandinavia) there are also strong trade campaigns. In Europe (particularly Latin countries) there are also more radical civil society "anti-globalization" protest movements (see Chapter 8).

In the United States—the source of much trade injustice—civil society campaigns are fewer and quieter. Most active are the environment groups, such as Friends of the Earth (FOE), Natural Resources Defense Council, World Wildlife Fund (WWF), and Sierra Club, which tend to focus on promoting environment standards in trade. A number of trade unions, particularly the American Federation of Labor, are similarly active—largely promoting core labor standards in trade agreements and opposing liberalization that would hurt their members' interests. Some church groups such as the Catholic-based Center of Concern campaign on the social aspects of trade and global governance issues, as does Ralph Nader's group, Public Citizen. In addition, a number of think tanks research and write about such issues, including the Institute for Agriculture and Trade Policy and the Institute for Policy Studies. However, the large development NGOs and church-based groups are rather silent. The advocacy section of the website of InterAction— the main umbrella of US development NGOs—contains nothing on trade, nor any links to trade campaigns in the United States (though it does have a link to the "Campaign to Preserve US Global Leadership").

NGOs may argue that the US public is not as interested in trade justice as their European (or indeed Canadian) counterparts, but which is the chicken and which the egg? In Europe, many years of trade campaigns have fostered popular concern. Especially in the light of an increasing global movement criticizing US isolationism and self-interest, it is high time to evolve concerted campaigning on these issues in the United States. Increased global tension is bound to go hand in hand with increased inequality and thus fuel anger toward the United States abroad. There needs to be a conduit for debate about economic justice issues into the US heartland in order to avoid it being seen simply as anti-US sentiment.

What motivates the public to join in with campaigns is not the impact world trade policies might have on Southern governments, but what it means to poor men, women, and children. This is the subject of the next chapter.

3.

How Globalization
Affects Poor People

The previous chapter concentrated on how globalization affects poor *countries*, but the strongest civil society criticisms concern its impact on poor people and on inequality. In this chapter we look first at what poverty means to different players—notably the World Bank and the poor themselves; next, we look at the vexing issue of distribution; and then we ask what impact globalization has had. The conclusions reinforce the findings of the previous chapter and make clear that reforming the management of globalization calls for major changes in global governance, the subject of the next chapter.

Supporters of globalization argue that it is the engine of growth that will give everyone a ride to prosperity; where poverty persists, it is because countries are missing the train or governments are bungling the economy. Rubbish, say the critics, a few countries have joined the rich countries' club and many more do the North's bidding—and their elite do nicely as a result—but for the masses there is just pain with no gain. Market openness subjects poor laborers to a "race to the bottom." No, say its supporters, it is a race to the *top* and everyone can win. Each group is so convinced of its case that it dismisses outright the other's view. This is a shame, for in reality both schools have good points.

The previous chapter showed how the management of globalization is biased against poor countries. But a quick look at countries that, for political or geographic reasons, remain largely outside the world economic community reveals how harmful to the poor that isolation can be. There are considerable benefits from globalization (though as we show later, its cheerleaders often exaggerate them).

This chapter looks behind these arguments. The task is made more complex by imprecision in both defining and measuring poverty. What does it comprise? And who is doing well or badly? NGOs have a tendency to dwell on the gravity of poverty today rather than past development achievements reducing it. More seriously, governments tend to dwell on the aggregates—such as average income—and forget about those falling well below that average. So it is important to start this chapter by asking, What do we know about the poor, and how can poverty be reduced? We need to understand the dynamics of poverty and what poor people themselves think in order to deduce how globalization could be better managed to put the poor first.

WHAT IS POVERTY?

We know with great accuracy how many people read newspapers or the latest novels, but we know only approximately how many are illiterate. We know exactly how many have cars, travel on planes and trains, or enter marathon races, but we have only rough data on how many are lame. We know how many own shares, but not how many millions own only the rags they stand up in. We know precisely how many have TVs or watch Hollywood movies, but we only roughly know how many are blind. We know exactly how many babies are fed on what variety of infant formula, but we can only guess how many die of malnutrition in their first year or two. The list of comparisons could go on. In short, we know a great deal about *wealth*, but we have scant knowledge about *poverty*.

Development assistance is a big industry ($53 billion from official sources in 2000, plus perhaps $9 billion raised by international NGOs). Virtually all the agencies and NGOs involved maintain that poverty reduction is their primary mission—but in truth all of us know little about it. We know a great deal about the assets, interests, and associations of the world's super-rich (in spite of their efforts to conceal this information), yet what we know about the poorest is sketchy, and few have taken the trouble to listen systematically to their interests or concerns. Most poverty statistics draw on a wide range of nationwide living standards surveys (LSS)—and these can be useful—but what they say about the poorest 10 percent in low-income countries is difficult to believe. Their total consumption from all sources, it would appear, is below what is needed just to keep a body alive when performing no physical activity (the basal metabolic rate—about 1700Kcal/day for adult men or 1300Kcal/day for women). Yet clearly they *do* survive, if only at the margins; but *how* they manage to do so is largely a mystery. They must derive more than the surveys detect from gathering, hunting, subsistence farming, and the informal sector, or they get support from relatives and neighbors. Or they may underreport income, perhaps from illegal activities.

Box 3.1 The bad news and the good news in the fight against poverty

The Crisis of Poverty—why the world needs to take action:
- 780 million people don't have enough to eat
- 1.2 billion people live on less than $1 a day (2.8 billion on less than $2 per day) according to widely quoted World Bank statistics
- 8 percent of children die before their fifth birthday
- 30,000 children die of poverty each day—16,000 from diarrhea or pneumonia alone
- 25 million people have died of AIDS (most in developing countries)
- 42 million are infected with HIV; over 70 percent of these are in Africa
- 23 million people died in wars in developing countries since 1945 (9,000 a week)

The achievements—to encourage us that an end to poverty is *possible:*
- The proportion of hungry people has fallen from 37 percent in 1960 to 17 percent now
- Infant mortality rates have halved in the last 40 years
- School enrollment has gone up 80 percent in the last 20 years
- It took 10,000 years of settled agriculture, till 1960, to reach an annual grain yield of 1 billion tons; it took just 40 more years to reach 2 billion tons; most of this increase was in developing countries and mostly due to improved technology, not increased acreage.
- 2,000 years after it is thought that the Romans introduced household water supply, 35 percent had access to safe water (1960); by 1990 this had doubled to 70 percent
- In the last 50 years, life expectancy in the South rose 21 years (from 44 to 65 years)—an increase of 5 months every year. Europe took 150 years to achieve a similar increase.

Sources: UNDP, World Bank, FAO, WFP, UNICEF, UNAIDS

The Concise Oxford Dictionary defines *poverty* simply as the "want of the necessities of life." But who determines what those necessities are; how little one has to have before it becomes a want; and whether people everywhere have the same needs? These are questions that tax poverty specialists throughout the world—and keep them in their jobs.

In my nine years in the World Bank I have been constantly amazed at how much trust is placed (by official agencies generally, not just the Bank) on purely economic assessments of poverty, and hence how many poverty specialists are economists, many of whom have had little personal contact with poor people. How credible would an agricultural specialist be, I ask, who has never been on a farm or talked with farmers? Poverty economists generally focus on *income* poverty, using LSS data to conflate all income (wages, farm yields, gathering, grazing, informal earnings, and so on) into an aggregate. For international comparisons this is converted into US dollars (using "purchasing power parity" exchange rates that adjust for different costs in different countries).

The World Bank estimates, thus, that 1.2 billion people—the very poor—live on less than $1 per day. These figures are quoted almost universally, as if they are incontrovertibly proven—but how accurate are they? You could say they are gospel truth—they are true, if you have that faith! Behind them, however, lie so many sources of error. Different family members give very different responses to questionnaires; surveys at different times of the year yield wildly different results; surveys need to be designed meticulously if they are to avoid missing important incomes or expenditures; they gather wrong data if those surveyed don't have trust in the researchers, if they resent the time detailed surveys consume, or if memories are not reliable; and statistics are often "refined" to tell the story the statistical agency wants to tell.

Such analysis is attractive to economists for two reasons. First, it allows trends on household fortunes to be compared with the macroeconomy; clearly to reduce poverty in the aggregate you need to increase aggregate income, or GNP. Since information about wealth distribution is sketchy or old in most countries, it affirms the conviction that rapid growth is what the poor need (a topic we return to later). Second, it quantifies poverty with comforting precision (often to several significant figures). Specialists I have spoken with admit the sources of errors and tend to reply, "Yes, but household surveys provide the only data we have." Is this good enough? It may be that the fisherman's estimates provide the only data about the size of the fish that got away, but it doesn't mean they are worth heeding.

I mustn't overstate. LSS does give some useful data, especially when compared with similar surveys in the same area conducted previously (and especially if effort is made to go back to the same families). But both sides in the globalization debate use them to substantiate their case, and I have come to regard them as too flimsy to bear this responsibility. Many, like myself, believe that measuring welfare *outcomes* (such as nutrition and health status, distance from schools or clinics, education attainment, and satisfaction with different public services) tells us more about the condition of poverty, but even this is only part of the answer. It assumes that we know what poverty truly *is*—a lack of defined welfare norms. But is this the whole picture? The only way to be sure is to find out what the poor themselves think are the important things to look at.

Early in my World Bank career I proposed a methodology for doing just this. For several years the Bank had routinely prepared country-level poverty assessments, mostly based on LSSs. I proposed *participatory* poverty assessments (PPAs) to supplement these, using participatory research to determine what poor people think are their most pressing problems, what they think of services and support they currently receive, and what priorities they identify for poverty reduction (Clark 1992). The approach quickly took hold, thanks in part to support we secured from the British government. The PPAs yielded useful information, and now most poverty assessments include at least some participatory research (Robb 1999), though the PPA findings aren't always acted on. In 2000 the World Bank published a major report summarizing the findings of all recent PPAs and a group of specially commissioned studies. It drew on interviews with sixty thousand poor people in sixty countries throughout the developing world (Narayan et al. 2000).

PPAs demonstrate that the poor are concerned about income, but they are concerned about many other issues besides, and poverty is highly heterogeneous (World Bank 2000c; Robb 1999). Besides income, the most common anxieties of the poor are:

- *Vulnerability:* they are acutely aware how susceptible they are to shocks through job loss, disease in the family, farm or livestock, drought or other calamity.
- *Lack of opportunity:* the poor may have no choice about whom to work for, borrow from, rent from, sell to, or buy from; poor children have little chance of the decent education that could help them escape the poverty trap.
- *Victimization:* they are discriminated against because of their gender, ethnicity, caste, and so on; government officials and services don't give them their entitlements; they are unfairly "taxed" or "fined" by corrupt officials.
- *Violence:* they experience high degrees of violence (including violence within the family); millions of people are victims of conflict.
- *Powerlessness:* they have nowhere to turn for redressing wrongs committed against them; they have little or no say in major local decisions that affect their lives.

Fighting poverty is about tackling these things, not just increasing average incomes; and it is about providing sustainability. Helping poor families double their income will be a poisoned chalice if that assistance increases the chance of ruinous following years. Poverty economists tend to seek improvements in averages while the defining life events of the poor are usually crises. To protect themselves, therefore, they usually spread their eggs around various income baskets and forgo the chance to hit lucky jackpots to ensure a secure livelihood. Diversity is the hallmark of their survival strategy, yet many aid agencies forget this as they promote their favored "quick fix."

FIGHTING POVERTY: EXPERIENCES OF THE WORLD BANK

I will now say something about how the World Bank views poverty and how this has evolved over the years. This is partly because the World Bank strongly influences the strategy of many governments and other aid agencies; partly because the Bank is controversial in CSO circles; and partly because I lived with this issue throughout the 1990s.

For decades the Bank has declared poverty reduction to be its overarching goal—though its critics (and many staff) have not always believed this. In the 1960s and 1970s the Bank largely emphasized helping countries to industrialize and grow. Through investment in infrastructure and exploiting its comparative advantages, poor countries could "take off." It wouldn't matter if the poor didn't benefit directly, because the society as a whole would prosper and eventually this wealth would "trickle down" to all. The experience, however, was often disappointing; the dramatic takeoff didn't happen, and the wealth generated stuck with the better off.

In the late 1980s, the Bank shifted toward promoting broad-based growth and targeted social development programs. This was encapsulated in a three-pronged strategy (described in the 1990 World Development Report on poverty):

- *Generate rapid economic growth:* emphasizing labor-intensive production to raise aggregate incomes and ensure broad participation in that growth;
- *Invest in "human capital":* improve education (particularly primary) and health services so that workers are more productive and have more opportunities; and
- *Provide welfare schemes and safety nets:* since many will not benefit immediately from growth, they may need welfare during the transition period.

To sustain rapid growth, the Bank argued, governments must provide an encouraging policy environment for enterprise, including reasonable taxes, minimal red tape, good infrastructure, secure property rights, low inflation, liberalized markets, controlled public spending, a competitive exchange rate to favor exports, and so forth. This strategy was the cornerstone of the Bank's work on poverty for most of the ensuing decade.

It is difficult to fault the logic of this case, but it is only a partial strategy. I used to speculate, in Bank meetings, what changes we'd need to make if our mandate became maximizing the wealth of the wealthy. We'd surely retain the enterprise-friendly policy environment and promotion of rapid growth. We'd want to ensure a stream of reasonably educated and healthy workers for the employers. And social safety nets for those laid-off and the destitute would keep the lid on social unrest. It is hardly credible that two diametrically opposite goals (minimizing poverty of the poor and maximizing wealth of the rich) could be served by the same strategy.

Growth is important, it should be stressed, and the three-prong strategy can claim much success. No country has been able to reduce poverty sustainably without generating sound growth and ensuring that the poor participate in it. The rapid reduction of poverty in Indonesia in the decade up to the East Asia crisis is a good illustration. This strategy is necessary but not sufficient. The *distribution* of income is also important. It is often the case (as in Indonesia) that when the economic winds

Table 3.1 Growth, poverty, equity, and social indicators in eight African countries

Country and years	Average economic growth per year	% change in poverty	% change in distribution	% change in primary school enrollment	% change in child malnutrition	% change in child mortality
Uganda ('92-'97)	4.8	-21	+	18	-4	-3
Ethiopia ('94-'97)	3.3	-26	+	6	-11	-5
Mauritania ('87-'95)	3.3	-40	++	13	-25	
Ghana ('92-'98)	1.6	-16	–	12	0	-15
Nigeria ('92-'96)	0.4	+56		4		+11
Madagascar ('93-'99)	-0.2	+1	++	16	-1	-21
Zambia ('93-'98)	-5.4	-3	–	-7	+3	-6
Zimbabwe ('91-'96)	-6.2	+35	++	3	-7	+31

Source: Christiaensen et al. 2001.

are fair, governments use public spending, tax policies, regional investment, and other instruments to ensure that the benefits of growth are
shared with the poor. In practice this doesn't always happen and the
lion's share of the growth goes to the better off.

Table 3.1 illustrates the relationship among growth, poverty, and
distribution in eight African countries in the 1990s. It shows that there
is an approximate correlation between growth and poverty reduction,
improved distribution, spending on social services and child welfare,
but not a perfect one. Most countries in recession saw increasing poverty and often deteriorating distribution and social indicators.

In recent years—due to findings such as these, the increasing weight
of PPA evidence, and pressure from liberal donors, NGOs, and others
working at the grassroots—the Bank has substantially evolved its three-
pronged strategy, making it more responsive to the priorities of the
poor, beyond income. In its *World Development Report 2000*, the Bank
set out a strategy for "attacking poverty," though it remains to be seen
how this will be incorporated into its operations.

Table 3.2 summarizes how the Bank's poverty strategy has evolved
over time through three stages. Each new stage represents a broadening—the principles and strategies of the previous stage are retained,
but new ones are added, with the result that the approach becomes
broader, as does its range of partners. Though it is a vast improvement,
it still has little to say about income inequality, to which we now turn.

Table 3.2 Evolution of World Bank's poverty strategy

	STAGE 1 1970s–1980s	STAGE 2 1990s	STAGE 3 current
Guiding theory	"Take-off" theory of the 1970s	*World Development Report of 1990*	*World Development Report of 2000*
Objectives of the strategy	Rapid growth, industrialization	Broad-based growth	Inclusion; comprehensive development
Key elements	Boost exports; develop infrastructure; sound economic environment	Employment; good social services; safety nets	Opportunity; security; empowerment
Main partners (ministries)	Finance and Planning	Labor, Health, and Education, as well as Finance and Planning	All ministries; local government; donors; firms; civil society
Target areas	Capitals	Areas of productivity	Poor regions

INEQUALITY AND THE DISTRIBUTION OF GROWTH

Economists and grassroots development workers vary considerably in how they view poverty, as we have discussed, but they are even more divided about the importance of inequality. Some argue that the critical objective is to move the poor above the poverty line. If the most effective strategy for doing so leads to the non-poor doing well, perhaps even proportionally better, this really doesn't matter; in fact, it is a bonus. Others respond that relative poverty is as important as absolute poverty. Poverty isn't just about what is needed to survive; it must be seen in the context of the country and the period. This argument is not new. In fact, Adam Smith (the father of conservative economics) described it in such relative terms in 1776, saying that poverty is about the want of the necessaries of life, but explaining this as follows:

> By necessaries I understand not only the commodities which are indispensably necessary for the support of life, but whatever the custom of the country renders it indecent for creditable people, even of the lowest order, to be without. A linen shirt, for example, is, strictly speaking, not a necessary of life. . . . But in the present times, through the greater part of Europe, a creditable day-labourer would be ashamed to appear in public without a linen shirt. (Smith 1776)

He went on to say that shoes would be regarded a "necessary" in England but not necessarily so in Scotland or France. The "basket of necessaries" he would have used to calculate a poverty line would include "those things which the established rules of decency have rendered necessary to the lowest rank of people."

In a low-income country it is typical for those at the poverty line to spend 80 percent of their income on basic food. In contrast, the Canadian poverty line, calculated in 2001 by the National Council of Welfare, includes a comprehensive array of "reasonable needs" for a socially acceptable life in that country, including basic cable-TV subscription. This would be the height of luxury for the wealthiest people in many poor countries. So what are the "necessaries" for dignified life in poor countries today? And do these automatically rise as the society as a whole gets richer? Those who answer yes to the last question often define a poverty line as a proportion (say half) of the average income, but this leads to the perverse conclusion that rich countries have higher poverty rates than uniformly poor countries, and in Canada the richest provinces have the highest "poverty rates" because the large number of wealthy people living there have driven up average incomes.

The only satisfactory approach is to establish, through participatory research, civil society consultation, and attitude surveys, what is regarded as necessary for dignified life, and then to calculate the income needed to afford these things. This analysis is still in its infancy.

Two things are evident: (1) growth is needed to reduce poverty; and (2) poverty reduction is much stronger when poor people participate in that growth. Box 3.2 illustrates how growth and redistribution both affect poverty levels, but do so differently, under different scenarios. There is strong evidence that social indicators relate to inequality as well as to poverty. US states with high income-inequality also have

---

Box 3.2 The importance of being equitable

The poor may benefit when a country's economy grows, but do they benefit enough? Classical economists argue that, if the growth is broad based, everyone's income will rise in step. True, but if the GNP (and everyone's income) rises 10 percent, the *absolute* gap between rich and poor grows, because 10 percent of the pittance the poor earn is very little, while a 10 percent increase for the rich is a lot.

This is best appreciated by looking at what happens to a typical wealth distribution, and to numbers falling below the poverty line, under different scenarios. The first diagram shows a typical plot of the proportion of the population (y axis) falling within a particular income range (x axis)—Curve 1. The dotted line is the poverty line for the country. The area to the left of this line represents the proportion of poor within the country.

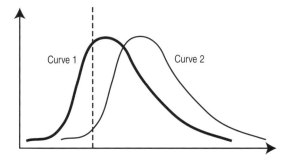

Curve 2 to the right shows what would happen if there were growth from which everyone received an equal dividend; this truly would be a rising tide lifting all boats, and poverty would be substantially reduced. But this doesn't happen. The next sketch shows a more realistic scenario: broad-based growth in which the rich and poor enjoy the same percentage increase in their income

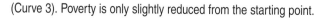
(Curve 3). Poverty is only slightly reduced from the starting point.

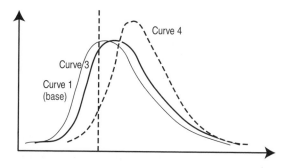

Curve 4

Curve 3

Curve 1
(base)

Greater poverty reduction could result from a similar aggregate growth, but one accompanied by a narrowing of the distribution, for example, through progressive taxation, transfers to the poor, or poverty-focused social services (Curve 4). In this third scenario the problem of poverty is largely solved, and it remains politically feasible, since the presence of some growth means that only the very wealthiest are actually worse off due to the redistribution.

Except in countries where most of the population is uniformly poor, effective poverty reduction requires as much attention to issues of distribution and increasing the life chances of the poor as it does to promoting growth.

high mortality rates, apparently because inequality tends to be found side by side with weak civic traditions and hence higher indicators of stress and community tension (*Scientific American,* July 2000).

Distribution is important, not just because it relates to poverty reduction, but also because it is pivotal to questions of the political economy. Nations are not at ease with themselves when social divides are conspicuous and growing. The belief that today's globalization heightens these divides motivates many in civil society to resist it. The spectacular wealth of the few and the multimillion dollar pay raises for TNC chiefs are viewed by ordinary people as simply *wrong*, yet governments do little about them—not even urge restraint. Only civil society makes the connections between globalization and immoral wealth (or immoral poverty). The connections, in truth, may be tenuous. Bill Gates lost about $6 billion during 2001 (arguably making him the poorest person in the world in income terms, while still being the richest in asset terms)—but no one benefited from that loss; his assets weren't distributed—they simply vanished. Conversely, when wealth is generated, it isn't necessarily at anyone's expense. But a system that allows some to make easy fortunes while denying even basic opportunities to most has to be challenged. And, thank goodness, civil society is doing just this.

Deregulation of financial markets has produced a cadre of super wealthy. UNDP reported in 1996 that the world's 358 billionaires had assets exceeding the combined incomes of 45 percent of world's population (Faux and Mischel 2001). The United States had thirteen billionaires in 1982—and 170 today. In the mid 1960s the income of CEOs in major US corporations was about forty times, on average, that of the production workers; now it is 419 times (Bauman 2001). Michael Eisner of Disney, for example, may receive a relatively humble base salary ($1 million a year in 2001), but this is dwarfed by his bonuses ($8.5 million in 2000) and share options (a world record $570 million in 1997) (*Forbes*, January 16, 2001, and May 13, 2002). During 2001, a year of US recession, the compensation of the boards of the largest two hundred corporations actually rose by 10 percent (*The Economist*, April 6, 2002).

In 1980s inequality grew in all major OECD countries except Italy; it grew fastest in the United States and the UK. In the United States the pre-tax income of the richest 1 percent grew 93 percent from 1977 to 1995, while productivity rose 22 percent. In this period the median worker's hourly wage (inflation adjusted) fell 3 percent for women and 13 percent for men. We now turn to look more systematically at distribution on a global level.

WEALTH AND POVERTY OF NATIONS

There have always been rich countries and poor countries, but the wealth gap between countries has been growing since records began. In 1820 the UK was the richest country, and its wealth (in GNP per capita) was just three times that of the poorest (then China). By 1870 this GNP ratio for richest and poorest countries had grown to 11, by 1913 to 16, by 1960 to 38, by 1985 to 52, and by 1999 to 74 (see Figure 3.1). If we compare not single countries but the richest twenty countries and the poorest twenty countries, we find that the ratio was 15 in 1960 but rose to 30 in 1999 (World Bank, 2000c). This accelerating divide during the current era of globalization is alarming but substantiates the anxiety projected by civil society.

Many Western economists argue that future opportunities are more important than past records. They maintain that when developing countries adopt sound economic policies they will grow and can start closing the gap with their industrialized counterparts. Some World Bank economists have optimistically stated that "economic power is shifting away from industrialized countries for the first time in more than a century. The economies of the new globalizers are growing far more rapidly than those of the OECD economies" (2002b). Really?

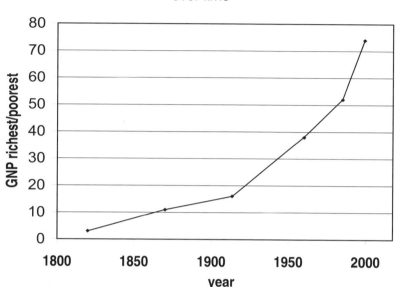

Figure 3.1 Ratio of richest to poorest country's GNP over time

It is true that the growth rates of East Asia (averaging 7.2 percent a year from 1998 to 1999) are much higher than for high-income countries (averaging 2.6 percent in the same period). But the starting points of these two groups of countries were very different. The GNP per capita in East Asia is $1,000, while that of high-income countries is $25,730. Hence the growth dividend averaged $72 a person in East Asia and $669 a person in high-income countries. East Asia may be *accelerating* faster, but it is premature to say it is catching up. It is like saying that a car setting off to catch up with a jet liner at full cruising speed is doing a good job because it is accelerating faster than the jet.

Even if East Asia is able to maintain indefinitely its current rate of growth (or acceleration), the absolute wealth gap between it and the high-income countries will continue to rise for fifty years, and it would take seventy-four years to catch up. Yes, it is encouraging that some countries are able to maintain rapid growth, but talk of catching up is an exaggeration.

The more rapid growth of East Asia (and to a lesser extent Latin America) means that the South collectively is occupying a slightly bigger share of the global economy (see Table 3.3). But this must be celebrated with caution. Throughout the 1990s, the high-income countries lost a 1 percent share of world economy to middle-income countries, but growth is largely the story of two countries—the United States and China. They have both expanded their economic share, while

Table 3.3 Share of world economy

Country/country group	1990	1999
High-income	79.3%	78.3%
Developing	20.7%	21.7%
low-income	4.2%	3.5%
middle-income	16.5%	18.2%
United States	26.0%	28.8%
Other high-income	53.3%	49.5%
China	1.7%	3.3%
Other developing	19.0%	18.4%

Source: World Bank 2000c.

other countries in their groupings have seen declining shares. During this period Sub-Saharan Africa's share fell from 1.4 to 1.1 percent.

What happens if we look at world population as a whole? In a unique analysis Branko Milanovic pools LSS data from ninety-one countries and shows that global income distribution polarized starkly from 1988 to 1993 (Milanovic 2002a). Average real incomes increased 5.7 percent during the period. But the richest quintile enjoyed a 12 percent increase, the poorest half saw no growth, and the bottom 5 percent saw a 25 percent fall. The richest 1 percent (50 million people) now earn more than the bottom 60 percent of the world's population (2.7 billion). In contrast, global distribution was relatively stable from 1960 to 1980 (Milanovic 2002b).

Within rich countries (such as the United States and the UK) the earnings gap has been rising over the past twenty years. In fact, the average hourly real earnings in the United States are now lower than they were in 1973 (before fringe benefits are included). From 1973 to 1993 the real pay of the bottom decile (poorest 10 percent) fell 21 percent for men, while the top decile's real pay rose 8 percent (for women workers the bottom decile rose 3 percent and the top by 29 percent).

GLOBALIZATION, INCOME, AND DISTRIBUTION

Having looked at poverty and discussed distribution, the important question now is, What is the connection with globalization? That the poor have become poorer isn't necessarily the fault of globalization.

Most live in countries or regions of countries that are quite marginal to world trade. But it does probably mean that globalization has helped make the rich richer. It is estimated that Americans now own about half of the world's entire financial wealth (*The Economist*, October 7, 1995).

Much has been written in recent years about the relationships among open trade policies, growth, poverty reduction, and income distribution. World Bank analysis by David Dollar and Aart Kraay (2001) paints an optimistic picture, using a large data set of trade, growth, per capital income, poverty rates, and income distribution over the last twenty years. They compare changes in poverty levels over time with changes in "trade openness" (defined as total trade, that is, imports plus exports, as a share of the country's GDP). They also compare these indicators with growth rates and conclude that some countries chose to take part in globalization, while others didn't; the globalizers have done well, while the others have fallen behind. These findings have been used in a major World Bank report (2002b) and have been widely quoted throughout the world by the advocates of economic integration, but could the data be interpreted in other ways?

Dollar and Kraay first compare growth and poverty (Figure 3.2). This demonstrates that the income of the poor generally rises pretty much in line with national income. This is relatively uncontroversial

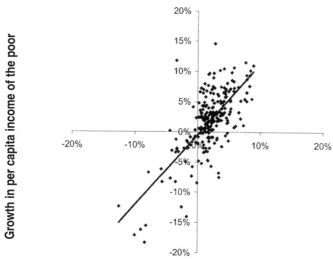

Figure 3.2 Growth in the poor's income compared with average growth

Growth in per capita income (overall)

Source: Dollar and Kraay 2001.

(but do remember the caveats about errors in poverty statistics), but it also means that the *absolute* benefits of growth go largely to the rich because of the unequal starting points of rich and poor. The "growth is everything" school has pounced on this correlation, however, to affirm its faith that poverty reduction is really just about maintaining high growth. It assumes a direction of causality that hasn't been proved. It is equally logical to conclude that the principal element of a growth strategy should be to reduce poverty (Rodrik 2001d).

The same data set reveals little correlation between growth and income distribution; in other words inequities do not apparently grow as societies as a whole become wealthier. But statistics about income distribution (usually measured by an indicator called the Gini coefficient) are even more prone to error than poverty statistics and tend to show much more sluggish change than is evident to people who work closely with the poor.

In comparing trade openness with distribution, Dollar and Kraay discern the opposite pattern to that which civil society generally asserts; they find a slight *improvement* in distribution as countries increase trade, but the correlation is not entirely convincing. Indeed, just changing a few points on their graph would lead to a different conclusion. Similarly they find a strong correlation between trade openness and growth (and hence poverty reduction). They conclude that a 10 percent increase in trade leads to a 5 percent increase in per capita income.

If we accept that growth and trade openness are correlated, what would it tell us? Openness is an *outcome*, as much to do with good fortune as good policy. Generally, countries are able to invest in export-oriented industries as they get richer, and hence trade openness will follow growth, rather than the other way around. What is irrefutable is that many countries have managed to break into international markets while others have remained relatively outside.

Dollar and Kraay argue that those remaining outside have fared relatively badly. They divide developing countries into two groups; the "globalizers," comprising twenty-four countries and 3 billion people, which doubled their openness since 1980; and the remaining "non-globalizers" (with 2 billion population) who reduced openness. They calculate that the average per capita GDP growth for the globalizers rose 5 percent in the 1990s (compared with 2 percent for rich countries), while the other group saw an actual decline (averaging –1 percent). The conclusion—integration is good for you—has been much quoted and underpins the policy advice that has long been given to developing countries. Since it contradicts a view offered by many in civil society, it warrants close scrutiny.

First, the list of globalizers includes many surprises. It includes China, India, Rwanda, Malaysia, Colombia, and Côte d'Ivoire—countries that are hardly classic examples of free trade—and Argentina, Zimbabwe, Nepal, and Haiti—countries that are not exactly economic paragons. It is particularly surprising that the World Bank bases a critical argument for capitalist trade on a group of countries dominated by those who are still communist (China and Vietnam) or adhere to strong central planning (India). In fact, given that the indicator used is the *change* in openness over the last twenty years, the group as a whole could be described as those countries that *resisted* integrating for the longest time and only started trading more once they had developed their internal markets. Conversely, some of the familiar free-traders (such as the East Asian "Tigers") are missing from the list simply because they moved into global trade before 1980.

Second, the non-globalizers include many countries to whom fate has been cruel: those depending on commodities whose price has collapsed (such as coffee producers), those facing particularly steep competition (for example, Zambia in copper exports), and those who suffer armed conflict.

Third, the performance of the globalizing group is totally dominated by four large economies—China, Brazil, India, and Mexico. These determine the statistics quoted by the Bank and, to all intents and purposes, the others in the group can be ignored.[1]

Fourth, if one looks at *today's* trade picture, rather than the change in trade over two decades, we find the unlikely conclusion that the globalizers trade *less* than the non-globalizers. For the "globalizers," as a whole, trade accounts for 42 percent of GDP (1999 data), while for all other developing countries trade is 60 percent of GDP (based on statistics from World Bank 2000c; Dollar and Kraay 2001). If the thesis is that *integration* (rather than *changes* in integration) is good for growth, the case hasn't been proved, and a different reading of the data suggests that countries that were cautious about free trade, and started integrating more recently, have done better than those who jumped in earlier.

It is also worth noting that the rich countries, which most keenly promote integration, are in reality rather *less* open than developing countries and are expanding trade more slowly (more slowly, in fact, than their economies are growing), as the following table shows.

Table 3.4 Trade as a percentage of GDP

	1990	2000
Developing countries	37.3%	51.2%
High-income countries	40.4%	38.5%

Source: World Bank 2000c and 2002c.

One of the *least* open countries is the United States, where trade accounts for just 23 percent GDP, compared with Iran (30 percent), Central African Republic (38 percent), and Sierra Leone (35 percent).

IS IT POLICY OR GEOGRAPHY THAT DECIDES?

It is important to distinguish between indicators of policy (like tariff rates) and outcome indicators (like the trade balance). A country may experience a sharp change in exports without changing its trade policy. For example, Zambia depends traditionally on copper exports, but in the 1980s more efficient producers entered the market and copper prices plummeted. Zambia had been the most open economy in the world in 1980, but now it comes well down the list without any significant change in policy.[2] If the purpose of analysis is to inform developing countries about their policy options, then one needs to track the impact of policy changes, not just changes in fortune.

Looking for patterns in openness, the clearest correlation is with size of population. The smaller the country, the more important is trade. Dividing countries into seven groups according to their population (ranging from small ones with populations of less than five million up to big ones with more than one hundred million), one finds that the importance of trade to the country falls steeply with the size of the country's population. This makes intuitive sense. Commerce is important for the generation of wealth and income; the smaller the country, the more one has to look outside one's borders for trading opportunities; they trade to survive. Large ones are better able to be self-sufficient; they have less need to import.

Table 3.5 Trade openness compared with population size

Population Range (million)	1–4	5–9	10–19	20–29	30–49	50–100	>100
Openness*	125.2	102.6	83.4	71.1	59.7	55.1	23.6
Number of countries	27	33	28	10	9	13	10
Average population per country	3.1	6.5	13.3	24.1	37.8	65.1	355.7

*exports plus imports of the country group as percentage of group GDP.
Source: World Bank 2000b.

Countries that are landlocked or affected by conflict tend to do less trade—again, an intuitive conclusion. It is also clear that *middle-income* countries tend to trade more. Low-income countries have the least opportunities; for exports they typically have to compete in the difficult raw commodities market, and they have little access to capital and technology for diversification or commodity processing. Middle-income countries, however, are able to invest in industrialization for both domestic and export markets. High-income countries have well-developed domestic markets; they import huge quantities, but as a proportion of their economy trade is quite small because domestic markets are strong.

CONCLUSIONS

The fairest conclusions are, first, that there is no clear correlation between open trade *policies* and growth or poverty reduction (in fact, growth seems to be higher where tariff rates are somewhat higher); second, countries tend to lower trade barriers as they become richer (but that is probably the direction of causality[3]); and third, large countries do well to industrialize first for their domestic markets, while small countries have to be more outward-looking (which can mean seeking regional rather than global integration).

The incentive to trade seems to have more to do with the size of the domestic market than political persuasion, though countries that are landlocked or in conflict have strong disadvantages. Conversely, the best economic performers today appear to be those who first concentrated on their domestic markets and were late converts to integration. All rich countries today also used trade protection during the initial stages of their growth.

This was the path of the Asian Tigers. South Korea, for example was a very poor, farming-based country in the 1960s when it was recovering from civil war. Its per capita GDP was below that of Ghana or Sudan. Its interventionist government set up or encouraged the establishment of strategic industries and protected them through import substitution policies. It also helped create a more equitable society by instituting land reform and investing heavily in education at all levels. Having built capacity by catering to the growing domestic market, the government then switched strategy to export promotion. Again by direct investment in high-potential industries, the government helped its industrialists foster niche markets, and the story of a miracle was born. The government realized that if export growth was to be sustainable, it should adopt a free-trade policy by removing barriers to imports, but it took this step from a position of trading strength.

China's foray into trade has been a similarly integrated process. The government has been the major investor in and owner of export companies. These are mostly quite insulated from industries catering for the domestic market. Due to the success of China's export processing zones, the massive inflow of FDI into export production, the managed exchange rate, and public expenditure that conceals subsidies, the government has been able to promote exports, protect its domestic markets, and gain admission to the WTO all at the same time—a feat that only one other country (the United States) has achieved.

Trade is important for developing countries, but it is much better to build that trade on strong foundations. Pressing developing countries to liberalize their imports and compete with one another in a restricted range of export markets won't help them build these strong foundations. A pro-poor trade strategy must start with industrialized countries removing barriers to third-world trade, and developing countries cooperating with one another, so that collectively they have more chance to build production capacity and more bargaining power in wider world markets.

Such arguments have been presented by the global economic justice lobby, and in particular the development NGOs and Southern advocacy groups (such as Third World Network). They are angry with the rosy pronouncements of the World Bank and others about globalization being good for the poor, when their own evidence from working in poor communities suggests widening inequalities and heightened risks. They are more prone to agree with Nobel economist Joe Stiglitz, who says that "globalization today is not working for many of the world's poor"; many agree with him, however, that the answer isn't to abandon globalization, because it has also brought great benefits. "The problem is not with globalization, but with how it has been managed" (Stiglitz 2002).

Part of the problem lies with the international economic institutions—the IMF, World Bank, and WTO—which help set the "rules of the game." In other words, the problem is with politics, and the failure of global institutions to serve the needs of the poor adequately. It is to these deficiencies of democracy and global governance that we now turn.

4

How Global Changes Affect Politics

From Delegative to Deliberative Democracy

The last two chapters looked at the economic consequences of globalization for the South and the poor, but the world is changing in other ways too, profoundly affecting democratic politics. Citizens are increasingly disinclined to see democracy limited to the periodic selection of representatives or presidents. They want a more direct voice in the particular policy debates that most concern them—as the plethora of independent advocacy groups, lobbyists, and think tanks in Washington, D.C., attests. Those policies are often the preserve not of national parliaments or legislatures but of supranational or sub-national politics or corporations. There is a "democracy deficit" in today's policymaking that impairs the management of globalization, as the last chapter concluded. We will now unpack these issues by looking at the newly emerging "marketplace of ideology," the symptoms and causes of the deficit, and the new challenges for global governance.

I experienced a taste of this debate at a recent reception. I was introduced to a backbench MP[1] as being with the London School of Economics' Centre for Civil Society. The MP turned quite aggressive, saying, "The only legitimate representatives of civil society are parliamentarians; why don't you study them?" I responded that the center *does* look at political parties and parliamentarians' associations, but that I disagreed with his argument. Many unions, churches, environmental groups, and others have millions of members and can claim some representation; anyway, *legitimacy* in a debate doesn't just depend on size or votes—it also derives from expertise and track record on the issue.

The MP grudgingly recognized that unions and others are different; *they* should be heard, but this shouldn't extend to every "one-man-and-a-dog outfit calling itself an NGO and having no accountability." On the contrary, I replied, *any* group has a right to speak—because freedom of speech is cherished in democracies. Problems only arise if the media, other CSOs, or parliamentarians promote a dubious group's cause, lending it unwarranted legitimacy without checking its credentials or its information. It's the column inches, not the title NGO, that is powerful. I explained that the public's increasing support of CSOs is partly due to dwindling faith in electoral politics delivering the democracy people want, that pressure groups are often better at hitting the issues of public concern. This was too much for my MP—and he sidled off.

What puzzled me was his defensiveness; he clearly saw NGOs as a challenge to his position in some way, perhaps competing with parliamentarians as conduits for citizens' wants and fears.

Was he right to feel defensive? True, civil society advocacy has much more influence than a decade ago, particularly in the international arena. And true, many advocacy groups are very small, but what is wrong with this? Those who keep chickens in their backyard have as much right to sell eggs as a multinational, providing they keep within the laws. There is no size requirement in the private sector—and there is no good reason why there should be for NGOs either. It is also true that many influential groups are not membership-based, are self-appointed, and are accountable only to their handpicked boards and their donors. But this doesn't negate CSOs' policy role. On any issue there may be many groups who have a view—a whole marketplace of ideas. Those who take or *shape* the decisions (including parliamentarians, the media, and governments) must act responsibly as they listening to and filter this diversity of voices.

Ignoring citizens' views is irresponsible, but so too is legitimizing an undeserving voice—perhaps for reasons of sensationalism or political rivalry. In this marketplace, as in commerce, the maxim is *caveat emptor*—let the *buyer* beware. Interest groups all parade their views, touting for customers. If they concoct facts, act maliciously, or falsely claim to speak for others they should be penalized—sometimes by law (when crimes such as fraud, libel, or incitement to racial hatred are committed), sometimes by peer pressure within civil society, and sometimes through ostracism from future policy dialogue. But if their facts are sound, their credentials honest, and they don't break any laws, then let them sell their ideas as energetically as they can. The onus is on the consumers of this advocacy to beware.

Was the MP correct about parliamentarians being the sole true voice of civil society? Manifestly not. If people start abandoning a public service for a private alternative, its defenders need to investigate what drives the defection, not challenge the legitimacy of the private providers. Similarly, if voters don't think electoral democracy answers all their political interests—and so turn to CSOs and away from parliamentary elections—the problem is with the democratic process not with the voters. MPs may have won elections—perhaps with a dwindling and unenthusiastic turnout—but are losing the confidence of constituents. *Caveat victor!*

RIGHTS AND RESPONSIBILITIES
IN THE IDEOLOGICAL MARKETPLACE

That pressure groups erode democracy is a charge increasingly leveled by those most comfortable with the status quo. After the street protests at the WTO meeting in Seattle in 1999, there was a chorus of such attack. *The Economist* (September 23, 1999), for example, said:

> The increasing clout of NGOs, respectable and not so respectable, raises an important question: who elected Oxfam, or, for that matter, the League for a Revolutionary Communist International? Bodies such as these are, to varying degrees, extorting admissions of fault from law-abiding companies and changes in policy from democratically elected governments. They may claim to be acting in the interests of the people—but then so do the objects of their criticisms, governments and the despised international institutions. In the West, governments and their agencies are, in the end, accountable to voters. Who holds the activists accountable?

The concern boils down to three issues: who elects the pressure groups; to whom are they accountable; and what right do they have to extract confessions from large institutions? The answers are actually very easy—though different for the "respectable" and "not so respectable" ones. The latter largely comprise amorphous groups of citizens that don't purport to be much else; they rarely engage in dialogue with their targets so aren't about extracting confessions; they are self-selected rather than elected (as freedom of assembly allows); and their accountability is as any citizens—if they damage property, intimidate people, or cause a public nuisance, there are laws that can be used against them (*policing* such laws is a more vexing question).

The elections and accountability mechanisms of the "respectable" groups are similar to those used in the private sector, and are largely internal. The larger, more influential ones, such as Oxfam, have management structures supervised by boards of trustees, who select the top managers and replace retiring trustees. Membership CSOs such as unions use direct elections to choose officers. While company boards care mostly about the "bottom line," their CSO counterparts focus on the "top line"—the headlines, column inches, membership, and public profile. Both are concerned about *sustainability*, and for both this means maintaining quality products and a good image. So pressure groups do care, not just about what their supporters think of them, but also about the opinion of the media, parliamentarians, and the public at large—hence they do need to be careful with their analyses and strategies. Of course, they aren't subject to nationwide elections, but neither are corporate chiefs or editors of newspapers, and *they* aren't reserved with their views.[2]

If activists do extract "admissions of fault" from companies and governments (as do journalists, of course), this is surely a measure of their effectiveness. No one wants faults perpetuated. When Cow and Gate broke ranks with other manufacturers in the marketing of baby milk in developing countries, this was because the NGOs had created a world view about the importance of protecting breast milk that the company thought it better to be part of than to oppose. When aerosol manufacturers started replacing the propellants they used well before laws compelled them to do so, this was because NGOs had won a global debate about the ozone layer. And when the World Bank accepted that it could, after all, spearhead debt forgiveness for poor countries without jeopardizing the world financial system, this was another policy change driven largely by pressure groups whose veracity is not now questioned.

Misgivings about pressure groups stem from an assumption that they seek to be more than most actually do. They don't aim to *replace* legislatures and political parties but to influence the decisions they make through argument. Hence, they can only be effective if democracy is working; they are *adjuncts*, not *threats*, to democracy. They achieve influence by persuading people to *use* the democracy at their fingertips—not just through their voting choices, but as consumers, shareholders, lobbyists, demonstrators, educators of their children, workers, employers, and investors. "Pressure groups demonstrate that individuals do matter and can meaningfully help shape society" (Secrett 1996).

While they don't usurp the institutions of *democracy,* in some Northern countries they have to some extent replaced the moral and mass leadership previously assumed by the church and trade unions. While pressure groups appear youthful, relevant, fashionable, and fun, unions and the church have lost their appeal.

On the surface there's a paradox. Popular newspapers remind us, in response to foreign threats, that we would die to preserve our freedoms, our democracy—yet we can't be bothered to walk five minutes to cast our vote. Are we only concerned about democracy in countries that lack it? Apathy plays a part, but also a transformation in what we mean by democracy. Though disenchanted by our politicians, we are getting keener on other conduits for our voice: pressure groups, taking part in demonstrations, confronting local officials or our boss, writing to the local paper, mounting petitions, and so on. Elected delegates are only a small part of today's democracy. The transformation under way, particularly in rich countries, is from *delegative* to *deliberative* democracy. David Held argues that this new dynamic of "cosmopolitan democracy" occurs because we now live in a world of overlapping communities of interests and fate, and hence a political system in which we are represented just according to our physical locality is anachronistic. Modern communications and the growth of civil society make possible more direct engagement between citizens and decision-makers (Held 1998).

This harks of the direct democracy of Ancient Greece, in which all native-born citizens (except slaves and women) could gather in the forum to speak and vote on any issue that concerned them. This was rule *(kratein)* of the people *(demos)*. As city-states grew, such decision-making became too cumbersome, and the practice of electing delegates to represent a constituency was born. Now, it appears, we can return to direct democracy.

This trend is triggering the controversy about the governance of pressure groups and other CSOs, but the more important question is why we are so disenchanted by the delegative processes. At the heart of decision-making, from local to the highest global level, lies a democracy deficit; this has been greatly exacerbated by the changes connected with globalization. CSOs have been prominent in exposing this deficit and seeking remedies—albeit ones that may assign too much prominence to their own organizations. The deficit has five aspects:

- *Ideology:* political parties have become less relevant to the political cleavages that concern most people (especially in rich countries); pressure groups and social movements are natural leaders in these newer debates;
- *Integrity:* parties in much of the world seem increasingly mired in sleaze and nepotism, often associated with their fund-raising and TNC links;
- *Representivity*: electoral candidates rarely reflect the diversity of the electorate;
- *Sovereignty:* most national governments experience dwindling autonomy as they become powerless to buck trends set by global powers (and in some countries the state has failed or has little authority in parts of the country);

- *Reach:* in the globalizing world, traditional institutions of democracy don't hold sway over the many decisions affecting everyday life made in IGOs such as the WTO, IMF, and global corporations.

The rest of this chapter looks at the symptoms of the ailment, how they have arisen, the role civil society plays in addressing them, and how principles of "good governance" could be applied to corporations and international forums.

SYMPTOMS OF THE DEMOCRACY DEFICIT

Public confidence in the democratic processes has waned over two decades, as is evidenced by falling voter turnout, declining membership of political parties, reduced confidence in politicians and governments, increasing citizens' actions against corporations, widespread hostility toward IGOs, and the rapid growth of the "global protest" movement (see Chapter 8). Few would abandon democracy or the chance to elect parliamentarians, but most are increasingly underwhelmed by the choices. Ironically, one of the world's most famous politicians, Winston Churchill, best summed up the current mood: "Democracy," he once said, "is the worst form of government—except for all the others."

Declining voter turnout

A University of California study showed that in eighteen out of twenty OECD democracies the voter turnout in the 1990s was lower than it was in the 1950s, excepting Sweden and Denmark, with the median change being a decline of 10 percent (*The Economist*, July 17, 1999). The turnout has declined most in countries where voter identification with parties is weak, such as the United States, Switzerland, and Japan, and holds up most in countries where there is strong class identification with parties, such as Scandinavia. In the UK general elections the turnout averaged 77 percent in the eight elections from 1945 to 1970, 76 percent in the nine polls from 1974 to 1992; it was 71 percent in 1997, and 59 percent in 2001. The turnout in US presidential elections averaged 80 percent in the eight elections from 1964 to 1992; it was 63 percent in 1996 and 51 percent in 2000. Less than half the electorate voted in the 1999 European Parliament election, and only 24 percent turned out in the UK. Even in the new democracies of Eastern Europe there are declining turnouts: in the Czech Republic from 96 percent to

74 percent (1990–1998); in Poland from 62 percent to 46 percent (1989–2001); and in Hungary from 75 percent to 57 percent (1990–1998) (data from www.idea.int).

Declining membership of political parties, while pressure groups grow

In the 1960s and 1970s people developed concerns about issues political parties appeared to ignore. They started to form and join pressure groups and social movements, particularly in the North—the start of deliberative democracy. These groups embraced civil rights, feminism, the environment, nuclear power, nuclear disarmament, the Vietnam War, anti-racism, and other causes. They grew rapidly and formed a new political culture of baby boomers that differed as radically from their parents' prewar political contours as their taste in music differed. Meanwhile, parties lost support, as they appeared increasingly old-fashioned and entrenched in old political thinking.

In *Democratizing Development* (1991), I pointed out that in 1971, when Greenpeace UK was born and when the British Labour Party had 700,000 members, no one would have credited that an organization concerned primarily with the marine environment could *ever* overtake Labour in membership. But that is what did happen—by 1990 Greenpeace's membership had risen to 320,000 and Labour's had slipped to 280,000.[3] The decline of the UK Conservative Party's membership has been even more dramatic. It was over two million in the mid-1960s and less than 350,000 in 2000. In some countries the decline of parties has been even sharper—a loss of two-thirds of all party members in France (Mair and van Biezen 2001).

A similar pattern is found in other industrialized countries. About 25 percent of the New Zealand electorate were party members in the 1950s, as were 15 percent of Italians and 10 percent of the French; by the 1990s this had declined to below 5 percent for all of them (*The Economist*, July 24, 1999). In many countries specialist parties have emerged that focus specifically on the "cosmopolitan" issues of public interest (Held 2002), particularly the Green parties. These have devoted memberships but mostly do not command large votes.

Pressure groups have a growing role, says the director of Friends of the Earth UK, only because the public is "dissatisfied with traditional political institutions and processes that drive public debate and decision-making." If the parliamentary process, the media, industry, and so forth "adequately represented the particular interests of citizens, ensured their direct participation in community affairs, and dealt with their concerns, there would be no pressure groups" (Secrett 1996).

There is less *identification* with parties today, as well as lower memberships. In 1960, 40 percent of Americans claimed to be either "strong Republicans" or "strong Democrats," but only 30 percent did so by 1996. In the UK the decline has been steeper; in 1964, 44 percent of voters expressed a "very strong" affinity with one party, but by 1997 this had fallen to 16 percent (*The Economist*, July 24, 1999).

Reduced confidence in politicians and governments

Opinion polls in a range of countries show decreasing respect for politicians. One survey of fourteen OECD countries (Putnam et al. 2000) shows that public confidence in legislatures has declined from the 1970s to the 1990s in eleven of them, for example, public confidence in the House of Commons in the UK halved (from 48 percent) from 1984 to 1995, while in the United States confidence that the government does the right thing halved over forty years (to 40 percent in 1998). Public trust and confidence in *politicians* declined in thirteen of the countries (all except Netherlands). Politicians are seen as making false promises, dishonest, just interested in getting votes, out of touch, and not caring. A 1998 survey of sixteen to twenty-one year olds in the UK found that 71 percent thought how they vote would not affect their lives.

Increased citizens' hostility to corporations

Transnational corporations have been popular targets for international civil society campaigns since the 1970s, not necessarily reflecting anti-capitalism but rather deep concern about the accountability and morality of large corporations. A prominent early campaign targeted Nestlé and other baby-milk manufacturers for their third-world marketing practices. This was followed by campaigns targeting companies profiting from apartheid in South Africa, pharmaceutical manufacturers, banks at the heart of the third-world debt crisis, companies using sweatshop or child labor, companies who deplete rainforests, and others (see Chapter 10).

Over time, campaigns have become more sophisticated and forceful as the spectrum of activities has stretched. Consumer boycotts, letter-writing campaigns, publicity events, and direct advocacy continue, but now alongside many other tactics. At one end of the spectrum there is violence to property (such as McDonald's restaurants and animal-testing laboratories), and at the other end there are ethical investors with multibillion-dollar portfolios earnestly negotiating reforms. TNCs are

Box 4.1 The baby-milk campaign and the birth of global campaign networks

Campaigns against unethical baby-milk marketing started in the early 1970s, as scientific evidence revealed high levels of infant diarrhea and death associated with the use of infant formula where water supplies are contaminated and where parents are too poor to use the right concentration of formula. High-pressure sales tactics spurred the rapid, inappropriate growth of third-world sales.

By the late 1970s there was massive public support for these campaigns in many countries, but few governments had taken decisive action. Governments in developing countries found the companies too powerful to restrain (and many politicians and health ministry officials were in their pay), while Northern governments thought it wasn't their problem and didn't want to appear anti-business. A turning point was a consultative meeting organized by UNICEF and WHO in Geneva in 1979; NGOs and manufacturers were invited as well as health specialists and government representatives. While getting all the stakeholders around a table on a controversial issue is standard practice now, then it was truly path breaking and daring. I attended for Oxfam.

Looking back on that event, I realize how much easier transnational campaigning has become, thanks to new and cheaper communications. Six NGOs who actively campaigned on the baby-milk issue were present; for years we had exchanged information by post, and even the rare phone call, but this was the first time most of us had actually met. We were able to discuss common strategy for the first time, and we found we liked each other! Today, the first step in any new international campaign is a meeting of the activists to map out a global strategy; they don't have to wait until a UN agency happens to invite them all to a meeting.

I also realize how powerful networks have become. At the end of the meeting we held a press conference announcing the launch of an international campaign. I wondered what impact this would have; after all, our group included well-known organizations like the International Organisation of Consumers Unions, War on Want, Oxfam, and the Inter-Faith Center on Corporate Responsibility in the United States. Surely journalists would be more interested in these, rather than the launch of a loose new organization that had neither office, staff, nor bank account. But I was quite wrong. There was lively coverage, and the International Baby Foods Action Network (IBFAN) was born. More impressively, IBFAN's launch immediately empowered NGOs interested in this issue throughout the world. They could join IBFAN, become part of a movement, and be globally connected. Again, this was radical innovation then, but old hat now. The second step in any international campaign today is to choose the name and logo for the global network.

taking ethics very seriously, if for no other reason than the desire to avoid a tarnished image in their home country.

Hostility toward intergovernmental organizations

Since the early 1980s there has been increasing CSO criticism of the environmental and social record of IGOs. Initially this largely came from international NGOs, and the main target was the World Bank. Later, trade unions, student groups, churches, and others joined in. The scope also broadened from specific World Bank projects to a critique of the underlying paradigm, in particular liberalization and structural adjustment, and the IMF—and later the WTO—became targets too as the global protest movement got under way.

In recent years CSO pressure has intensified greatly; protests greet almost any major international meeting of political leaders. Since the first anti-WTO protest in Geneva in 1998, specific campaigns have coalesced into an amorphous movement for global change. While specific issues are still cited (from World Bank–financed projects to the protection of intellectual property) the activists' main goal is the rejection of neoliberal politics and the search for a "different world." This is the subject of Chapter 8.

The rise of protest and the increasing sophistication of transnational civil society campaigns are changing the face of politics. The old left-right schism is now matched by a different divide: between parochialism and internationalism. Hence, Republicans and Democrats joined forces in 2002 to force a parochial decision to protect the US steel industry from imports. Those who condemned it were TNC executives (who fear a retaliatory trade war), consumers' associations (who know that products will be dearer as a result), churches, and development NGOs. While the Old Left often has sympathy with the global activist, and Old Right with the global corporatist, we increasingly find alliances between the globalists and the parochialists.

WHAT ARE THE CAUSES OF THE DEMOCRACY DEFICIT?

Democracy has never been perfect. In ancient Greece, where it was born and named, all freemen could attend forums to deliberate any aspect of public life. Universal franchise wasn't in vogue until well into the twentieth century, much later in most developing countries. But for a brief window after World War II, at least in Western Europe, the institution of democracy probably hit its peak. Then a decline set in as its deficiencies became increasingly apparent and it became devalued in the eyes of voters (or *non*voters, as we increasingly are). Civil society can play an important role both in exposing the deficiencies and in addressing them.

Deficiency of ideology

The main political parties in most rich countries remained locked into traditional left-right divides—particularly over the ownership of the means of production—long after they ceased being voter priorities. Citizens are more concerned about *what* is produced and for what sort of society. Recently, there has been some modernizing of parties. None in the North can appear credible these days if they don't have clear policies on the environment, gender, human rights, and an array of other CSO-promoted issues.[4] Likewise, in the South, opposition parties prioritize issues of accountability, participation, and corruption. But the way in which parties adopt such policies, parade them while in opposition, and then neglect them once in office appears reactive and insincere. Parties in power are managers of huge enterprises, and like their counterparts in business or other walks of life they need to handle many issues consistently and maturely. Yet they appear to lurch from one priority of the moment to another, capturing plaudits (and votes) where they can, and "fighting fires" as disasters loom.

The British Labour government came into office in 1997 proclaiming its priorities to be "education, education, education." But as crises erupted, this seemed to be forgotten; the absorbing issue of the day became first the Millennium Dome, then foot and mouth, then trains, and so on—often issues that would never motivate people to vote. This is the *appearance*; the reality is different. All governments juggle a vast array of issues, but the media is fixated on scandal, the humiliation of ministers, and the hideous spectacle of Prime Minister's Question Time, in which political gladiators slog it out to hoots of derision or glee from the assembled MPs. The media play their part in tarnishing democracy. The United States tells a similar story. Bill Clinton won in 1992 by defining *the* issues as "the economy, stupid" and "jobs, jobs, jobs." Once in office the ideology evaporated as Whitewater-gate, the embarrassing failure of health reform, and other crises dominated.

Most mainstream parties in mature democracies are aging; they were born in a different era. Times have changed, and so have ideologies—particularly with the end of the Cold War—but the parties have a hard time letting go of old thinking. They bolt on new voter interests as extras without defining new cleavages. And there is increasing convergence around some of the traditional battle lines, such as state versus private ownership of the means of production, the role of the state, the provision of health and education services, private-public partnerships, distributive taxation regimes, and many other issues. The election of a government is now more about choosing whom voters trust most to manage budgets and civil servants than ideology.

As the costs of winning elections increase, in some countries (notably the United States), political success owes more to the ability to raise money (or already being rich) than to oratory or political conviction. George W. Bush's campaign funds for the 2000 contest amounted to $191 million (Hertz 2001). Democracy US style is being reduced to the choice every four years between one multimillionaire and another as president.

Civil society has done much to define the landmarks of the new political topography: the environment, global warming, feminism, homosexual rights, human rights, corruption, globalization, and so on. Responsible pressure groups can help all parties develop policies that are forward looking, realistic, and compelling. They can help parties in power implement their policies and mobilize public support for them. And they can also help opposition parties identify flaws in government programs, so improving parliamentary debate. In these ways CSOs help strengthen, not undermine, democracy. Civil society has also been behind actions to reform campaign and political party contributions.

The "Third Way" philosophy espoused by center-left governments in recent years attempted to define a compelling new ideology, and its gestation was helped by a number of independent think tanks and other CSOs. It espouses the importance of market forces and an unfettered private sector (including improving state services). It recognizes the potential of globalization but encourages maximum devolution to the local level. It attests to the importance of sustained growth but also social inclusion and equality of opportunity. It emphasizes creating work opportunities rather than welfare. And it charts a stakeholder approach in which all players, including civil society, actively participate in policymaking (Giddens 1998). These are powerful ideas, but so far they have not captivated voters, who largely see the Third Way as a compromise between Old Left and capitalism.

Deficiency of integrity

Parliamentarians do have constituencies to represent, but they are also members of national legislatures and so must promote decisions for the national good. However, much of their time is spent on parochial matters—especially when elections loom. An infrastructure project of great national importance may be resisted fiercely simply because constituents don't want it sited near them. Conversely, powerful legislators can swing program resources to their constituencies, even if they would be better used elsewhere (the "pork barrel" effect). Or decisions that might be good for the nation (and the world) as a whole may be blocked due to strong local vested interest, as happened when US Congressmen for steel communities forced in protectionist tariffs. Local realities are important in politics, but ultimately legislatures should reach decisions that best suit the whole nation, not simply aggregate a series of local imperatives. Overemphasizing local issues is a crude strategy of politicians to cling on to office.

The motives of parliamentarians are more seriously tarnished in other ways, however. They take wild delight in calling for the resignation of their opposite numbers, even for trivial errors. They give voters the impression that they just want to maximize their power and diminish that of their opponents. And through their fund-raising strategies and sycophancy toward anyone wealthy, they convey an impression that any political principle can be sacrificed for a price. In many countries (from Italy to India) there is such a profusion of parties that only coalition governments are possible. This often leads to a haphazard array of policies built around political expediency rather than national priorities. As elections near, this deficiency becomes clearer as parties in office offer sweeteners to coalition partners and voters alike.

Civil society can compound some of these deficiencies. In particular, local pressure groups will hound their representative to protect local interests (*they* don't have anything other than a local mandate, after all). But CSOs can also redress the weaknesses—for example, through watchdog activities that subject legislators to broader accountability than local elections and that expose the sleaze and unflattering processes of politics.

Deficiency of representation

In most national elections the candidate slate is overwhelmingly middle-class, heterosexual, able-bodied males from the ethnic majority. Only 15 percent of the world's parliamentarians are women (Inter-Parliamentary Union website). In the UK, while 52 percent of the electorate are women, most mainstream parties still select few women candidates; only 9.2 percent of MPs were women in 1995. This is now changing, after the Labour Party introduced quotas for women candidates in the 1997 election, when 101 women were elected, increasing the proportion of women MPs to 19 percent. Labour's decision may have had more to do with gaining power than feminism. For a long time it enjoyed less support among women voters than among men. If women had voted in the same way as men, this would have reversed every postwar election defeat for Labour until 1979 and would have won them the 1992 election (*The Economist*, April 15, 1995). Fielding many more women candidates helped focus the campaign on social issues such as health and education, helped win Labour the election, and for the first time on record, gave Labour higher support from women voters than men.

With the exception of the Scandinavian countries, most legislatures are far from having gender and ethnic balance, distancing voters from the electoral process. CSOs such as EMILY's List (which supports women Democrat candidates in US elections), the 300 Group (which campaigns for gender equality in British parliament), Shevolution (which helps women contest for legislatures in transition countries), and equal opportunities campaigners have elevated diversity issues in government as well as other institutions. By helping generate greater diversity, they contribute to making politics seem relevant to a wider public.

Deficiency of sovereignty

Contemporary institutions of democracy were designed around the assumption that the highest political decisions are made at the national level. This pretty much applied until the 1970s. True, countries often cooperated in fighting wars or reaching trade deals, but these were voluntary agreements to pursue common interests. National sovereignty was the hub around which democracy revolved. The world has moved on since then, however. The most important decisions affecting voters are often made outside their nations' borders—through bilateral agreements, regional blocs, international forums, or simply the pressures toward global policy conformity.

Larry Diamond (1993) speaks of the "globalization of democracy," a near universal diffusion of popular demand for political freedom, representation, participation, and accountability—yet there is at the same time an erosion of democratic institutions and norms in many developing countries. Bilateral agreements between equally balanced powers can reflect a balance sheet of interests. But when, as in the real world, economic and political power is increasingly polarized, such agreements aren't between equals. Mexico can hardly change its trade policy without reference to its NAFTA partners, but the United States doesn't have to give much thought to the impact of its decisions on its neighbors. Similarly, in regional blocs (whether EU, NAFTA, MERCOSUR, ASEAN, or SADC) the appearance of collegiality belies the reality that power is not equally divided.

In regional and global processes there is also parochialism. Decisions are intended to benefit all countries, but in practice negotiators are fixated on issues of domestic concern. Politicians may make fine speeches about global challenges, but when it comes to action, most think first about the impact on their voters. The issue may be global and long term, but the political response is short term and parochial. The powerful players press policies that benefit their country most and block decisions that cost them most. The European Union demonstrates this. In key appointments it is beset with squabbles about the nationality of candidates, not their caliber. Decisions concerning key policies and the location of key institutions are resolved by compromise among the strongest national interests.

Smaller or weaker partners have a tough choice in international forums: Give way to the dominant nations or retreat into isolation. As cross-border transactions occupy an increasing role in today's business world, isolation becomes increasingly unviable. This requires conforming to global economic policy norms. Legislatures and voters, therefore, no longer decide on critical aspects of policy or even influence them. Governments of *other* nations effectively make such decisions. On such policy issues, democracy has become irrelevant. It is ironic that just when *formal* democracy extends to many new areas (Eastern Europe, Latin America, Africa, and East Asia), *substantive* democracy—the ability to participate in decisions affecting everyday life—has been eroded by the loss of autonomy of national states (Kaldor 2000).

This lack of policy choice is not just in regard to formal international agreements. In the globalizing world it is becoming less realistic to maintain policies that are significantly different from powerful neighbors or trading partners. If tariff structures differ, smuggling will be rampant; if taxation or labor policies are different from the norm, FDI and foreign companies will be lost; and if exchange rates are managed in ways that buck global norms, then speculators are likely to savage the foreign exchange reserves. Many governments have lost the use of exchange rates, capital controls, or money supply as tools of economic policy since these are left to market forces. Overwhelmingly, the instrument of choice is interest rate management, but even this is becoming less effective. It seems dangerous to be out of line with what the US Treasury and IMF think one should be doing, otherwise there could be a loss of confidence; moreover, the increasing use of interest-rate derivatives has reduced the impact that a rate change would have. Also, while traditional banks follow interest rates set by central banks, electronic money does not necessarily do so; hence, the power of central banks to set rates diminishes.

Many governments have decided that it is easiest just to accept defeat and go with the flow. This is the easiest option but not the safest, as the East Asian Economic Crisis demonstrated. The roots of Thailand's problem were hot money and property speculators. It had accepted capital account openness because this goes with trade openness and the neoliberal wisdom of the Washington Consensus about how economies ought to be run. Thailand's macroeconomic regime was a textbook case of going with the flow. But this meant it had entered a world in which a significant proportion of its liquidity could enter or exit its economy at the click of a mouse on Wall Street.

When investors started pulling out, the currency wobbled and the government intervened to stabilize it. But currency speculators turned the situation to their advantage in ways that magnified the financial crisis. They realized that the government didn't have enough foreign exchange to prop up the bhat. When Thailand sought IMF assistance, it was told that the Thai banking system and its lack of transparency was the problem. True, to a point, but the banks were just the transmission mechanisms through which hot money translated into harm. There is a parallel with the gun reform debate in the United States. As homicides and accidental shootings soar, curbing gun sales makes better sense than programs to improve the discipline of gun owners.

Civil society at the national level generally presents the most effective accountability pressure on governments who embrace globalization uncritically. Some CSOs are isolationists, some are nationalists, but many (perhaps most) are simply saying they want a different path toward regional and global integration, one that safeguards the interests and security of the vulnerable. Acting transnationally, civil society networks inject into international bodies (such as the World Bank, WTO, and IMF) concerns of communities that are critically affected by their decisions but whose governments are unable (or unwilling) to make such representation. And a global movement of CSOs is calling for a different management of globalization, based on global economic justice—offering more opportunity and less threat to the weak, and narrowing rather than widening disparities.

Deficiency of reach

Some decisions affecting citizens' lives slip outside the democratic orbit because they are reached in government forums outside their country or in corporations, not governments.

TNCs are enormous economic powers. BP's turnover is larger than the GNP of all least developed countries combined. The top two hundred have combined sales equivalent to more than a quarter of the world's GDP though employing only 0.6 percent of its work force (still an impressive 18.8 million people) (Curtis 2001). The top three hundred TNCs account for over a quarter of the world's assets (Hertz

Box 4.2 Addressing the democracy deficit in international institutions

IGOs have enormous impact on people's lives, particularly in the South, yet escape the democratic challenge, scrutiny, and accountability to which domestic institutions with far less impact are subject. They are technically answerable to member governments, but those whose populations are most affected by their programs have the weakest voices (and are often more concerned about landing funds than the needs of the vulnerable), while those with powerful voices make little social use of this accountability. Even in UN agencies power rests with those who contribute the most funds.

This deficit is found in the multilateral development banks (MDBs). Outside the United States, governments make little use of their national agencies to probe what the institutions do or to assess the quality of their work. True, they have seats on the boards of executive directors (EDs, particularly in the South, *share* a seat), but EDs tend to rely on information generated by the IGO, many go on to take jobs in it, and there is an unwritten rule among Southern EDs *never* to criticize other countries' projects. EDs rarely commission independent investigations, except in response to intense NGO pressure. Such lax scrutiny wouldn't be tolerated in a comparable institution at home. Some independent scrutiny is done by the World Bank's Inspection Panel, which receives and investigates grievances from anyone claiming damage as a result of World Bank–financed operations and reports directly to the Board, not to management. It is trusted by NGOs but seen by some as being too close to NGOs and too critical of the Bank (Wade 2001b).

The US government alone plays a fairly active watchdog role, though usually focusing on US interests (for example, concerns raised by US CSOs or US firms seeking World Bank contracts). Its aid agency (USAID) monitors a list of upcoming projects that are environmentally or socially sensitive; both the US Treasury and the Environment Protection Agency track such projects and sensitive policies; the General Accounting Office regularly investigates specific topics; there are occasional hearings on Capitol Hill about controversial issues (usually CSO prompted); and Congressional committees sometimes scrutinize issues and negotiate changes. No other government is as diligent—or meddlesome, depending on your point of view.

In truth, the most regular outside scrutiny is by civil society. This fills an important gap but is biased toward finding fault; complaints may be anecdotal and sometimes distorted; research quality may be poor; and what is often forgotten (or downplayed) is that they are government, not MDB, projects. The MDB is technically just the financier, though in practice is heavily involved in the design. Developing countries complain that more invasive scrutiny would violate their sovereignty, though perhaps a multilateral independent scrutiny mechanism might be more acceptable and would do much to close the democracy deficit in these institutions.

2001). And sales of the top five hundred TNCs have grown sevenfold since the early 1970s, while their employment has been virtually flat.

In 1970 there were 7,000 TNCs; today there are 63,000, with 690,000 subsidiaries (often located in the 2,000 EPZs in the South). Two-fifths of world trade comprises internal transactions within TNCs—often to capture tax advantages through "transfer pricing," that is, selling artificially cheap or dear so as to shift profits to a gentler tax regime. Tax avoidance is a high art. Rupert Murdoch's News Corporation, for example, pays only 6 percent tax on its profits worldwide (Hertz 2001); until 1998 it had paid no tax at all in the UK (where it controls 41 percent of newspaper readership) despite having accrued £1.4 billion in profit since 1987 (*The Economist*, March 20, 1999).

One or a handful of TNCs dominate almost any given sector globally. Nestlé and General Foods dominate the coffee trade; five companies provide 65 percent of pesticides; four companies dominate corn, wheat, tobacco, tea, and rice. In total, ten companies control over 60 percent of the global food chain, including seeds, fertilizers, pesticides, processing, and shipment (Korten 1995). TNCs wield great political as well as economic power, partly due to political party contributions, partly to their coziness with OECD governments. Hence, at the WTO ministerial meeting in Seattle, the 111–member US negotiating team included 96 members from the private sector (Curtis 2001).

National laws don't easily constrain a company that can shift effortlessly from one playing field to another. And governments are only concerned about misdemeanors on home soil, not the overseas wrongs of nationally registered companies. Little international law (and no specific intergovernmental bodies) applies to TNCs. When governments seek to regulate them, they face fierce opposition. For example, when the Massachusetts state government resolved not to do business with companies trading in Burma for human rights reasons (in response to CSO pressure), a group of TNCs went to the WTO disputes process. Similarly, when the European Parliament agreed unanimously to ban synthetic hormones in beef in 1996, the US government (under pressure from its meat and chemicals industries) took the case to the WTO (Hertz 2001).

Civil society, working internationally, is highly relevant to this deficit. As watchdog, it identifies illegal or immoral practices and mounts public campaigns to shame offenders. It promotes shareholder action to change corporate policy. It lobbies for laws against egregious practices such as corruption (and has promoted international action against bribery and money laundering). In the absence of agreed global practices, civil society works with leading industrialists to establish and police voluntary codes of practice (more than 60 percent of the top UK companies now have such codes [Curtis 2001]). It promotes ethical investment practices. And it exposes and campaigns against undue business influence in governments and international organizations (see Chapter 10).

TIME FOR "GOOD GOVERNANCE"

Though a latecomer to the field, the organization that has done the most in recent years to analyze the strengths and weaknesses of Southern governments and to assist reform is the World Bank. During the 1980s the World Bank pressed governments in economic difficulties to reform their policies. Many undertook structural adjustment programs, backed by loans from the World Bank and the IMF. Apart from the serious social costs that many (including myself) have written about and the social unrest generated that often led to the programs being abandoned, it is clear from the World Bank's evaluations that many of them failed *economically* simply because the government didn't implement the reforms it promised to. Sometimes the government wasn't serious (it wanted the first tranche of money but wasn't committed to the reforms), but more often it was simply weak—its officials couldn't handle the tasks, the relevant departments didn't coordinate, supervision mechanisms weren't in place, and information systems weren't up to the job.

Until the mid 1990s, though it had much to say about *policies*, the World Bank regarded how governments *behaved* as out of bounds. Its mandate forbids political considerations (just economic and development factors). However, the experience of adjustment shows that one can't separate these factors; moreover, having good governments is more important than having good projects—in fact, without the first you're not likely to have the second. This led to a new emphasis on good governance (not good *government*, which would imply political bias, favoring Western style democracy) to improve governments' effectiveness. The World Bank describes four pillars of good governance:

- *Transparency:* full public disclosure of all government plans, budgets, evaluations, minutes of meetings, and so on, unless commercial confidentiality or national security requires otherwise; public disclosure of draft proposals and reports, to encourage public debate (unless this would jeopardize the deliberative processes within government); legislation to increase transparency within the public sector.

- *Accountability*: ensuring that elected representatives and government officials are adequately monitored and held to account; ensuring legislatures have adequate processes and resources for this; cooperating with independent accountability mechanisms, both formal (such as government audits) and informal (such as the media and citizens' watchdogs); laws and institutions to combat corruption.
- *Rule of law*: providing a clear framework of rules and laws (compatible with international conventions on civil and political rights, and so on) that delineate what citizens can do and how the state protects them; ensuring that this framework is predictably applied, without favoritism or prejudice; ensuring all citizens are adequately compensated if they lose through any government program.
- *Citizens' voice*: enabling citizens to choose representatives, by elections and by opting to join representative organizations, such as trade unions; guaranteeing citizens' rights of free speech and free association; enabling all citizens to express views on decisions that affect them; consulting citizens in policymaking (World Bank 1992).

This set of principles would ensure that governments are honest, fair, responsive, efficient, and concentrate on citizens' priorities. It would also ensure that citizens are well informed about their rights and about government actions, that they are empowered to be active citizens, and therefore that they have confidence in the democracy.

The very same framework should be applicable to IGOs and TNCs, though their managers resist it. When pressure groups hound institutions for information, pipe up with questions at shareholders meetings, lobby executives with their views, demand meetings with top officials, trigger critical media enquiries, and mobilize citizen protest, in essence what they are doing is promoting good governance. If these principles were adopted formally and with good grace, the heat of opprobrium would probably lessen. The current shrillness is because the public thinks that these large institutions are not accountable (however fair that view is). If there were formal and independent accountability processes, the officials responsible for them would probably be much less hostile and less media-hungry than pressure-group activists.

Campaigns on the World Bank have largely been about good governance (and have been well described in Fox and Brown 1998 and P. Nelson 1995). NGOs have successfully pressed for an open-disclosure policy, which makes public many previously confidential documents. NGOs scrutinize World Bank activities to see if its policies, particularly social and environmental, are properly followed—and demand remedies when they are not. They encourage national (mostly OECD) legislatures to scrutinize and debate World Bank activities. NGOs have urged that policies be clear, predictably applied, and regarded as institutional law. They have been instrumental in creating the Inspection Panel. And they have pressed the World Bank to go ever further in consulting civil society and using participatory approaches. The reform process has been far from smooth. Some NGOs have been overly harsh, and some reforms are deeper in rhetoric than substance—but the World Bank is undoubtedly better equipped today for the task of poverty reduction than it was a decade ago, and much of this is due to pressure from international networks of NGOs who challenge it.

Some TNCs are undergoing equivalent experiences today. They are no longer private entities making decisions in private. A new era of corporate ethics and citizen accountability means that their CEOs are becoming increasingly answerable to the public. The proliferation of independent channels of information (from the serious to the scurrilous) enables activists and the media to probe what TNCs are doing and to make it impossible to trace leaks; institutions, therefore, might just as well learn to be open. TV and journalism are increasingly penetrating, and senior executives cannot avoid the cameras. It has become easier for activists to get shareholders, the media, and others to adopt their campaigns. The more TNCs avoid contact with pressure groups seeking to "extort admissions of fault," the more it looks like they have something to hide, and so the greater the risk of street protests.

There is a global trend toward stakeholder accountability and corporate citizenship—a trend that smarter TNCs realize is better to join than to fight. Hence, companies like Nike, GAP, and BP are now working with CSOs, for example, doing social or environmental audits of their activities, resolving controversial activities, and discussing new policies (we return to these issues in Chapter 10). But civil society isn't the only answer. Corporations and institutions can do much directly to improve governance. They can establish ethics or social and environment offices to serve as internal watchdogs and to liaise with external critics. They can publish more information about their activities. They can engage with ethical investment companies, including negotiating improvements where the investor identifies problems. They can hire advisors with relevant experience. They can commission academics or other independent parties for social and environmental audits of their operations. And they can appoint people of unquestioned integrity to their boards and management to guard ethical standards. Nestlé, for example, has been pilloried for twenty years by NGOs for flouting the internationally agreed-upon code on baby-milk marketing. It is now appointing an ombudsman to investigate and advise action on specific allegations of violation, hence for the first time giving an official conduit for complaint. If this proves to be effective, Nestlé may at last find peace with its critics.

There are real reputational advantages for an institution to engage actively with civil society. There are difficult choices about *which* groups and how much weight to vest in these processes, but these are teething problems. Getting to know the CSO community is like getting to know the media. A previously media-shy organization would be daunted by its first press conference. The press pack, like civil society, includes troublemakers and the constructive, the flippant and the serious. Regular experience quickly teaches how best to handle the media, whom to give exclusive interviews to, who to trust with fly-on-the-wall documentaries, and even who to ask for advice. The same applies to civil society.

CONCLUSIONS

This concludes Part One—how globalization has affected countries, people, and democracy—and why these issues are of such great importance to policy- and justice-oriented CSOs. We now turn to Part Two—looking at how globalization has affected civil society itself and provided it a framework of opportunities to expand its influence on the world stage. CSOs face a difficult choice. One direction leads to greater confrontation, more aggressive street demonstrations, more youthful hostility vented toward authority and more polarization and unease in our societies. The other direction, equally challenging, leads to negotiations and working for institutional reform—public and private.

There is no doubt about what will happen. Because of its plurality, civil society will surely go *both* ways. Deliberative democracy knows many styles of deliberation. Hence, the future of contention is largely in the hands of the institutions themselves. The more responsive they are to dialogue, the more confident CSOs will be in constructive engagement. But if they ignore groups who want to engage, then those groups will lose prestige and support, leaving street activists the stronger. Conversely, NGOs who get coopted into ethical dialogue for show only undermine more radical reform efforts. An alternative scenario is the reform of *delegative* democracy, such that national legislatures link internationally and agree upon a formal governance framework for

IGOs and TNCs—but I doubt this will happen any time soon. Politicians the world over are too myopic, unable to see further than the boundaries of the constituencies they represent, and unable to think beyond the time scale of the next election.

Part Two

How Global Change Affects Civil Society

5

This Is the Age of a *Civicus*— The Rise of Civil Society

The last two decades have generated enormous changes in world economic affairs, including those described in Part One of this book, but equally profound has been the transformation of civil society. The same technical and political opportunities that have shaped business and economics have enabled the sector to grow meteorically in size, influence, and resources, and its roles have multiplied. In the realm of international policy it is particularly powerful. This chapter charts this ascendancy, offers definitions and descriptions of the sector, discusses the growth of transnational CSOs and activities, explains why and how advocacy has become more prominent, describes the emerging tactical diversity, and concludes with a note on the dilemmas tactics can pose, based on my own experience inside and outside the World Bank. Subsequent chapters in Part Two look at specific areas of transnational civic activism, particularly those relevant to global change, and at the challenges and backlash that come with the ascendancy.

The proposition developed here is that there is an emerging community of CSO activists—a *civicus*[1]—who are, with varying degrees of formality and design, networking globally to tackle common issues that concern citizens and citizenship throughout the world. In the absence of established democratic channels for such citizen influence, this is both timely and powerful.

POWER SHIFT

The end of the Cold War brought a redistribution of power among states, markets, and civil society; governments are choosing, or being forced, to share power in many ways (economic, political, social, and cultural) with businesses, IGOs, and CSOs (Mathews 1997). This presents civil society growth opportunities in both service provision and shaping policies—including tackling the "democracy deficits" of Chapter 4. Social changes have led to a more individualistic world, many argue, in which we emphasize personal interests more than national interests, identifying with CSOs that best fit our interests. These and other factors have heightened public trust, awareness, and use of civil society.

CSOs confront enormous opportunities today, thanks to the transition toward democracy and more liberal values in most of the world, cheap information and communications technology, the relative ease of world travel, and an abundance of resources for civil society. The growing use of English as the medium of international (and especially Internet) communications has also made transnational networking easier.

Hence NGOs and other CSOs have often been faster than governments to respond to new global challenges and been able to strengthen the fabric of democracy where it is creaking with age or still in fragile infancy. They have been able to organize transnationally in advocacy and shaping public opinion. This isn't just because technology makes it easy or that coordinating globally advances their cause. Working transitionally also gives voice and international solidarity to citizens in countries where civil society is ignored or repressed, and it parades a strength CSOs are discovering to organize globally yet be embedded locally— hence being able to offer swift policy proposals and analysis in response to world events. This makes CSOs popular with the media and liberal politicians, and makes intergovernmental processes look sclerotic in contrast. However, it has surfaced questions as well: For whom do these pressure groups speak? How democratic are they?

Before looking at issues of its growth and diversity, it is timely to define civil society more precisely and to discuss what it offers in the context of the globalizing world.

What civil society means: from demos to "demos"

Civil society is, simply, the associational activity of people outside their families, friends, and work places that is not for profit-making purposes (the private sector), nor for governing (the government, or public sector). Association means the voluntary coming together of people to pursue their own interests or wishes—either physical coming together for common activities or a more spasmodic or remote form of association. What is important is that people *feel* that they belong.

Civil society, then, spans a wide spectrum from the ancient Greek notion of *demos*, "members of a given public" (from which the word *democracy* derives), to demos in the sense of street protests. Scholte

(2001a) points out that in modern times the members of a given public can be an affinity group (ethnic, sexual orientation, occupation, class, or gender, for example) as well as a group of people within a nation.

Civil society comprises organizations (that may or may not have legal recognition) and less tangible institutions such as neighborliness, clan loyalty, or the tradition of free speech. CSOs include interest groups (ranging from cultural and sports societies to gangs and crime syndicates), churches and other religious organizations, professional associations, trade unions, mass organizations and social movements (such as peasants associations or the feminist movement), pressure groups, and NGOs[2] of various kinds. Civil society also includes new organizational forms such as the "dot-causes"—the web-mediated associations to promote specific political interests (see Chapter 8).

There are gray areas of overlap with both the private and public sectors, as Figure 5.1 illustrates. People join cooperatives for multiple reasons, but if the dominant one is to increase incomes, as with big-scale farmers' cooperatives, such business partnerships are closer to the private sector. Similarly, business associations such as chambers of commerce are not businesses, but their primary purpose is to advance the profit-making aims of their members. Overlapping with the public sector are organizations that are nonprofit and independent of government, but which are instigated and often financed by government (quangos, such as the BBC in UK), or which are privately instigated but exist essentially to secure government contracts. Political parties are also a gray area; some have characteristics of pressure groups (such as the Green parties of Europe), but parties that form governments are closer to the public sector. There are also areas of overlap between the public and private sectors.

Figure 5.1 shows the circles as the same size, but in reality the three sectors will have very different weights, according to the country. In the United States all sectors are strong, but the private sector is probably most powerful (the government doesn't find it easy to take actions that business is opposed to) and civil society the weakest—though influential in many areas. In Nordic countries the public sector is strongest, but there is also a vibrant private sector; civil society is not so influential because of high levels of public trust in the other sectors. China, in contrast, has a huge public sector, a small but growing private sector, and a very weak civil society sector, because most associational life is subsumed under the Communist Party—an organ of the state. In Somalia it is the reverse: the government is very weak (or nonexistent in some areas), the private sector is surprisingly strong, and civil society is also quite strong (though dominated by disruptive clan structures).

Figure 5.1 The three sectors of society

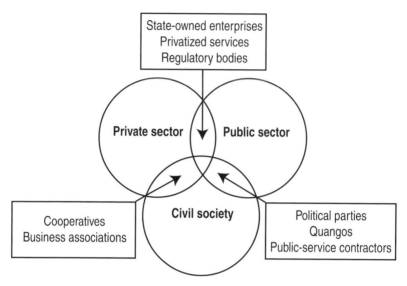

The foundations for a healthy civil society are the freedoms of speech, association, and religion; predictable rule of law; peace; democracy; effective and capable government; a permissive, enabling, and not controlling policy environment; substantial literacy; a sizeable middle class; and a participatory political culture (Clark 1995). Where civil society is strong, many organizations compete for the attention and support of citizens—as in the private sector, where firms compete for our custom within the marketplace. Civil society is hence also market-based, albeit driven by non-market values. In this marketplace the currency is not money but associational commitment; instead of goods and services, civil society markets the "Three 'I's":

- *Interests:* such as sports, public services, or mutual support;
- *Ideas:* such as environmental conservation or microcredit;
- *Ideologies:* such as religions, human rights, or anticapitalism.

As in the conventional marketplace, association has many motivations. We join a trade union to *defend* an interest or an environment pressure group to *promote* an interest. Motivations can be altruistic (supporting public charities), selfish (joining a tennis club), or antisocial (belonging to racist gangs or the Mafia). Not all of civil society is "civil" (Holloway 1997); however, there is a strong correlation between associational activity and harmony. In US inner cities, youth living in neighborhoods of high church attendance and other civic engagement are more likely to finish school, avoid drugs and crime, and get jobs than youth in other areas—even after controlling for race and other characteristics of the youth (Putnam 1993).

An important function of civil society (of primary concern to this book) is providing a nucleus of independent political activity; hence, the term grew in prominence during the popular struggle against East European authoritarianism and the eventual fall of the Berlin Wall (Carothers 1999). Civil society provides the political space for shaping the rules governing aspects of social life, including laws, public actions or attitudes, and the social order as a whole; this group of actors includes conformists (business lobbies, philanthropies, and so forth), reformists (most pressure groups and NGOs), and radicals (such as social movements and religious revivalists) who seek radical change (Scholte 2001a).

A strong civil society provides the means by which interests of citizens are represented in relation to the state and market. But what does *strong* mean? Robert Putnam emphasizes membership of societies and time spent out of the home in associational activity, and laments that—at least in the United States—this has steeply declined in recent decades (Putnam 2000). Others are unconvinced by his methodology

Figure 5.2 The three transnational sectors in the international domain

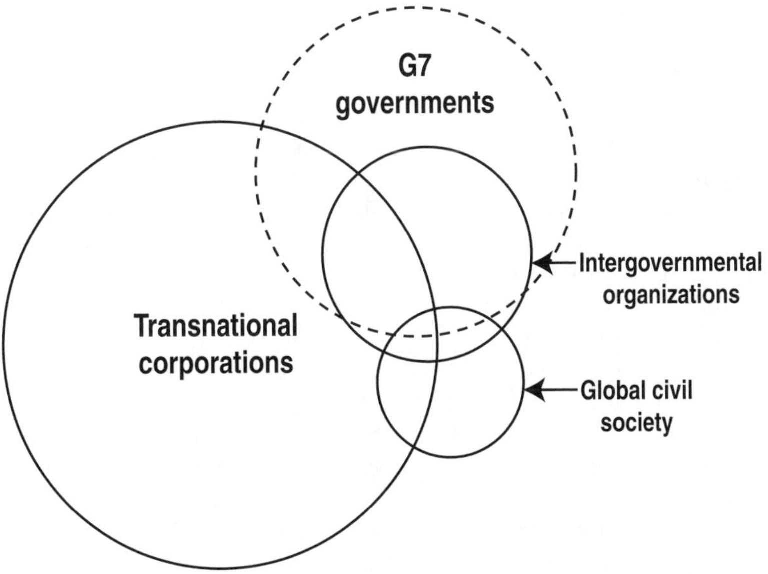

and conclusions (Woolcock 1998; Harriss and de Renzio 1997). Association is a powerful force in development, but its strength can't be measured by people hours (no more can capitalism's strength be gauged by time spent in factories and offices); it depends on many social, economic, and political factors.

Civil society, then, is a marketplace, but it is also the result of market failures. It provides goods, services, protection, and associational opportunities that aren't offered by either the state or private sectors (or at least aren't offered in the same way), and it *pulls* these sectors in directions their constituencies want.

Figure 5.2 illustrates that in the international domain TNCs are strongest; most governments (except the United States and the G7) are very weak; IGOs are fairly strong but are dominated by the G7 (which is therefore shown as a backdrop to the IGOs) and sometimes by powerful TNCs. Civil society is organized increasingly strongly at the transnational level; besides its operational activities, it seeks to influence IGOs, and it makes some dents in TNCs.

GLOBAL—AND GROWING

Civil society increasingly answers needs and delivers services at the national level, but its achievements and growth in the international domain of recent years have been most striking. CSO pioneers have learned to work together across national frontiers tackling global problems and shaping global policies. This entails more than sharing information and coordinating activities; it has meant joint strategy planning and global campaigns. The nature of the globalized world provides the need; modern communications provides the opportunity. In *Democratizing Development* (1991) I wrote that it is time to turn the old peace movement slogan on its head—it is time to "think locally, and act globally"; NGOs, I urged, must build global campaigns on global issues, fueled by information from their local bases on the grassroots social impacts of the issues they follow.

Much has changed in the eleven years since then. There are now many impressive examples of global advocacy and many confident groups in the South asserting leadership in these campaigns. At its best, international advocacy is reinforced by grassroots action in countless communities around the world and by impressive field research; access to decision-makers has been "democratized" so that Southern groups are increasingly able to speak for themselves in addressing international sources of power. The slogan might now be: "*Think* locally and globally, and *act* locally and globally!" But not all global citizen action

is at its finest. Often the elite leadership retains power, Southern stakeholders are not consulted, haphazard anecdotes provide the foundation for sweeping generalizations, and simplistic world views and
straightforward prejudice color judgments and deceive followers.

Opinion is divided about the significance of global civil society. The
Centre for Civil Society at London School of Economics considers it
important enough to be the subject of a new annual series (Anheier et
al. 2001). John Boli and George Thomas think international NGOs are
molding new global political and social norms, and are serving as "en-
actors and carriers of World Culture" (Boli and Thomas 1997). Others
ask what is transnational about them—pointing out that CSO actors
may travel a lot but still largely influence *national* level institutions and
policies; civil society exists in relation to the state. Sid Tarrow questions whether there really is any "global civil society"—just "rooted
cosmopolitans," national civil society actors with international out-
looks who have a lot in common with peers in others countries (Tarrow
2002).

Some argue that international CSOs are not a new phenomenon.
The International Typographical Union (a professional association) was
established in 1852, the World Alliance of Young Men's Christian Associations started in 1855, the International Committee of the Red Cross
was formed in 1863; by 1874 there were thirty-two such organizations, including the Socialist International (John Foster 2001). One of
the easiest to measure indicators of the growth of *global* civil society is
the number of international organizations (that is, those operating in
multiple countries). The Brussels-based Union of International Associations has been counting these for many years. It estimates that this
number rose slowly to about 1,500 in the mid 1950s and then accelerated after 1975 to reach 9,789 in 1981, and 24,797 in 2001.

Of course the *number* of international organizations in itself means
little; a swarm of midges carries little weight (though it can be irritating). The rapid growth is partly a reflection of today's very low transactions costs for setting up and running an international organization.
Travel is cheap and ICT at hand. Because the Internet is virtually free,
"members" needn't be asked to pay—just log on. Whether an organization should branch out into other countries was once a serious strategic dilemma; now it can seem a trivial question. In fact, it is *easier* for
small, new groups to establish themselves from the start as international organizations than for large existing NGOs with well-established
memberships, boards, offices, and other infrastructure to do so.

Another useful growth indicator is the number of NGOs with consultative status at the United Nations (the UN's founding charter provided for such consultation through its Economic and Social Council).

While this number crept up slowly to about one thousand in 1996, it shot up to over fifteen hundred in 2000, and the following year over eight hundred applications were received. The UN bureaucracy simply cannot handle this volume of applications. Now some of the larger NGOs—wanting to be apart from the crowd—are seeking a higher status with more access. NGOs have seen the major UN conferences as particularly important occasions to lobby, learn, and network. This started in the late 1970s with NGO presence at environmental and women's conferences, and accelerated steeply with the Rio Earth Summit in 1992. While initially the purpose was lobbying and reaching journalists, the NGOs also organized their own parallel events and these became the main focus. Through them, it was possible to reach common positions, shared strategy, and even a common culture; this contributed greatly to the birth of global activism. While eight thousand NGO delegates went to the UN women's conference in Copenhagen in 1980, and eleven thousand attended the Nairobi equivalent in 1990, over forty thousand went to Beijing for the 1995 women's conference.

Though many small transnational CSOs (TCSOs) are effective, it is the big, global organizations that have achieved most influence. They experience a "virtuous circle." When they make an impact, the media like to report it; people identify with the David versus Goliath fights against environment despoilers or global poverty, hence membership goes up (of course some of the Davids are now pretty big!); funders like being associated with winners and so readily provide money. This enables the organization to develop new campaigns, hire new staff, and strengthen its media outreach. New successes are charted, receiving yet more media coverage and growth spirals.

The NGO growth phenomenon is like that of big corporations. As organizations get larger, they start to search for new pastures and new activities; the trailblazers achieve advantage and grow faster than their more conservative peers. In time, a few brand leaders come to dominate any given sector. What is true for coffee and TVs is true for NGOs. About eight organizations dominate the environment field, four or five the human rights sector, and about ten NGO networks the development sector.

Some environment groups have enjoyed particularly strong growth. WWF grew from 572,000 members in 1985 to five million in 2001. It now employs thirty-three hundred staff and has an annual budget of $350 million. Greenpeace's growth spurt was somewhat earlier; it reached over four million members globally in 1994 and an annual budget peak of $179 million in 1991. As early as 1986 it had linked its network of thirty national offices through an international computer network—well before most TNCs did so. After 1994, Greenpeace experienced a downturn due to internal problems, competition from other environment groups, and competing concerns such as AIDS and globalization. It now has just 2.5 million members but still a budget of $142 million, and eleven hundred staff. Friends of the Earth comprises sixty-eight autonomous national groups with, collectively, over one million members, five thousand local groups, and a budget of over $200 million.

In human rights, Amnesty International now has over one million members in 160 countries and employs four hundred staff (Power 2001). Jubilee 2000, the NGO promoting third-world debt relief, orchestrated the world's largest petition (with twenty-four million signatures). In 1998 it also mobilized sixty thousand supporters to form a human chain around the G7 Summit venue in Birmingham, UK, in order to generate the political will for debt relief. The French-based pressure group ATTAC (Association pour la Taxation des Transactions financiers pour l'Aide aux Citoyens), has mobilized thirty thousand paid-up followers to campaign for a seemingly arcane proposal for a new tax to curb capital mobility (see Chapter 11). This may be the first popular campaign in history *for* a new tax. (We will turn to operational development NGOs in Chapter 7.)

Box 5.1 Corruption and the growth of Transparency International

Bribery has increased with international commerce. It is estimated that TNCs alone shell out $80 billion a year in bribes (considerably more than international aid). An NGO bringing together development professionals and ethical business people was formed in 1993 and called Transparency International. Its focus is largely combating corruption in developing and transition countries and "grand corruption"—the wholesale bribery of governments by Northern actors.

By 1997, TI had become well known internationally and had put the corruption issue firmly on the international agenda by advocacy about the general climate for transparency and combating corruption. Its best-known work is its "corruption perception index," which ranks countries according to business people's perception of the need to use bribes to work there. It employed just four senior staff and eight program officers. Over the following years it grew rapidly; it now has almost one hundred chapters throughout the world, comprising business leaders, journalists, academics, churchmen and others. Forty professional staff in their Berlin headquarters support the chapters and TI's global programs. TI also acts as the secretariat for the International Anti-Corruption Conference.

Source: Fredrick Galtung, in Florini 2000.

It is not just NGOs who have moved into the global arena and grown. Trade unions well know that the major issues they deal with—TNCs, economic shocks, the labor market—are not nationally bound. Of increasing importance are the global union federations (GUF) of unions in a similar trade. For example, Education International is a union for teachers' unions throughout the world; its significance in education policy internationally is due to it representing over thirty-five million teachers worldwide. The International Union of Food and Allied Workers (IUF) represents farm and estate workers and food factory staff around the world, helping its members negotiate with food giants such as Nestlé. These GUFs have existed for many years, as has the International Confederation of Free Trade Unions (ICFTU—the umbrella of all these umbrellas), but their power and influence has increased significantly in recent years, as we discuss in Chapter 6.

CSOs' objective in moving into global arenas isn't simply to grow, of course, but to make an impact on issues that are determined at international levels. What counts is how effective their advocacy is.

THE ADVANCE OF ADVOCACY

International campaigns to shape international policy are not new. The Anti-Slavery Society—which started in the UK in the eighteenth century—made a pivotal contribution toward that cause. But of late, civil society's influence in international policy has become remarkable. The plot has changed, as has the setting, and a whole new cast of leading actors has emerged on this stage. Whereas previously the field was largely left to the specialist advocacy groups, it has now broadened in at least three ways.

First, many CSOs that previously concentrated on specific operational or representational work have come to see advocacy as pivotally important. Development NGOs such as Oxfam have gradually expanded policy work because they realize that, however important their projects, poverty will only be eradicated by tackling the structural inequalities and anti-poor policies that fuel it. Human rights groups like Amnesty International—partly at the insistence of their growing Southern membership—are diversifying from specific examples of human rights abuse to "promotional work," addressing the underlying policies in which this abuse breeds. And trade unions similarly are moving beyond representational work and collective bargaining with specific employers to influencing policies shaped by the WTO, IMF, World Bank, and others that critically affect workers' conditions and the labor market everywhere.

Second, articulate and effective Southern groups and CSOs from the transition (former Eastern bloc) countries have burst onto the stage. These include small but highly influential advocacy and communications groups, such as Third World Network, Focus on the Global South, and Social Watch, and umbrella groups that link mass organizations of marginalized people throughout the world, including Via Campesina (comprising peasant farmers and plantation workers) and People's Global Action.

And third, new types of organizations that bring issues of globalization to life for new constituencies have emerged. These include groups like Jubilee 2000 and its successors, which appeal to church members and people concerned about social justice in both North and South, and the Internet-based "dot-causes" and radical protest networks, which reach large numbers of young people who would not readily identify with more established groups but who care passionately about the direction the world is taking—but also many anarchic groups attracted by the prospect of a good fight with the police.

Transnational action on environmental issues has been the longest and strongest—dating from 1972's first parallel NGO forum to a UN event (the Conference on the Human Environment in Stockholm). International networks emerged in the 1970s and 1980s; while the early causes were largely conservation issues (such as the protection of whales), they gradually evolved to incorporate social concerns—thanks in part to pressure from Southern groups and to specific events such as the Bhopal and Chernobyl disasters. The discovery of the hole in the ozone layer, the sabotage by the French government of the Greenpeace ship *Rainbow Warrior*, and the emerging scientific consensus on climate change spurred public support for international environmental activism. In the United States, membership in Greenpeace and Environmental Defense Fund doubled from 1985 to 1990, and membership in Natural Resources Defense Council almost tripled.

The success of CSOs in influencing policy is inspiring ever bolder action. NGO lobbying is widely credited with securing the landmine treaty (Florini 2000), debt relief for the poorest countries, the Rio Earth Summit agreement on controlling greenhouse gases, approval for the International Criminal Court (Almeida 1999), Antarctica being declared a world park—protected from mining (Runyan 1999), scuppering OECD's plans to launch a Multilateral Agreement on Investment, and securing major changes in projects and policies of the World Bank. In the United States, pressure group effectiveness is increased by the revolving door that allows academics and NGO leaders to move into significant government positions and back. Some leaders of the influential Campaign for the Non-Proliferation Treaty had themselves been in previous administrations, for example. Such exchange is much less common in the UK, where the civil service is a caste system of its own, though we are now starting to see some personnel flow.

The former director of Oxfam, David Bryer, advocates advocacy and lists several important guidelines:

- Target issues that are subjects of moral outrage;
- Ensure there is a foundation of solid research based on the NGOs' experience of how the issue affects people's lives;
- Present clear and well thought out change propositions;
- Get to know the institutions to be influenced and how to "press their buttons";
- Use opportunism and risk-taking;
- Build up strategic alliances;
- Develop a campaign momentum (that is, short-, medium-, and long-term objectives);
- Ensure that the information contains a good deal of human interest; and
- Be prepared for flak (Bryer and Magrath 1999).

Others observe that not all global campaigning lives up to such high standards; sometimes, sweeping campaigns are based on shoddy research and thin anecdotes (Harper 2001). Inaccurate academics rapidly lose credibility, but this isn't always so with NGOs. The media love them if they offer good headlines and don't expect them to be right every time—or fair. They will still cover their campaigns providing they offer good copy. When Greenpeace pressed Shell not to dump the Brent Spar oil rig at sea but to dispose of it on-shore (a much more expensive option) to avoid polluting the North Sea, Shell finally gave way. Later, Greenpeace admitted its calculations were wildly wrong, but this didn't damage its reputation as much as a heated internal wrangle and staff firings over its strategy of opposing French nuclear tests in the Pacific. (I conclude this chapter with my own reflections on over-the-top campaigning at the World Bank.)

It is a difficult call. NGOs aren't always well equipped for thorough research, and the events they try to affect may be fast moving. Most think it is better to take opportunistic chances to achieve real change and be approximately right rather than to be scrupulously accurate and miss the boat. Some take it too far, however, and sound off on the flimsiest evidence and worry about the consequences later (the "load, fire, aim" school); others deliberately exaggerate to excoriate a favorite target. "There are those," Charles Secret of Friends of the Earth once told me, sighing, "who never let the facts get in the way of a good campaign." He strongly urges high standards of pressure-group ethics.

IGOs are not the only targets of international campaigns. Engaging and influencing TNCs has become increasingly important and offers many pressure points (see Chapter 10). Many NGOs that engage with corporations have consciously shifted from *problem*-focused advocacy (emphasizing media attacks describing the company's faults) to *solution*-focused advocacy (seeking to persuade the company to try out new approaches). This demands greater technical knowledge of the issues at hand and a preparedness to develop NGO-corporate links. TNCs are getting more open to this in order to avoid what they see as the increasing risk of "reputational loss." Hence, Greenpeace has promoted "Greenfreeze" (a hydrocarbon refrigerant to replace halogen-bearing chemicals) since 1992; WWF joined forces with Unilever in 1997 to create the Marine Stewardship Council for regulating and monitoring sustainable fishing; and NGOs have cooperated with industry in the certification of sustainable timber (Smart Wood) and environment-friendly products (Green Seal) (Runyan 1999).

Evidence of the seriousness with which large corporations view the challenge coming from CSO critics is the effort they are making to be seen to be embracing positive social and environmental strategies. Many are joining programs of "corporate citizenship," establishing their own ethics or environment offices, employing seasoned NGO campaigners as advisors, increasing charitable contributions, or setting up their own foundations. There has been a rapid growth in the number of corporations who issue "sustainability" reports alongside their annual reports (Zadek 2001). Whereas seven TNCs issued such reports in 1990, 194 did in 1995, and 487 did in 2001 (*New York Times,* March 28, 2002). Though these reports are deficient in that they are produced in house (and therefore are unlikely to be objective), lack any common standard, and are not "audited" by any independent body, this is an impressive start.

Diversity of tactics

A wide range of tactics has been used in international campaigning: high-level lobbying, media work, public education campaigns, protests and other forms of direct action, boycotts, presenting testimony to parliaments, defending court actions, *taking* court actions, shaming campaigns, and so on. This array embraces three broad goals:

- Seeking to win the argument: showing that something being done at present is wrong, or that there is a better approach that could be taken;

- Seeking to demonstrate that there are large numbers of people who demand and expect change (and that at least some of them are well informed);
- Insinuating or inflicting damage: this can mean physical damage to property, or preventing activities, or damaging reputations through negative publicity.

Events such as the "Battle of Seattle" include all three tactics. Groups such as Oxfam and Jubilee use lobbying and media briefings to argue the case for change. Trade unions and churches mobilize people on the street for mass demonstrations. And radical groups try to disrupt meetings or "dismantle" symbols of global capitalism (such as MacDonald's restaurants). I call these the head, heart, and fist schools of action (Clark 2002).

Keck and Sikkink have analyzed a range of transnational civil society campaigns to understand what tactics and strategies have been most effective. They conclude that successful campaigns have shifted political debate through using four key political tools: *information*—ensuring its reliability; *symbolism*—dramatizing facts and using symbolic events; *leverage*—threatening sanctions (for example, boycotts)—and setting targets for changes; and *accountability politics*: monitoring compliance and scrutinizing ethical standards (Keck and Sikkink 1998).

DOES THE CRIME FIT THE PUNISHMENT?

I conclude this chapter on a personal note—one not easy to write—reflecting on whether international campaigns ascribe too much blame to intergovernmental organizations. Having spent the last nine years working for one of them, the World Bank, I have seen sweeping improvements triggered by these campaigns, but also the growing cost. I could easily be seen as having a bias—but *what* bias? Take your choice. I joined the World Bank because I criticized it, not because I admired it. Previously I headed Oxfam's campaigns and development policy work; I was its chief IGO lobbyist and led Oxfam's criticisms over structural adjustment, resettlement, and other issues. Together with a small, international group of NGOs, I helped form the World Bank reform campaign. And since working at the World Bank I've not significantly changed my views on the issues we addressed. In the last nine years I've commonly (but not always) agreed with the NGOs in their disputes with the World Bank and have helped them to press their case. I recognize that many important reforms wouldn't have happened without their ceaseless efforts. But at the same time I worry that too much CSO attention focuses on the IGOs and on the World Bank in particular.

Why have IGOs become such favorite targets? They certainly have influence on the world stage, their market liberalization favors international capital, numerous specific actions (projects, adjustment loans, and individual decisions) have seriously affected vulnerable populations, and most of their staff members have little contact with poor people. So they are fair game for criticism, but this can be overdone. My concern isn't that their staff get too hard a rap (they can take care of themselves), but that more appropriate targets, particularly in the G7, get off too lightly. The rhetoric of some of the protestors and pressure groups gives the impression that the IGOs set the rules of world trade and economics, dominate financial flows, and tell governments in the South exactly what to do. This is wildly overstated.

To begin with, in resources the World Bank is puny compared with commercial banks and governments. The entire fifty-seven-year history of World Bank lending amounts to no more than is exchanged on world money markets every eight hours. True, the Bank (and more often the IMF) offers a "seal of approval" triggering loans from governments and commercial banks, but this can also be provided by major finance ministries, export credit agencies in the G7, or commercial bank syndicates. True, the Bank often sets liberalization as a condition for structural adjustment loans, but evaluations reveal that these loans usually continue to flow even when the government doesn't implement the conditions.

The World Bank, in reality, has much less influence with governments than is commonly supposed. Governments in dire economic straits or of very poor countries perforce listen to it carefully (but probably have weak capacity to follow what it says), but most governments—particularly of middle-income countries—take the messages they like and discard the rest. Were the World Bank ten times stronger, it would still be farfetched to suggest that countries like China or India would set policies at its behest.

True, the World Bank tries to influence policy reform, but this includes improving basic social services, consulting citizens, tackling corruption, and allowing NGOs to exist and operate freely—not just market liberalization and privatization. The Bank usually simply helps governments do what they want to do, including, sometimes, controversial programs, for example, projects that displace people or damage the environment. These are often subjects of NGO campaigns—which is fair—but those promoting them should be more honest in portraying the government in question as the main protagonist, not the World Bank.

Why does it matter? It matters partly because it is wrong to ignore egregious activities of Southern governments, but more importantly because *Northern* governments shouldn't be let off the hook. It is G7 governments, not the World Bank, who determine the rules of international economics; it is the US Treasury that largely decides whether bail-out packages are offered to countries in crisis, not the IMF; and it is the United States and European Union who shape the rules of world trade, not the WTO.

Too little effort, in my view, is spent tackling Northern governments and educating their publics about their part in global economic injustice. Sometimes, especially in the United States, it seems that NGOs have a blind spot—that the government-NGO relationship is too cozy, dulling such criticism, and governments are all too happy for the blame to be deflected elsewhere. This struck me particularly as I listened to Hilary Clinton speak to a mostly NGO audience at the Beijing women's summit in 1995. As her eloquent speech concluded, she baldly blamed globalization for many of the problems she had described. This got a loud cheer, but I found it simply incredible. Was her husband's government not the greatest ever promoter of globalization? No one seemed concerned by this hypocrisy; they relished the affirming message that the dark forces of liberalization (evidently *not* including her husband) wreak havoc among the poor. Four years later her husband voiced sympathy with WTO demonstrators in Seattle, saying he too wanted labor standards enshrined in the WTO. Another loud cheer—but the statement was later retracted (*The Economist*, December 11, 1999). The great wrong of such double-speak is that it encourages people to believe that the problem is global integration, not the highly selective and self-serving way in which integration is allowed or denied by powerful governments (as described in Part One).

Overemphasizing IGOs is a form of scapegoating. Slogans used in international demos and protest websites often pin on them blame for all global injustice. History is replete with examples of great wrongs stemming from oversimplified and overly selective blame casting. The wrong that stems from excessive targeting of IGOs is the erosion of multilateralism. The United States and other Northern countries have become more insular and more xenophobic since the end of the Cold War because there's not such a clear need to "hang together." This is bad news for UN agreements, UN specialist agencies, interest-free World Bank loans to low-income countries, and new global initiatives such as climate treaties and the International Criminal Court. And it is bad news for developing countries seeking access to foreign markets. Instead of multilateral trade agreements we are seeing an increasing array of bilateral agreements, forged by the United States and European Union in particular, that further weakens prospects for truly global agreements. Countries of strategic importance will be OK, but the rest can go whistle!

Northern CSO campaigns shouldn't ignore the very real struggle between poor and elite in the South. To do so suggests a communality of interest between hapless Southern stakeholders (citizens and their governments) against irrepressible neoliberal enemies. In reality, the Southern elites—to whom governments listen much more attentively than the poor—are usually the keenest for privatization (it presents business opportunities), for market openness (it presents export opportunities and cheaper imported luxuries), and for financial liberalization (so they can tap foreign capital or ship their own money abroad). An unwillingness to blame either governments or national business elites for poverty and inequity denies the paths to poverty reduction that have been the mainstay of social reform in rich countries, such as progressive taxation and welfare benefits. It is also latently racist—treating Southern leaders as not responsible for their own actions.

I should stress that many CSOs give a much fairer balance. Oxfam's recently launched trade campaign is clear about the need to target the European Union and the United States. And Ann Pettifor, former director of Jubilee 2000, describes how the debt campaign shifted target as it became more acutely aware that the real culprits were the G7 leaders and finance ministers. She believes that NGOs who only target IGOs have "unwittingly colluded with the world's most powerful leaders in this strategy, by targeting, almost exclusively, the IMF and World Bank and vesting great power in civil servants like the President of the World Bank" (Pettifor 2001). Taking on domestic targets may be dangerous. CSOs may experience government reprisals and loss of conservative supporters; they risk being labeled as partisan; and politicians may criticize them as unpatriotic, while they wouldn't bother to defend an IGO (another reason that multilateralism is under threat).

I discussed the issue of casting blame with a civil society meeting in Manila in 2002. One CSO leader responded: "It doesn't matter whether or not the World Bank is guilty of everything it is blamed for. The impression is there, and the impression is reality." I profoundly disagree. The same logic would hold the Jews guilty for all the Nazis' charges. Although all who spoke on this issue in the seminar were critical of the World Bank, several came up to me afterward to agree with me and criticize the slavishly "black-and-white" views of their colleagues. I asked why they hadn't said this during the meeting, and they replied that they would have been given a hard time if they had. The NGO community can ostracize those who buck the established norms. Many in civil society know that the true picture is more complex, but it isn't in their interests to defend an institution that they know has many faults. Unfortunately, multilateralism itself is a casualty of this unchecked scapegoating.

CONCLUSIONS

Democracies have seen a strong power shift toward civil society over the last decade. This influences politics everywhere but is particularly potent in the international arena—due to its "democracy deficit." There is, accordingly, an upswing of transnational civil society activism— with increasingly sophisticated advocacy—but alongside this goes new challenges and responsibilities. Some targets are "easy" and over-flogged, while others present dangers and are neglected.

These are tough obstacles for any CSO, especially if acting alone. Networking with other like-minded groups heightens credibility, reduces risk, and preserves political support. In particular, creating transnational alliances and expanding the diversity of partnership can be immensely empowering. It is to these issues we now turn.

6

Civil Society
in the Network Era

All over the world CSOs are changing what they do and how they work in response to their shifting, globalizing environment. This applies to development NGOs, human rights organizations, environmental and other pressure groups, trade unions, consumers' organizations, and faith-based groups. Though their cultures and functions vary greatly, they face a remarkably similar range of problems and choices; this is a finding of our recent work at the London School of Economics (Clark 2001; Clark 2003) and is the subject of this chapter.

We first use organizational theory to explore parallels with the private sector and discuss the significance for CSOs of the "network age." Then we describe the different types of organizational structures CSOs adopt to improve their effectiveness. Next we ask how they are dealing with the related governance dilemmas and what changes in focus and culture stem from working globally. We then discuss the important question of learning to work with new strategic partners, looking at the specific challenges faced by particular types of CSOs. Throughout the chapter we draw lessons from the experience of some of the major pioneering civil society networks, including three case studies: the international labor union movement, Amnesty International, and the international consumers' movement. Later we look at specific challenges faced by development NGOs (Chapter 7) and new organizational forms of civil society (Chapter 8).

CAN BUSINESS STUDIES TELL US ANYTHING?

Organization theory—developed by those studying why some firms do well and some poorly and whether this relates to "organizational form"—provides an interesting lens for viewing modern currents in

109

civil society. It describes the modern private sector through three stages of development.

First was the rise of the *unitary form* (U-Form), typified by the large factory of the industrial revolution. As such firms grow they employ more people and expand their plants in the locality; owners employ managers to help run the business but keep a tight hold on all important decisions and knowledge. The second stage is the emergence of the *multi-divisional form* (M-Form), typified by conglomerates that branch out into new products or new locations (perhaps overseas). Much authority is delegated to chief executives of the quasi-autonomous units; but strategic decisions and information flow among units are managed by corporate HQs. It is estimated that while only two of the top one hundred US companies were M-Form in 1929, eighty-four were by 1999; these companies were better able to capture efficiencies of scale and scope (Anheier and Themudo 2002). The third and most recent phase is that of the *network age* (N-Form), in which companies delegate more power to the unit level, develop more fluid matrix ways of working, and view information as their most powerful tool. They encourage copious and rapid horizontal exchange among staff throughout the corporation and with specialists outside—even competitors. Leaders are concerned less with hierarchy or controlling information than with ensuring that networks are built and information is exchanged smoothly.

Networks have clear advantages of adaptability and problem-solving. They can reach decisions faster and more swiftly discover and adopt new techniques developed elsewhere, but established firms set in old ways find it difficult to shift to this new mode. Big advantages are reaped both by those who loosen the reins and take the leap and by new market entrants—hence the enormous upheavals we see today in the world of big business, including surprise takeovers and changes in pole positions. The transition from U-Form to N-Form means increasing flexibility and unit-autonomy while decreasing hierarchy, but also less predictability and stability.

There is a direct parallel with civil society. The U-Form describes the large charity, nonprofit hospital, or Catholic church. The M-Form is represented by many of the biggest CSOs, such as CARE, national unions, Greenpeace, or the Rotary Club. The N-Form, as with firms, includes innovative CSOs undergoing change and new entrants. Many advocacy-oriented CSOs are emphasizing networks with strategic partners. Examples include Friends of the Earth International, Oxfam International, and Amnesty International. New entrants include Jubilee 2000, the landmines campaign, the umbrellas of national mass movements such as Via Campesina, and the "dot-causes" such as the Free Burma campaign.

How they adapt to the network age is CSOs' organizational test of today. Those who succeed are likely to make more impact and gain most public support—though they can also experience problems (see the Amnesty case study). Those who don't are likely to stagnate. And all must compete with new entrants, whose chief strength is that they lack the organizational baggage of established CSOs. Drawing parallels from smart corporations, the N-Form can help CSOs with four challenges:

- *Working globally:* developing North-South links and international campaign strategies; speaking with a single, loud, global voice—albeit with national variations in how they work and what they work on;
- *Managing information:* establishing two-way information systems so that campaigns are well informed by ground realities and the grass roots are empowered to be full and active campaign participants;
- *Managing strategic partnerships:* strengthening links with *new* as well as traditional allies, even if there is little in common beyond the issue at hand, because the scope of global challenges goes well beyond the boundaries of individual CSOs;
- *Responding rapidly:* as ICT has speeded up news and current affairs, CSOs able to respond rapidly to political opportunities derive a valuable premium; this is often difficult for established CSOs.

We now look at the challenges CSOs face as they evolve new organizational structures to improve their effectiveness as they enter the network age.

GETTING THE STRUCTURE RIGHT

CSOs working internationally are wrestling with what structure best helps them with the growing range of tasks they feel they need to do (see Lindenberg and Dobel 1999). The tradeoffs are between maintaining a coherent "brand" worldwide and permitting local autonomy; between ensuring quality control and capacity for quick response; between wanting rapid expansion and retaining standards of style and ethics; and between professional ethos and fostering grassroots voluntarism. CSOs generally tackle these through one of five structural choices:[1]

- *Centralized organizations:* global organizations with global HQs (secretariat) and national offices in other countries, albeit having considerable autonomy at the local level (examples: the Catholic church, Greenpeace, and Human Rights Watch).
- *Federations:* networks comprising national members with a common name and charter but also national self-determination; they have strong global boards, comprising members' delegates, making binding decisions; and their secretariats are largely responsible for implementation (examples: Amnesty International, Anglican Church, Rotary Club, and WWF).
- *Confederations:* looser structures in which the members are autonomous but agree to a set of common ground rules and work together on specific activities in which there is mutual advantage (examples: Public Service International, Oxfam International, and Friends of the Earth International).
- *Informal networks:* fluid networks on a self-selecting basis; any group having broadly similar aims can join, but membership bestows few advantages (other than information and "belonging") and demands few responsibilities (examples: International Baby Food Action Network and Jubilee 2000).
- *Social movements:* not true organizations but loose networks or affinities of *people* rather than CSOs; an increasingly powerful form of civil society on the global stage (Cohen and Rai 2000); CSOs may gain strength by enmeshing themselves in a movement (examples: the women's movement, today's protest movement).

International secretariats are typically very strong and the locus of key decisions in centralized organizations, strong but largely for servicing members and professional implementation of agreed upon programs in federations, relatively small and decentralized in confederations, very small and voluntary in informal networks, and nonexistent in (indeed, an anathema to) social movements. In confederations and networks there is an inherent tendency for members to put their own organization and national context first.

An inherent weakness in global civil society is that it is never truly global. With some notable exceptions, such as the Catholic church and the Red Cross, they tend to be strongly oriented to countries that are Northern (usually Anglo-Saxon) and where English is commonly spoken. Country representation tends to parallel civil society strength, which in turn depends on the tradition and legal environment for associations, the form of government, motivation for social change, and other factors. In some countries, such as France, association tends to be for personal rather than societal purposes (for example, worship, trade unions, or cooperatives).

GOVERNANCE CHALLENGES

As CSO networks grow, they find it increasingly difficult to reach decisions that satisfy everyone. Activists are frustrated both by top-down decision-making (Greenpeace has experienced this) and by losing critical opportunities because democratic processes are slow (see the Amnesty case study). Unless deliberative processes change when new Southern or transition country members join, the previous power base may persist, leaving the new members feeling like second-class citizens.

When a network is entirely Northern, it might be riddled with self-doubt about its legitimacy on Southern issues. WWF, for example, has few Southern members and so a largely Northern board; it decided to redress this by including some Southern program officers in its board. But those staff members are unsure about their status and how much to speak out. Oxfam International has a different approach to the dilemma—inviting some large Southern NGOs to become full members and instituting associate status for major advocacy partners that don't meet the operational criteria for full membership.

Use of the CSO's name can be another vexing issue. Many are understandably protective, since they may have spent years building up their good name; they will expel members who misbehave and take legal action to confront misuse of the name. All sections of Amnesty the world over, for example, must use the name and logo; its "brand" is its key strategic asset—being, to human rights, what Microsoft is to software.

Jubilee 2000, however, took the opposite approach. Set up as a UK NGO network in 1996, its founders soon decided to develop global reach. Rather than defining a membership charter and inviting groups to apply (or setting up subsidiaries directly), they simply invited all groups working on debt to *be* Jubilee 2000 in their country and decide for themselves what that meant. In practice it worked surprisingly well initially; a strong network emerged (some using the Jubilee 2000 name, some not); most supported the Jubilee 2000 petition (which remains the world's largest); and most welcomed the coordinating role played by Jubilee 2000 UK. However, serious problems emerged from the lack of global governance or unifying platform. A Southern network emerged, calling itself Jubilee South, which urged a more radical platform. This caused confusion and tension, especially as many assumed this was a unified voice of Southern debt campaigners. Jubilee 2000 had become globally famous due to the pragmatic and effective campaign launched by the UK group. But by not protecting its name, it effectively handed a powerful calling card to another group with a very different platform (Pettifor 2001; Greiner 2003). Eventually, the North-South and reformist-radical tensions significantly split the movement, eroding both its legitimacy and dynamism (Bauck 2001).

The opposite problem arose in Oxfam International, many of whose members have a completely different name at home (such as NOVIB in Netherlands, Community Aid Abroad in Australia, and Intermon in Spain). This has led to confusion and diluted impact. An Oxfam statement may get little coverage in a country where it has little name recognition. All Oxfam members have now agreed to a phased process of moving to the common name and logo. The same issue arises in Friends of the Earth International (FOE-I), but it has no intention of harmonizing, strongly emphasizing local autonomy. Its global campaigns are on a sign-up basis; if the majority agrees to a campaign (and there are no strong objections) it is approved, but each member decides whether to take part in it.

CHANGING HOW YOU WORK CHANGES WHAT YOU DO

When CSOs form international networks they may have a common unifying interest but not necessarily shared views on strategy. New Southern partners may have very different agendas and working styles. If strong Northern CSOs keep hold of the reins, the network is likely to fail; the CSOs must learn to accommodate one another by adjusting the network's focus and culture. Many have found this both difficult and exciting.

Most international CSO networks were initially Northern; they invited Southern members much later, by which time there was a well-established organizational culture and strategy. FOE-I, for example, started thirty years ago with four Northern national groups (US, UK, France, and Sweden). It gradually expanded but stayed largely Northern and strictly environmental. In about 1990 FOE-I decided to accelerate network growth, particularly within developing and transition countries. It now has sixty-eight members, of whom over half are from these regions. The new members have challenged the network in various ways, notably by emphasizing a sustainable development rather than a "green environment" perspective. The mandate and focus challenges experienced as a result of Amnesty's growth provide another powerful example (see case study).

Changes in focus and style may also respond to global changes. Labor markets, for example, have changed greatly over the past thirty years (see Box 6.1), hence trade unions must also change. This has spurred the formation of global networks, because labor market policies are shaped

Box 6.1 Labor pains

In Western countries the trade union movement entered the twentieth century like a lion—the most powerful example of civil society action to redress injustice and transform political debate. While it would be unfair to say that it left the twentieth century like a *lamb*, it had lost many of its teeth.

In the United States, the UK, Japan, and Germany union membership has fallen 30 percent since 1980; a similar story is found throughout the OECD. The Trades Union Congress now represents just 7.3 million workers, 5 million fewer than it did in 1980. For the first time, white-collar workers exceed blue-collar workers. Five factors probably account for the decline:

1. A steady switch in employment from the public sector and nationalized industries to the private sector, where unionization rates are traditionally lower. On average, 60 percent of UK public sector workers are unionized compared with 19 percent in the private sector.

2. A shift within the private sector from traditional manufacturing industries (where 28 percent of the UK work force is unionized) to the service sector, with a large numbers of small work places difficult for unions to recruit.

3. UK unions' loss of battles in the 1980s with Mrs. Thatcher's Conservative Government, which damaged the morale of the movement. Unions in other countries were similarly emasculated.

4. Changes in the nature of employment and the labor market over the last twenty years (due to globalization, new technology, more women entering the work force, etc.). There is no longer a clear divide between those with and without jobs. Many now work part time, on temporary contracts, and in many countries, in the informal sector. Unions generally represent full-time, formal-sector workers with open-ended contracts; these are in sharp decline. Other groups of workers don't think unions cater to them.

5. Loss of public appeal due to all the other factors, but it is more than this. Unions seem old-fashioned and a part of the mainstream political processes with which people have become disillusioned. The decline is particularly pronounced with young workers. In the UK, whereas in 1983, 44 percent of workers aged eighteen to twenty-nine were union members and 57 percent in the 40–plus age group, the comparable figures fell to 18 percent and 33 percent respectively by 1998. Globally, 20 percent of all workers are under twenty-five, but they comprise only 9 percent of union members. The loss of young blood is of great concern to Western trade unions.

Work places with unions have better pay and conditions, smaller wage differentials, less gender and race gaps, and fewer accidents. In some countries union membership has risen strongly, and there are signs that membership decline has reversed in the UK and Australia.

Note: UK statistics taken from the Trades Union Congress.

internationally. But in forging closer networks with Southern unions such networks encounter new priorities that barely arise in Northern countries—such as informal sector growth, structural adjustment, and child labor.

The more progressive unions are, like NGOs, making major changes in what they do—but they are driven by a greater sense of urgency. They are forming stronger global networks, putting increasing emphasis on advocacy and campaigning (beyond traditional collective bargaining and representational work), and they are networking with NGOs and other CSOs outside the union movement. Globalization, the East Asia crisis, the perceived threat posed by the proposed Multilateral Agreement on Investment (which unions and NGOs successfully opposed), and the huge protest at the Seattle WTO meeting all helped to convince rank-and-file members that they should put more effort into working globally.

Although they feature less in the media than the environmental groups, students, and anarchists, unions mobilize more participation in modern demonstrations about globalization than any other group. For example, they mobilized two-thirds of the demonstrators at the Seattle WTO protest (see Chapter 8).

New working styles also drive changes in culture. Organizational growth and an increased focus on policy work tend to make CSOs' activities more professional, often reducing the influence of grassroots members and national-level staff, especially as resources expand (from membership dues or greater capacity to raise funds).

The Internet facilitates affinity groups within CSO networks; hence, old subdivisions (global network, national chapters, local groups) are no longer the only way of dividing the pie. Amnesty, for example, now has global groupings of lawyers, medics, teachers, and youth, as well as those working on the death penalty, homosexual rights, and rights abuse in specific countries. A similar pattern occurs in Oxfam, Greenpeace, Friends of the Earth, and other CSO networks. Activists may now feel more identity with their affinity group than with their national chapter. And as these compete with one another, pressure groups arise within pressure groups. Networks find they can achieve much more overall by encouraging affinity groups. This parallels the experience of firms; dense networks permit more effective information flow, which is highly prized in an age where information is power.

GETTING NEW PARTNERS

If information is one magic ingredient of the network age, partnership is the other. In CSOs, as in the business world, strong and diverse partnerships correlate with success and innovation and are most likely to be found in organizations that are adaptable and good at problem-solving. Most well-known NGOs today have excelled at partnership building; it opens new doors for activities and influence and expands achievements, thus generating good publicity, wider name recognition, and organizational success.

This is illustrated by the growth in voluntary donations, as opposed to government contributions, to the major UK development NGOs (statistics from Charities Aid Foundation). Save the Children Fund, whose strongest UK partnership has traditionally been with the royal family, did well in the 1980s, when donations grew almost 11 percent per year, compared with 3.7 percent for Oxfam and 3.2 percent for Christian Aid. In the 1990s Oxfam was most creative in developing global and national partnerships. The other two NGOs stayed with their traditional partners and approaches. Donations to Oxfam rose 8.5 percent a year from 1990 to 1996, while Christian Aid's grew sluggishly (1.6 percent) and Save the Children Fund's declined 6.2 percent a year. Save the Children Fund's total income greatly exceeded Oxfam's in the 1980s but is now considerably smaller. Though there may be other factors at work, this shift in fortunes is partly due to the more modern image and wider public appeal of network-oriented NGOs.

The network age does not just mean working with like-minded groups in neighboring countries, it means building radically new partnerships—inside or outside civil society—to tackle issues that would be immovable without those alliances. But partnerships are not easy to build for organizations that are characteristically competitive. The large operational NGOs compete with one another for public donations; the big advocacy groups compete with one another for membership. Partnership is generally, therefore, easier with peers in *other* countries (such as in the Oxfam International network) or with organizations in different fields. For example, trade union–NGO partnerships are increasingly significant.

Business links

NGOs (especially environmental groups) have increasingly forged partnerships with the private sector, generating a whole new discipline of "corporate citizenship" (Zadek 2001). Many examples involve NGOs helping or pressing TNCs to introduce more sustainable or ethical approaches; the NGOs typically provide the standards and the certification (which protects the corporation's reputation).

NGOs can, of course, conduct unilateral audits, but these would be limited to firms they can access. Hence, the Center for Responsibility in Business, an accreditation agency in New York, uses auditable standards to assess companies' employment practices; by April 2001 it had positively certified sixty-six manufacturing facilities around the world (Gereffi et al. 2001). A more collaborative approach is to develop codes with the companies and then to provide independent monitoring of compliance within overseas subsidiaries and suppliers. Oxfam GB and Levi Strauss developed such a partnership in 1997 regarding the company's Dominican Republic suppliers. This engagement was productive and encouraged Levi Strauss to evolve a further-reaching ethics policy (Zadek 2001).

Such partnerships do not always experience smooth sailing, however. The clothing industry, NGOs, and unions came together to form the Apparel Industry Partnership in 1995, prompted by the Clinton Administration after some sweatshop factory scandals had surfaced. It agreed to a code of conduct governing pay, conditions, and workers' rights, and created the Fair Labor Association in 1998 to implement and monitor this code. Industry pressure led to weak standards and the main union involved walked out, condemning the venture. The NGOs who remained received much public criticism (Gereffi et al. 2001). The association continues to exist, however, and is generally seen as objective in its certification work and reports.

In the sustainable forestry field there have also been numerous partnerships with varying degrees of success. The Forestry Stewardship Council (an initiative of WWF and Greenpeace) was launched in 1993 to certify timber harvesting and the whole distribution chain. Most timber users found the standards too onerous and so developed their own easier regimes, such as the Sustainable Forestry Initiative. Campaigning by consumer groups and environmentalists, however, discredited such industry efforts, and some retailers (such as Home Depot and Lowes) have insisted on the higher FSC standards (Gereffi et al. 2001).

CSO partnerships can help shift companies toward more ethical and sustainable values. A similar approach has been used to promote changes within IGOs. For example, WWF and the World Bank created the Forest Alliance partnership agreement to promote the designation of protected forests. Similarly ActionAid and other NGOs were influential in encouraging the World Bank to form the Business Partners in Development program.

Some particularly powerful partnerships have been formed in the public health field. The Rotary Club has raised $400 million to date for the polio eradication program (implemented by the World Bank and WHO in partnership with a wide range of NGOs and scientific institutes). And a more recent campaign against the parasitic disease lymphatic filariasis (elephantiasis, which affects 120 million people) comprises multilateral agencies (WHO, World Bank, and UNICEF), seven bilateral donors, twelve major NGOs, nine academic centers, and two pharmaceutical companies. GlaxoSmithKline agreed to provide the key treatment drug (albendazole) free of charge for twenty years, forgoing $1 billion—probably the single largest act of corporate philanthropy to date.

These examples illustrate that partnerships are powerful but not always easy. A disease such as elephantiasis cannot be eradicated without up-to-date scientific knowledge about the disease and the timely supply and correct dosages of drugs; the logistical challenge of integrating the program into the health-care systems of eighty countries is vast, and a mammoth public motivational campaign is needed to ensure that the 120 million infected, *and* the 1.2 billion at risk, come for medication five times each year. All the players in the partnership have critical but very different roles.

Such partnerships require leaps of vision, can be fraught with ethical dilemmas, and can be readily misconstrued by rivals or supporters. It is tempting for all CSOs to stay with the familiar, and large organizations can be particularly reluctant to work with others because of the high gravitational pull of their own mass.

Faith partnerships

The slowest CSO sector to build partnerships comprises the faiths. Competition for the loyalty of believers is the foundation of their existence; hence, they emphasize *differences* with other religions rather than communalities. There are common interests, however, concerning the right to worship, other human rights, peace, education, poverty, the environment, and social justice. Over the last one hundred years there have been spasmodic and short-lived attempts to develop interfaith partnerships, starting with the First Parliament of World Religion held in Chicago in 1893. In recent years this cooperation has accelerated. In 1993 the International Interfaith Centre was set up in Oxford, UK; in 1996 the United Religions Initiative was launched at a major conference in San Francisco; in 1998 the World Faiths Dialogue on Development was launched; in 1999 a Council for the Parliament for World Religions met in Cape Town; and in August 2000 the Millennium World Peace Summit (the "Faiths' Summit") brought one thousand senior religious leaders together in New York from all the leading faiths (Boehle 2001).

This gathering momentum, however, is ringing alarm bells in some quarters—in particular the Vatican. Cardinal Joseph Ratzinger (widely regarded as the diviner of correct procedures within the church) recently responded to discussion of the declaration "Dominus Iesus" by warning clergy to be wary of religious pluralism. His has not been the only voice on this topic.

North-South divides

Often the most difficult aspect of partnership building is managing North-South relations, particularly in NGOs (also in trade unions and the consumers' movement). Southern NGOs in international alliances often feel like second-class citizens—welcomed as sources of information and legitimization but not as equals (Ashman 2000). This imbalance leads Northern NGOs to emerge as mediators between the global and local levels, due to their greater access to intergovernmental processes. This gives the impression that "civil society of rich countries— especially the United States—is more important politically than that of the poor countries," thus diminishing democratic processes in the South (Vianna 2000).

Southern NGO leaders, such as Aurelio Vianna of Brazil, call for higher partnership standards based on Southern needs, reciprocity, and true exchange. The tendency of donors to fund *Northern* partners in transnational CSO networks and their reluctance to share these resources exacerbate inequalities and tensions (Jordan and van Tuijl 2000).

NGO campaigning on the Amazon in the early 1990s, for example, was dominated by resource-rich Northern environment groups that stressed only the rainforest conservation issues. In Rondonia the local NGOs united to present a challenge to their Northern peers about the need to include social concerns of forest inhabitants when depicting the issues of their state. Eventually the international campaign broadened, but some of the strictly conservation groups pulled out of the coalition (Rodrigues 2000).

Union–NGO partnerships

Unions and NGOs see mutual advantage in cooperating in global campaigns due to their different strengths. NGOs often have higher profile than unions (even though they may represent few members) and are often more successful communicators. Though unions at the national level often have little to do with NGOs, most of their international umbrellas regularly work with NGOs. For example, the chemical workers unions and Greenpeace jointly lobbied the worldwide chemical industry federation to institute stricter safety and environmental controls in the production of chlorine-based chemicals (Leather and

Harris 1999); unions worked with NGOs in the campaign against the Multilateral Agreement on Investment and are prominent in ATTAC's campaign for the Tobin Tax. NGOs and unions have also worked together to promote improved labor practices—sometimes including setting up unions in factories supplying retail giants such as Nike, Reebok, and Adidas.

Relationships are not always smooth, however, due to major policy differences. NGOs often see unions as preserving formal-sector jobs and wages in the North at the expense of others more vulnerable. The strongest differences have been with Southern advocacy groups concerning whether labor standards should be incorporated into WTO rules. Most unions think so (though agreeing that sanctions aren't appropriate for enforcing social clauses), but groups such as Third World Network and Southern consumers' groups believe this would be a back door to Northern protectionism and that such clauses would hurt the very workers their proponents claim to be concerned about. The unions reject such criticism and accuse those promoting them of being elitist and lacking a mass base. These simmering differences were the subject of a special union-NGO round-table meeting in Bangkok in 2001 (Focus on the Global South 2001).

These major differences clearly make for uneasy alliances, as does the underlying conviction of many unionists that advocacy NGOs don't really represent anyone but themselves. They resent NGOs' greater maneuverability (many can make impromptu decisions while unions must refer them back to their members), which makes them powerful in fast-moving campaigns, and feel the need to keep a wary distance. This has been magnified by political and tactical differences since the 9/11 terrorist attacks, particularly in the United States. US trade unionists have strongly supported the "war against terrorism," while the more radical NGOs who have been allies on issues concerning globalization are seeking to direct the energy of the protest movement into a peace movement against this military response. Analysts are divided as to whether cooperation has been shelved permanently or just temporarily (Davis 2002).

CASE STUDY 1:
GLOBAL UNIONS: THE FORCE OF ARGUMENT
PLUS THE ARGUMENT OF FORCE

Trade unions form national umbrellas to influence national policy, but they have also formed global union federations (GUFs)—umbrellas of unions in particular trades or sectors. These are increasingly important in the transitions the Labor movement is experiencing toward working transnationally and dealing with issues of globalization. The GUFs also have their own umbrella (the International Confederation of Free Trade Unions, ICFTU) and a think tank in the OECD (the Trade Union Advisory Committee). Together, these form the Global Unions movement. They have become more prevalent in recent years in lobbying the IGOs (especially the European Union, OECD, WTO, World Bank, and IMF) and as key players in the protest movement about globalization. Though individual unions have become weaker in most countries, global unions are a growing force.

Many GUFs have also facilitated exchange between unionists in different countries who have a common (TNC) employer. Some employers, such as Vivendi, have agreed to enter global negotiations over their employment policies (there were twelve such framework agreements as of 2001).

The GUFs have been through considerable change. When their task was largely solidarity work and sharing information between national-level unions, they could maintain small offices covering quite specific trades, but as their role expanded to become more proactive and demanding, they required more professional staff and decentralized offices. Since they are resource-poor, this has required pooling; hence, there have been a number of mergers. Now there are just ten GUFs, some of which embrace a wide range of related trades. The newest GUF, Union Network International (UNI), for example, was created in 2000 out of various prior union federations covering post and telecommunications, banking and financial services, insurance, retail, media, entertainment, graphic design, and information technology industries. It represents fifteen million members and is, in effect, the union of the new economy.

Globalization is also critical for Public Service International, the worldwide umbrella of 560 unions representing public-sector employees (other than teachers). Working internationally doesn't strengthen their leverage over employers, who by definition are at the national level, but it enhances the effectiveness of their advocacy, particularly concerning the impact of adjustment and privatization on public-sector workers and pressure on the IGOs to respect hard-won workers' rights when advising governments on labor market policies. PSI is the most decentralized GUF, with twenty-five regional and sub-regional offices.

Decentralization and new membership, mostly from developing or transition countries, has been a major challenge for PSI and other GUFs. PSI almost tripled its membership in the last fourteen years with little extra funding (the new members are poor). This has triggered significant changes in its style and activities, with more emphasis on campaigning and lobbying. Southern trade unions, such as those in the Philippines, have pressed hard for GUFs to take up issues of "flexibilization" of labor contracts and support for informal sector, migrants, and other unprotected workers.

Because of the world changes they face, a sweeping review of the global union structure was initiated in 2000. A review group was established to propose new ways to address the global challenges, restore membership, attract young workers, support informal and unprotected workers, elect women into leadership positions, and coax TNCs into global negotiations. The review has reinforced the importance of global unions and international organizing around issues of the global economy (ICFTU 2001). The ICFTU group of unions now represents 156 million members (almost twice its 1982 representation), of which almost half are from developing and transition countries. There is a smaller "rival" organization (the World Confederation of Labour) representing Christian Democrat trade unions, with which ICFTU collaborates on some activities.

CASE STUDY 2:
THE TORTURE OF AMNESTY

No NGO is more concerned about internal democracy or more scrupulously professional than Amnesty International—and it pays a high price for its principles.

Amnesty International was launched in 1961 and now has more than one million members in over 140 countries and territories. It is the world's most democratic NGO. Its London-based international secretariat has more than 320 staff from over fifty countries. It has more than 7,500 approved local groups (and many informal ones) and numerous specialist networks in nearly one hundred countries. There are nationally organized sections in fifty-six countries, with another twenty-three on the way. The growth of sections in recent years has been due mostly to new Southern and transition country Amnesty Internationals. Its activities are determined by its mandate—a charter of Amnesty International's convictions and agreed upon strategies (Power 2001).

During its first decades Amnesty International was accustomed to being the only significant NGO in the human rights field and considered its independence from others an aspect of its impartiality. During the 1980s and 1990s other human rights groups formed (notably Human Rights Watch). Amnesty International was initially rather suspicious and territorial, but the emergence of these groups has fostered a global human rights movement, attracting a more diverse following. This has not only elevated rights issues on the international political agenda, but it has helped Amnesty International, since it remains the "brand leader." Amnesty International plays an active part in the movement and now frequently develops partnerships with other human rights groups, unions, religious groups, and development NGOs, for example, in the recent campaign for the International Criminal Court.

No network demonstrates the dilemmas of decision-making more clearly than Amnesty International. Many within the organization and friends outside say that it is in crisis because its governance, though democratic, is hidebound in procedure. Its careful democracy was designed for a time when it had few sections, mostly in industrialized countries, and a common culture. All major decisions, such as changes in mandate, are taken at the International Council Meeting of all sections every two years, with votes weighted according to the number of groups in each section—and there is a strong preference for achieving consensus or at least avoiding major splits. Consequently, on controversial issues an issue may be held over from one meeting to the next, or a compromise reached. In a fast-moving world such delays can be damaging. Debates about mandate can also be highly technical and inaccessible to most new or smaller members, especially if they are not fluent in the languages used.

One of the most difficult recent controversies centered on whether Amnesty International should campaign on gay rights. Most OECD groups argued strongly in favor, while many in developing countries contested that this could make them unpopular or even illegal. The landmines issue also presented a difficulty; Amnesty International missed opportunities to contribute to the global campaign because at the time the mandate did not include this issue. Amnesty International's leaders recognize that decision-making has become too slow for the modern age and too technical to maintain popular appeal. Amnesty International is currently considering a range of options for "changing the way we change" (Amnesty International 2000).

Amnesty International's major "competitor," Human Rights Watch, has no such bottlenecks. It is not ruled by a mandate but can take up any cause in which a human rights connection is evident (whether political, civil, economic, or social). Human Rights Watch is also a centralized organization, governed by a primarily US board. It is weak on participation and empowerment but has built a reputation as a highly effective human rights NGO.

Mission creep

Amnesty International's founding mandate was clear: the release of prisoners of conscience, whether held on religious or political grounds.

In its first three decades there were a few extensions—to permit campaigning on the death penalty, extra-judicial killings, torture, cruel treatment and disappearances—but there has been a mandate explosion since 1990, reflecting in particular the interests of new Southern groups. Dozens of new clauses have been introduced, covering topics as diverse as armed opposition groups, laws on wars, homosexuality, female genital mutilation, human rights promotion and education, forcible exile, fair trial, the International Criminal Court, and landmines. The mandate now is no longer a crisp mission statement of Amnesty International's values but a legalistic tome of which few in the organization have a good grasp and which many see as a millstone, preventing Amnesty International from being able to respond flexibly to world events as they arise.

This has far from ended. As more development interests have come into Amnesty International, and as a greater variety of affinity groups have been formed, new mandate changes are constantly being proposed, particularly relating to social and economic rights. Proponents argue that globalization has diminished the strength of nation-states; other actors, such as IGOs, are gaining political power; and armed opposition groups often have de facto control over territories and their populations. Hence, they argue, it is no longer sufficient to focus on violations perpetrated by governments.

And as Amnesty International increasingly seeks to work in partnership with other NGOs, it comes under pressure to lend reciprocal support to their campaigns, which also contributes to mission creep. In addition to Amnesty International's traditional campaigns on specific human rights abuses, Amnesty International is increasingly involved in education and campaigning in support of broad human rights. Furthermore, Southern members are challenging Amnesty International's founding principle against working on "own-country" issues. The principle was designed to ensure impartiality and to avoid becoming embroiled in partisan politics, but Southern members find this anachronistic. For them, participation in Amnesty International only makes sense if they can work on national issues and take a full part in the human rights movement in their country.

CASE STUDY 3:
CONSUMING MATTERS—
THE INTERNATIONAL CONSUMERS' MOVEMENT[2]

Consumers unions emerged in Northern countries in the postwar boom years of the 1950s. Their emphasis was on providing rigorous

and unbiased information to their members to help them in their purchasing choices. In 1960 the leading five formed the International Organization of Consumers Unions (IOCU), which mirrored its founders
in its emphasis on product testing and fixing testing standards. It also
set the norm for consumer groups until the 1980s. However, the emergence of Southern consumer groups (initially gradual but rising to a
flood in the 1990s) changed the culture of consumer activism, introduced new ways of working, and triggered a "reinvention" of the international organization. Though tensions are evident, IOCU provides
a model of a relatively smooth transition to new member priorities as
different global realities impinge.

In its first fifteen years, IOCU's growth in size and influence was
largely North-driven, but then it started to promote Southern membership and by the 1980s began to adopt new activities and working styles
reflecting this diversification. It even stopped product-testing work,
giving more space to global campaigns on policies affecting consumers, especially where national governments cannot readily make individual decisions. It had five members in 1960, 110 in 1986, and had
grown to 263 members in 119 countries by 2002. Most members are
now non-OECD, and there are growing numbers of activist groups—
very different in style from the middle-class membership groups in
Northern countries. As a result, IOCU has changed what it does, how
it works, and its culture.

Its new members encouraged an emphasis on consumer-justice campaigns. The first of these were mounted jointly with NGOs. They include co-founding the International Baby Foods Action Network in
1979; campaigning for safe, affordable medicines in 1981 (Health Action International); and creating the Pesticides Action Network in 1982
to curb the use in the South of hazardous farm chemicals that are banned
in the North. IOCU also successfully pressed for the establishment of a
UN list of hazardous products, designed to alert Southern governments
about products that have been banned or strictly restricted in the North,
which might therefore be dumped by manufacturers on Southern markets. Much of its international advocacy has been conducted through
the United Nations, including its support for the development of national consumer-protection laws.

These changed emphases became reflected in changes in its governance structure. The apex of this is the world assembly—the three-
yearly meeting of all members.[3] This approves overall direction and
elects both a world council and a president. The council meets every
year but delegates authority to a smaller executive committee that meets
more frequently for tactical decisions. The assembly appointed IOCU's
first Southern president in 1980. The assembly and the council have

guided the reinvention process, shifting the emphasis from product information and testing work to activism and strengthening national members (especially in the South), from value for money to consumers' rights, and from member coordination to building a global consumers movement. They also decentralized the secretariat to support these changes, so that most staff now work at regional level. And they agreed to a name change to Consumer International in order to reflect that fostering a global consumers movement is now the main aim.

While the culture of the organization has changed successfully, there are tensions. Northern groups tend to be politically middle of the road, while Southern groups tend to be more radical; Northern groups have mass memberships, while Southern groups are small and depend on foreign funding; Northern groups emphasize consumer choice and information-based work, while Southern groups prioritize basic needs and rights-based advocacy. And Southern members tend to resent that the original five founders still dominate the body and always have a seat on the executive committee.

CONCLUSIONS

In civil society, as in the business world, the N-Form presents today's most powerful organizational challenge. Since most CSOs operate at a local or national level, networking is particularly important for those who seek to influence policies that are substantially determined internationally. It is also vital in operational activities where goals can only be achieved by working transnationally (such as the global health campaigns). The networking pioneers are the most effective CSOs in this arena, but they experience major bumps in the road, as the case studies illustrate. Tighter federations allow more efficient resource deployment (for example, the GUFs) and greater access to and use of IGOs (for example, Consumer International). Membership diversification heightens credibility but also brings challenges of decision-making, culture, and mission creep (for example, Amnesty International); it can also surface North-South divides. Global networking, however, enables policy influence that would hardly be possible otherwise (for example, Jubilee 2000), and has heralded new approaches to global responsibility (for example, the business ethics cases). Considerable discipline on the part of the CSOs is called for and perhaps a shift in their core emphasis (for example, FOE); this presents greater difficulty in some sectors than others. Networking with nontraditional partners is very important (for example, the GUFs and Consumer International), but faith-based CSOs find this particularly difficult. Often the whole becomes more than the sum of the parts as networks seed the emergence of wider social movements (all three case studies).

We will now look at how such issues play out within the civil society category that is most concerned with achieving global influence—the international development NGOs.

7.

Retaining Relevance

Twenty-first Century Strategies
for Development NGOs

International development NGOs (INGOs) are the giants of civil society. They may have fewer members or supporters than large trade unions, and fewer staff and "outlets" than the major religions, but in terms of budgets and global reach they rule the roost. How have they acquired this clout, and are they content having done so? Who are the key players? What are the key dilemmas they face today? And how is their contribution likely to evolve in the future? These are the questions to be explored in this chapter.

Because of the public and media support they enjoy in the North, INGOs have immense moral authority. Though most have been relatively inactive in policy advocacy, some have moved increasingly into this arena. They have found not only that their impact can be very considerable but—contrary to their fears—rather than see support and income decline as a result of such political activity, they actually enjoy increasing support. This is leading their more conservative peers to question whether they are being left behind, whether they too need to use their field experience to influence policy if they are to stay relevant in the modern age.

Collectively, INGO growth over the last three decades has been striking. In 1980 they channeled $3.5 billion from North to South, while by 1999 this had grown to about $15 billion, according to one estimate (Development Initiatives 2000), including about $7.2 billion by US NGOs (1997) and $7.3 billion by European NGOs. Of all North-South aid (official and voluntary), the NGO share probably doubled in this period, as voluntary giving increased and official aid declined. The rapid growth in the number of INGOs and international grants from foundations and other factors make it difficult to be precise about the contributions NGOs make, but they have clearly grown considerably. The following table indicates this growth in real terms (however, note that the 1999 figures are calculated differently and are estimates).[1]

Table 7.1 NGO and official aid to developing countries (constant 1990 $ billion)

	1970	1980	1988	1999
Total NGO Aid	3.64	5.2	6.9	12.4
Private donations to NGOs	3.58	3.6	4.5	10.7
Official grants to NGOs	.05	1.6	2.4	1.7
OECD official aid	29.5	42.1	51.4	46.6
NGO aid as percent of all aid	11.0	11.4	12.3	21.6

Sources: Clark 1991; OECD Development Assistance Committee (various); Lindenberg and Bryant 2001; Development Initiatives 2000; UNDP 2001. US$ GDP deflators from World Bank.

This growth is due to increased disposable income (and guiltier consciences) in rich countries, the near-monopoly of television as the conduit of mass communication (and NGOs can help TV producers access Southern stories as well as provide good television), the media's thirst for national heroes to help dramatize events, celebrities' desire to be associated with such heroes, and official aid agencies increasing focus on poverty reduction and preference for nongovernmental conduits for their aid.

So are INGOs satisfied with what they have achieved? Up to a point. Their incomes continue to rise, as do staff numbers, but there is a creeping malaise. The odd scandal aside—usually the product of a disgruntled staff member or a right-wing media probe—all seems healthy. Southern governments accept them more and even offer collaboration or contracts (frequently at the bidding of official donors). Perhaps the nagging qualms stem partly from the very comfortable situation they have reached. Is it the comfort of a staid and rather corpulent middle age?

This unease shows in self-flagellating writing by some NGO leaders (see, for example, the collection of papers in Lindenberg and Dobel 1999, and Fowler 1997) and the strenuous efforts most major INGOs are making to "reinvent" themselves. Their concern shouldn't be overstated. Most INGO chiefs are optimists—proud of their programs, confident in their staff and partners, and convinced their NGO is making a difference—but they *know* this is a rosy view and so think it beneficial to expose themselves occasionally to a dose of healthy cynicism and parade doubts before one another. They also know that the world is fast changing, and hence so must they. Global change offers huge new opportunities, which we will discuss later, but first we will sketch the anatomy of the sector.

THE TOP TEN TNCS OF AID

In the business world a handful of TNCs commonly dominates any given sector—whether cars, coffee, computers, or cosmetics—thanks to the rapid growth of brand leaders coupled with mergers and take-overs. A similar pattern applies to relief and development NGOs, but here they are transnational *charities*.

There is one critical difference. With NGOs (and most CSO categories except unions) takeovers and mergers are rare. An NGO may wither to nothing, but it is rarely wound up, and few go bankrupt. Leaders of NGOs in decline generally prefer to scale back and hold on rather than be taken over, and the stronger NGOs are not interested in taking over problems. Growth in INGOs is through organic growth, not mergers. However, NGOs do seek economies of scale and would like to punch a heavier weight.

Networking is the solution. Hence seven independent organizations in different countries came together in the 1980s to form a loose network, Oxfam International, albeit dwarfed by the founder, Oxfam UK. Initially they just exchanged information and ideas and coordinated emergency relief, but in the early 1990s they decided to make it an active confederation for joint advocacy and program harmonization. NGOs in Netherlands and Spain were invited to join, even though they weren't named Oxfam; Oxfam Ireland was "given independence"; and the network formed two new Oxfams in New Zealand and Germany. It recently invited BRAC of Bangladesh to be its first Southern member.[2]

The biggest INGOs have evolved international networks of different forms in recent years. CARE, for example, was originally a US NGO, principally financed by the US government; it later established offices to do fund-raising in other Northern countries. These grew and their purposes evolved such that some (CARE Canada in particular) became substantial NGOs in their own right, with their own overseas programs, though channeling the bulk of their income through CARE US. In the 1990s the structure changed from a unitary organization with CARE US as both parent and its largest operation into a nominal confederation (CARE International), in which each CARE is technically independent, and there is a single CARE program in any program country, managed for the network by one member (the lead agency). Given that CARE US so dominates the group, it remains close to a unitary organization but with flexibility allowing other CAREs to lead programs in countries of particular interest to them.

Plan International and World Vision are clearer unitary organizations, though delegating much autonomy to the national-level agencies that are responsible for fund-raising, donor relations, and development education. In contrast, Save the Children is a very loose network, comprising twenty-six child-oriented NGOs—all with similar names but little else in common. The Protestant and Catholic NGO networks offer similar independence.

Médecins Sans Frontières, which changed course halfway through its evolution, combines both approaches. Originally a French NGO, from 1981–85 it helped establish independent organizations (with the same name and a common charter) in various European countries. MSF then switched to having "delegate offices" in other Northern countries, raising funds to channel through MSF France, and mobilizing doctors and other volunteers for MSF programs. WWF is another hybrid. Like Amnesty, it has a strong secretariat serving its membership.

Box 7.1 provides a sketch of each of the ten major networks. It includes WWF, because the distinction between operational environment and development NGOs is no longer clear-cut. In some countries (but not all) WWF emphasizes sustainable development rather than species and habitat conservation and hence gives equal attention to social and environmental needs. Similarly, many development NGOs work on issues of habitat conservation and environmental pressures.

Collectively these networks had an income of approximately $4.64 billion in 1999, which means that they command about 31 percent of all INGO aid for development—a concentration approaching that found in the private sector. There has also been a steep increase in US foundations' grants for international work. The 50,532 independent US foundations gave almost one-tenth of their grants to international programs in 2000 (or $2.5 billion), though two-thirds of this was to US or other Northern-based CSOs for their international work rather than Southern CSOs. The major contributors are Bill Gates, Ted Turner, and the Ford Foundation. This group of US foundations tends to work closely together and could be seen as an eleventh network.

TNCs and the super-charities have one big structural difference. In the business world they are undoubtedly single corporations, albeit in network mode with considerable autonomy delegated to subsidiaries. At the apex sits one chief executive and one global board. CARE, Plan, and World Vision are similar, but other INGOs are confederations or loose networks of independent NGOs, not single conglomerates. They increasingly coordinate their strategies and advocacy to heighten power and influence, but they remain collections of independent NGOs.

Increasing exchange within and between these networks facilitates more concerted strategies. This could accelerate the adoption of innovations and strengthen advocacy in both North and South. If they realize their collective strength, they will be a formidable development force. They command a total budget close to the GNP of Nepal ($5.3 billion), or the soft-loan arm of the World Bank ($5.2 billion in 2000), and more than the entire UK aid budget. They have universal name recognition throughout the North and most of the South. They have excellent media relations and highly professional communications staff. Most devote more than 10 percent of their income to advertising, media work, and other public relations, hence their combined communications budget is about $500 million. This is more than the US public contributed to all Democrat candidates combined to fight the last election ($275 million, compared to $466 million for Republicans). Among them, they have hundreds of millions of members or supporters (115 million volunteers for the Red Cross alone) and employ approaching 100,000 staff worldwide.

This is unparalleled civic power, but it is partly *unrealized* because until now they have been wary of using their clout for fear of losing support, and they don't work in concert. If they did, they could transform thinking about development and international relations and be an inspiration to the rest of civil society.

Suppose one-fifth of their communications budget was contributed to a global campaign (for example, to do away with Northern farm policies that devastate opportunities for Southern farmers—see Chapter 11). This would have dramatic impact on public opinion that policymakers would find hard to ignore. It would also balance what the food and agriculture industry spend lobbying to retain and increase their privileges ($52 million in 1998 in Washington [Nestle 2002]). In truth, nothing like this sum would be needed, but if such an investment *did* lead to significant policy change, it would mean more for poverty reduction than decades of direct project funding.

Box 7.1 Vital statistics for the leading INGO networks

CARE

Global size: approximately $550 million in 2000; ten member agencies plus CARE International (Brussels); ten thousand staff, of which 95 percent are locally hired. The United States government provides about half the global budget; much of the rest comes from other governments and multilateral agencies.

Founded: 1945 as US organization—Cooperative Agency for Relief Everywhere—initially providing relief to refugees and others after World War II; later broadened to relief/welfare in the South, then to development. It executes many projects for governments and donor agencies.

Members (and percent contribution to total income): the United States (79%), Canada (15%), Australia, Austria, Denmark, France, Germany, Japan, Norway, and the UK.

International structure: CARE works as a single organization; each program in the South is managed by one of the ten CAREs as lead agency. It is akin to a unitary organization.

World Vision

Global size: $600 million (1999); works in ninety-two countries.

Founded: 1950 in the United States by an evangelist.

Members (and percent contribution to total income): the United States (68%), Canada (12%), the UK (6%), others (14%).

International structure: World Vision remains close to a unitary organization but goes further than most INGOs in giving strong autonomy to program offices in the South. World Vision International was formed in 1971 as a member agency network. Since the late 1980s the program officers have sat on the WVI council, which meets every three years. The board (which meets regularly and is more powerful) has some Southern representation. WVI maintains strong control over all partners.

Save the Children

Global size: $368 million (1999); twenty-six members.

Founded: 1919 in the UK in response to World War I.

Members: the United States and the UK are largest (both had incomes of approximately $140 million in 2000). Save the Children–US is over 50 percent US-government funded, Save the Children–UK is about 60 percent privately funded.

International structure: It is both the largest and most informal INGO network. The International Save the Children Alliance (ISCA) was established in 1988 and until recently served mostly information and coordination roles; in the mid-1990s a secretariat was established in London; the first CEO was appointed in 1998. Save the Children members appear unwilling to forgo further autonomy to build a stronger alliance.

Oxfam

Global size: $504 million (1999); twelve members; works in 117 countries.

Founded: 1942 in the UK (as Oxford Committee for Famine Relief) to bring relief to Greek citizens suffering as a result of the Allies' war effort. It started to establish Oxfams in other countries in the 1970s but soon decided that these should be independent.

Members: the UK, Ireland, Netherlands, Belgium, Spain, Australia, New Zealand, Canada, Quebec, the United States, Hong Kong, and Germany.

International structure: Until the early 1990s, Oxfam International was a very loose network, though Oxfam UK coordinated relief programs for all Oxfams. In 1992 the agencies decided to strengthen Oxfam International for advocacy and to explore program harmonization. A secretariat with a CEO was established in Oxford with sub-offices for advocacy in Washington, Geneva, and Brussels.

Plan International

Global size: $311 million (2002); fifteen members; 80 percent of income from child sponsorship.

Founded: 1937 as Foster Parent Plan to help children victims of the Spanish civil war. Plan works in forty-two program countries.

Members (and percent contribution to total income): Netherlands (25%), Germany (11%), the United States (14%), Japan (9%), the UK (11%), Canada (10%), Norway (7%), Belgium, Australia, and six others.

International structure: A corporate HQ, initially in the United States, now in the UK, is responsible for all program work. All national Plans are fund-raisers. Total staff is 5,859 (5,358 in program countries, 422 in national organizations, and 79 at HQ).

Médecins Sans Frontières

Global size: $304 million (1999); six full members; thirteen support members (and Médecins Sans Frontières International based in Brussels).

Founded: In France during Biafran war (in response to the Red Cross not being allowed to provide relief without government approval). Médecins Sans Frontières maintains distance from all governments and emphasizes its "witness" role. It has twelve hundred volunteer doctors in sixty to seventy countries at any given time.

International structure: Full sections were set up from 1981 to 1985 in Belgium, Switzerland, Netherlands, Spain, and Luxembourg. Then only support offices formed (Australia, Austria, Canada, Denmark, Germany, Greece, Hong Kong, Italy, Japan, Norway, Sweden, the United States, and the UK). Full members share the same charter, act independently, but are loosely coordinated by Médecins Sans Frontières International.

WWF

Global size: $350 million; five million members; thirty-three hundred staff.

International structure: Network of largely independent national conservation organizations, mostly Northern based (though there are WWFs in some larger Southern countries); serviced by a large Swiss secretariat (WWF-I). To diversify and expand the Southern voice, for the last five years WWF has included program offices in the deliberating processes, though these have less weight. The largest offices (WWF-US, WWF-NL, and WWF-I) dominate decision-making.

Red Cross (International Federation of Red Cross and Red Crescent Societies)

Global size: $230 million in 2001 from international appeals.

Founded: 1919 (though the Swiss International Committee of Red Cross started in 1869).

International structure: Now the world's largest humanitarian NGO, with 178 member societies and 115 million volunteers. The largest donor societies (with percentage of total international appeal contributions) are the UK (14%), Sweden (10%), the United States (9%), Norway (8%), Japan (7%), Finland (4%), Canada, Netherlands, and Germany (each 3%).

Association of Protestant Development Agencies in Europe (APRODEV)
Global size: $470 million; about 40 percent private, and the rest from the European Union and other official sources.
Members: Fifteen Protestant church–based NGOs in eleven countries (Denmark, Finland, France, Germany, Hungary, Iceland, Netherlands, Norway, Sweden, Switzerland, and the UK).
International structure: Very loose association with a small secretariat in Brussels, largely for making joint statements on policy issues and liaison with the World Council of Churches.

International Cooperation for Development and Solidarity (CIDSE)
Global size: $950.5 million (2000) for 7,781 projects (32 percent Africa).
Members: Fourteen Catholic church–based NGOs in Europe (Austria, Belgium, France, Germany, Ireland, Italy, Netherlands, Spain, Switzerland, the UK) and one in Quebec.
International structure: Very loose network.

DILEMMAS OF DEVELOPMENT NGOS

INGOs are at a crossroads. The road ahead has a surface that appears to be deteriorating. Continuing on their present tack in today's globalizing world will confront them with the ever-clearer logic for the operational work to be assumed by Southern NGOs, leaving them just with fund-raising at home.

The road to the right is wide, straight, and freshly surfaced. This is the path toward deeper partnership with governments and donors, with NGOs as contractors providing public goods and services. This path has great income-growth prospects but is otherwise unattractive. Since governments worldwide are keen (or urged) to roll back their production and service roles, some NGOs will become progressively like the for-profit service sector TNCs, who are scrambling, thanks partly to the WTO, to scoop up the opportunities of privatization in the South. NGOs will increasingly compete with private-sector providers and drift from their primary emphasis on the poor.

The road to the left is narrow, winding, and leads into the hills. It is clearly the most difficult and least financially rewarding, but it heads to where the poorest people and greatest development challenges lie. This is the justice trail, along which the NGOs consciously side with the poor in their fight against exclusion and return home as ambassadors for global economic justice.

Each INGO will choose its own path (and its strategy can combine elements from all three), but the overall sector will be strongly influenced by the slant of the largest and best known. Their leaders, therefore, have responsibilities going beyond the boundaries of their own organizations. As they stand at the crossroads, they must ponder five key dilemmas. (In the following I draw on various essays in Lindenberg and Dobel 1999; Lindenberg and Bryant 2001; and my personal experience.)

The dilemma of scale

Many INGO chiefs come from a private-sector background. They are accustomed to income growth being a proxy for success. True, their projects can offer hope to extremely poor communities, and with more money they can work more good. But in their mission statements their aim is to eradicate poverty itself. This entails not only more and bigger projects (what I called in *Democratizing Development* "islands of prosperity in oceans of destitution") but reshaping development itself.

Jubilee 2000, on a shoestring budget, probably contributed more to poor countries financially than all operational NGOs combined by wresting for them up to $100 billion of debt relief from unwilling G7 governments and IGOs and by ensuring that much of this was redirected to basic services in those countries. And as successful NGO projects lift many out of poverty, millions more may be in the "down elevator" due to conflict, environmental degradation, HIV/AIDS, financial crises, or rising unemployment—perhaps linked to globalization. To strive for poverty eradication requires NGOs to attack such root causes and to be more humble about their place in the development firmament.

There is a popular view that INGOs are a major source of funding for Southern governments and people. The following diagram sketches, very approximately, the range of North-South resource flows of relevance to development (some figures are accurate, some are informed guesses, and others, such as debt service, are omitted for simplicity— the notes offer explanations). The picture reveals how small are NGO flows in the general scheme (or, for that matter, official aid). Remittances are a much bigger source of people-to-people flow.

Aid is more important to least developed countries, but even here trade and government programs contribute more to national development. Harnessing these larger resource streams for effective poverty reduction is a greater challenge for INGOs than boosting their own

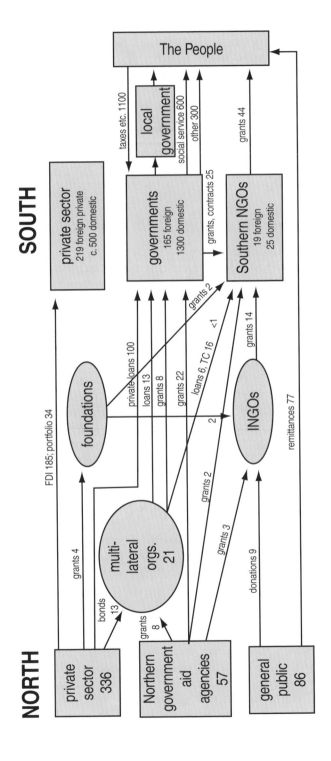

Figure 7.1 North-South flows of development finance (schematic, all figures are $billion, see notes)

Notes (all figures in US$ billion per year)

Private-sector financing: comprises about $185 billion of Foreign Direct Investment (mostly to South-based subsidiaries of industrialized country firms) and $34 billion in equities and bonds. Private banks lend a varying amount, typically perhaps $100 billion, to Southern governments. Private institutions also invest in IFI bonds, so financing their $13 billion non-concessional loans. Wealthy philanthropists contribute through foundations to global causes. Much of this (perhaps $4 billion) goes to the South through NGOs.

Public-sector financing: governments give bilateral grants, low-interest loans, and technical cooperation (gratis specialists, ranging from bankers to volunteer teachers) amounting to $22 billion, $6 billion, and $16 billion respectively in 1999. In addition, they channel about $8 billion through the multilateral agencies (for grants or low-interest loans to developing countries, and a small amount of grants to Southern NGOs). Government aid agencies also channel about $3 billion (more during major emergency appeals) to NGOs of their countries and increasingly give grants directly to Southern NGOs.

Northern people: give $6–12 billion to NGOs for their work in the South (estimates vary). Remittances by overseas workers to their families back home constitute a much bigger flow (estimated by IMF to be about $77 billion, but much from workers in the Gulf and so forth rather than people based in the North).

In the South: domestic investment is about $1,500 billion—firms receive perhaps one-third of this and also mobilize FDI and so on. Government domestic revenues average 20 percent of GDP ($1,300 billion for all developing countries), of which about $1,100 billion is direct and indirect taxes and $200 billion is state enterprise earnings, fees, fines, and other income. Roughly two-fifths of public spending goes to social services (health, education, social security, welfare, housing, etc.). Perhaps one-fifth is returned to the population as other goods and services and two-fifths goes to central purposes such as maintaining the civil service, industrial investment, national infrastructure, and defense. The figure for the provision of government grants and contracts through Southern NGOs is a total guess (based on assuming that one-quarter of all bilateral and multilateral loans and grants is channeled through Southern NGOs and that this is half of the total government financing through NGOs).

Sources: World Bank, UNCTAD, IMF, OECD-DAC, and data used elsewhere in this book.

growth. Yes, they should mobilize new support, but not if it means diluting their attack on the *root causes* of poverty and their battle for *inclusion*.

The dilemma of politics

INGOs tend to avoid political controversy, and hence few have honed their advocacy skills, though some Oxfams and church-based NGOs are notable exceptions. Yet in tackling poverty's root causes, advocacy skills, not their money, are their most powerful weapon. Projects can dent the structure of poverty, but reforming global policies can tear it down.

INGOs are unique in providing distinct people-to-people bridges connecting rich and poor worlds. This gives them both the clearest possible viewpoint on the realities of poverty and ready-built constituencies for campaigns. Yet most INGOs use this privilege only for fundraising. The large US INGOs do little to tell fellow citizens unpalatable home truths: how their country's self-serving approach to world affairs fuels poverty, how the United States' cavalier disdain for international agreements courts widespread disappointment and anger, and how the greed of some Americans is driving global inequalities to dangerous levels. Many European NGOs are similarly silent about their nations' complicity.

INGOs are becoming more advocacy-oriented, but they tend to choose soft targets (such as World Bank and WTO) rather than their own governments and TNCs. This is particularly evident with US INGOs. Other G7 countries have vibrant trade justice campaigns to which INGOs contribute, but not the United States. Why are US INGOs silent on the injustice to Southern textile or farm workers posed by US protectionism? Why didn't they protest when their government, prompted by US food giants, forced the European Union to end trade privileges for a group of poor banana producers?

Why are INGOs so timid or so conservative? Their environmental counterparts, in contrast, wouldn't hesitate to lash out at corporate or government despoilers. Ironically, tropical turtles, tigers, and trees have bolder defenders in the North than Southern people. The answer is that environment and development groups, by quirk of history, have different crude yardsticks of success. The former count membership—and well-publicized David versus Goliath battles do wonders for this—while the latter count income. Much of this income comes from government, business, and conservative supporters. The different starting points lead to different organizational cultures, particularly at leadership levels. Environment groups tend to be led by populists who are good at media work and politics; INGO heads are typically from business and strong management backgrounds. Environmentalists whip up anger among supporters against world wrongs and urge them to vent this through policy demands. INGOs cultivate compassion toward the poor and urge charity.

Politically sanitizing suffering is not just missed opportunity; it is abdication of duty. INGOs have a duty to bear witness. Information technology makes it possible for them, as never before, to inform the media, teachers, politicians, government officials, and others about the dynamics of poverty and the diverse ways their society contributes to them. This must be careful, fair, and accurate. Yes, there will be a backlash (see Chapter 9) and some income sources may be lost, but this is a modest price for doing what is right.

This duty has become even clearer after 9/11. While those who committed the atrocities were middle-class young men with international educations and pilot's licenses, the applause for their action—and perhaps some material support—was from poor communities throughout the South. In a world in which communications are global, instantaneous, and ubiquitous, it is no longer safe—let alone morally defensible—to live with such polarization of wealth and life opportunities. A truly "strategic defense initiative" would be for Northern countries to declare war on poverty and inequality, with INGOs as their guides.

The dilemma of the state

NGOs are named for what they are *not*—governmental organizations. But, paradoxically, many large relief and development NGOs seek ever-closer links with official agencies. Much of their funding comes from official aid, and in addition they increasingly act as contractors, managing projects for official agencies and for Southern governments. Besides inhibiting their advocacy, this trend raises two important questions. First, the priorities of donors and governments may not be toward the very poorest but rather the middle poor or even aimed at national growth through exploiting the most productive regions. Surveys show that there is generally a higher density of NGO work in and around the major cities and more prosperous zones than in the poorest areas, and there is a tendency of official donors to concentrate resources where economic returns are highest.

Second, what is the ideal state-NGO relationship? Governments around the world, not just those in the South, are redefining their roles and retreating from many aspects of production and service delivery to concentrate more wholeheartedly on things that *only* governments can do—legislation, creating a healthy policy environment, managing the economy and national investments, defense, social protection, and so forth. The last entails ensuring people have *access* to—not necessarily delivering—basic services. These trends offer chances to private firms but also to INGOs. Those who seize them are increasingly having to compete with for-profit companies, and this will become more so as the WTO's General Agreement on Trade in Services starts to take effect, and governments must offer a level playing field to all potential service providers, ending the slant toward local providers. Hence service INGOs may be drawn increasingly into public-private partnerships alongside commercial competitors, which may deflect them ever further from their poverty mission. This is not inevitable, however. When governments are serious about poverty reduction (as in Vietnam and Uganda), there are powerful opportunities in collaboration.

The dilemma of networks

As noted, NGOs have similarities to companies. They compete with one another for supporters, funds, and idea leadership. This serves well the purposes of growth and reach but not necessarily advocacy and innovation. The challenge of the network age is to shift from competition to cooperation—not in all things, but in strategic areas. The director of Oxfam America predicts that "the most innovative INGOs of the future will have moved from the hands-on operational style of the 60s to a highly complex and diverse set of institutional partnerships, joint ventures and networking relationships. Their development work . . . will be largely managed by their Southern partners [who] will largely define the work agenda" (Offenheiser et al. 1999).

Networking could allow mutual learning and more rapid diffusion of innovations, construction of common defenses against common threats, more efficient fund-raising in new markets, economies of scale (including in procurement of drugs and hardware, and combining field offices), and improvement in staff morale and supporter confidence. Most important, it offers new opportunities for advocacy. If all the main development INGOs were to pull together—for say two years—on a major (but soluble) development problem, they could profoundly influence that issue and so, perhaps, poverty itself. This could have more lasting impact than their direct programs (an idea that is expanded in Chapter 11). But such campaigning is scarcely conceivable today. Communications budgets are jealously guarded for fund-raising—and this entails competing with other NGOs, not cooperating. What a blockage to tackling the really big challenges of development this presents! New thinking is about building networks to make the whole greater than the sum of the parts, to solve problems collectively using all tools available, and to communicate messages that excite and empower. It is about *bold* thinking, not old thinking.

A familiar Third Way political axiom is the need for "joined-up government"; that is, for departments and ministers to cooperate across bureaucratic divides, finding synergies in tackling the most pressing problems and avoiding energies being dissipated through conflicting strategies. The INGO world today needs "joined-up altruism." Most NGOs state similar missions; by pulling together they could influence policy changes well beyond the reach of individual NGOs. In doing so, they could expect increased public respect, even if they lose a few donors. With bold thinking, big challenges can be seized—but only by a leap into a mindset of cooperation.

The ethics dilemma

As INGOs have grown in prominence and official funding, they have increasingly become subjects of probes and accusations. This trend could grow as NGOs give more weight to advocacy and court powerful detractors. INGOs must, therefore, promote high ethical standards both within their own agencies and in the sector as a whole.

Within an individual NGO this entails tackling the challenges of governance, culture, and focus, especially accountability to Southern partners and to the communities it aims to help, not just to donors. It entails procedures to ensure responsiveness to the priorities of the poor, and it calls for building up the capacity and confidence of Southern CSOs—even if this may reduce its own "shelf life"—because sustainable development, ultimately, relies on internal not outside agents.

Even deeper challenges lie in promoting ethical standards within the wider INGO sector. Networking could play a critical role. For example, InterAction (the US umbrella of INGOs) has devised an ethics code for its members ("Private Voluntary Organization Standards," 2001), but this largely deals with internal matters, such as probity, media images, child sponsorship, and equal opportunities. It has nothing on listening to the poor, respecting Southern partnership, or "downward accountability." Country-level INGO networking is also important in program countries for setting standards, ensuring coordination, and monitoring, especially where the state has failed or is weak. There have been ugly examples of poverty problems being compounded when NGOs fail to coordinate strategy and intelligence (for example, during the Rwanda ethnic conflict) (Anderson 1996). This has prompted the International Federation of the Red Cross to initiate a code of ethics for agencies working in complex emergencies.

It is timely for INGOs to elaborate jointly ethical standards throughout the spectrum of their work and devise self-regulation mechanisms to give them teeth. While a reluctance to cooperate is one hallmark of old thinking, another is a reluctance to criticize peers openly and with integrity when this is warranted. We return to these issues in Chapter 9.

CHANGING FOCUS—THE FIGHT AGAINST POVERTY

Though INGOs vary greatly, they all state an overarching priority of poverty reduction. How they seek to contribute to this mission, however, differs from one to another and varies over time. Just as David Korten has described four generations of voluntary development action (1990), we can discern an evolution in INGOs' approach to their poverty mission. What I suggest here builds on Korten but keeps the focus on INGOs. I see changes as shifts of focus more than generational leaps, since NGOs tend to broaden from one activity to encompass new ones rather than abandon the old and jump to the new. Most INGOs still do relief and welfare work when that is needed, but many have broadened to self-help development, and some to empowerment activities.

During the 1970s and 1980s, INGOs increasingly recognized that relief and welfare are insufficient and that they should also assist development—particularly through self-help approaches and supporting Southern partner organizations. There was a focus shift from poor *individuals and families* to poor *communities* (see Table 7.2).

In the 1990s, more progressive INGOs emphasized the "bigger picture": macro issues such as governments' commitment to poverty reduction, sustainable development, social justice, and inclusion agendas. Though operationalizing this new thinking hasn't been easy, it has brought home the need to strengthen institutions that the poor can access and trust, and it has led many INGOs to focus on new issues, such as debt burdens or the unaffordable price of HIV/AIDS drugs. The shift in focus is toward *poor societies*.

For relief and welfare, INGOs work in refugee camps, orphanages, NGO-run schools, and other institutions that are largely *outside* communities and are run by exogenous actors. INGOs' natural partners are local charities and missionaries. And the root causes of the destitution are natural disasters, wars, disease, disability, or other calamities.

In community-based development, however, different factors apply. INGOs have to move (sometimes literally) into the slums and villages where poor people live. The goal transcends immediate needs to *long-term* poverty reduction. To be sustainable the communities must be in the driving seat; that is, development must be participatory. Hence, partners very close to poor people are needed, such as their

Table 7.2 The shifting focus of INGO activities

Target → / Strategy ↓	Poor individuals	Poor communities	Poor societies
Objectives	Relief and welfare	Self-help	Equity, building institutions for *inclusion*
Operation goals	Meeting basic needs	Participation, sustainable poverty reduction	Rights-based development, voice, and empowerment
Local partners	Charities; missionaries	Community-based organizations, local NGOs	Civil society, progressive people in power
Local bases	Orphanages, refugee camps, schools	Village- and slum-level institutions, co-ops	CSO networks from local to global levels
Sources of problems	Nature, wars, ill-fortune	Local elites, resource poverty, etc.	Social injustice, weak institutions, bad governance
Typical instruments	Needs assessment, cost-effective business plan	Participation—from project planning to implementation and evaluation	Advocacy to ensure CSO views are reflected in national development plans, "scaling-up" innovations
Key allies	Local religious institutions	Community leaders, existing community organizations	National and international media, unions, progressive politicians
Key INGO strengths	Fund-raising, logistical skills	Local knowledge, listening skills	Persuasion, access to influence, linking skills (from bottom to top, North to South, academic to practitioner)

own community-based organizations (CBOs) or local NGOs. This exposure generally leads to a different, more political, view on poverty. People are poor not just because of calamities, but because the local elites annex the best resources, services, and development opportunities. Landlords, moneylenders, merchants, and politicians also exploit them.

When INGOs shift focus to a more holistic view, looking at *poor societies* at the national level, they make further adjustments. They need to have one foot in poor communities and one at the national level to enable them to link the daily reality of poverty with national debate about equity, inclusion, and social justice. They must collaborate with civil society leaders and progressive intellectuals who spearhead this debate, seeking to empower the poor through elevating their voice and rights regarding state institutions. They must work with diverse segments of civil society at both local and national levels to tackle issues of social injustice, weak institutions, and poor governance.

This shift of focus requires developing different instruments and different skills. Humanitarian activities fundamentally require good logistics, planning, management, and—of course—fund-raising skills back home. Self-help programs call for strong listening skills and a commitment to, not just training in, participatory development. They also necessitate strong local knowledge to assess where threats and opportunities lie and to identify community leaders and organizations with which to work. The inclusion agenda calls for accurate research, persuasive advocacy, and imaginative linking skills. Bridges are also needed with national or local government agents, the media, academe, and donors if the objective is to change state programs or to mainstream new approaches.

I am not suggesting either that NGOs are all making the same linear thought progression and are simply at different stages, or that the earlier stages are less important. Each INGO knows its comparative advantages and how its competencies differ from those of others. It wouldn't do if all NGOs thought and acted alike, because needs are so diverse.

INGOs increasingly see their role as *two*-way. It is no longer appropriate simply to raise funds in one country for humanitarian use overseas, returning just with information for fund-raising. INGOs are expected to play their part in heightening world understanding of the development challenges through policy debate, media work, development education, and advocacy.

Plan International recently sought to join the small number of INGOs that receive block grants from the British government's Department for International Development, not just funding for specific projects. Plan had a good case, especially since its global HQs are in the UK (making it the largest British-based INGO), but it wasn't successful because, DFID said, even though its field work was competent (and had indeed been funded by DFID for many years), Plan wasn't yet sufficiently part of the UK development policy debate. This is ironic.

When I was newly in charge of Oxfam campaigns, some of our trustees and managers feared that moving into campaigning might lose Oxfam support, including, perhaps, the strong funding from the aid ministry. Now the opposite is the case; an NGO is penalized if it isn't energetic in lobbying and policy work.

CONCLUSIONS, MASS CUSTOMIZATION, AND SOME THOUGHTS ABOUT THE FUTURE

Twenty years ago most successful INGOs concentrated on what they thought they did best, whether relief, self-help, conservation, microcredit, or advocacy. Now leading NGOs are seeing the need to do all these things and take a holistic view of development. Much of this chapter, indeed of this book, is about the imperative for NGOs to engage more systematically in policy debate at national and international levels to correct injustices and promote inclusion. We concentrate, therefore, on advocacy. But INGOs will always largely be about operations, not campaigns, and so before concluding this chapter let us weave the logic of its main threads into an operational message.

INGOs can look to industry for ideas. Throughout most of the twentieth century "Fordism" was the watchword: companies sought to devise a product for which there would be a vast new market and produce it as cheaply as possible through capturing every possible economy of scale. In this way Ford managed what rivals thought impossible—to produce a car for the ordinary family—by paring back to basics, standardizing to the ultimate degree, and *mass production*. This contrasted with the *customization* offered by up-market tailors and others to their richest clients.

In recent years a new production approach evolved. Customers of cars, computers, hi-fi, and other consumer durables want a fairly cheap product, but with *their* specifications: the choice of gearbox or air-conditioning in the car and its furnishings; how much memory the computer has, the speed of its chip and modem, and so forth. The manufacturers who offer little choice are losing ground to those catering to picky customers. Smart companies are going for *mass customization*. They produce a standard skeleton and invite customers to handpick the rest from a wide range of options. The components are all mass produced, but they are assembled according to the individual customer's specifications.

There is a development parallel. Government and donor programs are often disappointing because they offer a uniform product universally. In the real world, situations and needs vary. A national program may work for some but not be well-suited to female-headed households, ethnic minorities, the landless, people living in mountainous or other difficult areas, the very poor, or other vulnerable groups. The services might be more suitable if they could be "customized" to individual communities. It would be difficult for a government ministry to do this; with its wide geographic responsibility it understandably takes a "one size fits all" approach. But NGOs who work closely with the poor are well placed to help communities adapt the services to their own requirements, using local knowledge, participatory planning, and advocacy skills.

For example, the basic package of an agricultural program might be the provision of improved seeds and fertilizers, and training for farmers about growing the new crop. But where the land-holding is very small, the packages may need to be divided into smaller units; where a river is close to hand, diesel pumps for irrigation may improve yields; women farmers may need additional help to market the crops they grow; in some areas animal traction makes sense, but elsewhere not; where soils dry quickly, inter-cropping will allow the new variety to grow in partial shade; where there is a tradition for common land, it makes sense to adapt the scheme to a communal basis; and so on. The basic model may have universal relevance, but it is truly useful only if it can be adjusted to the local realities.

This suggests a sort of Third Way for INGOs—a path between total independence (with numerous worthy but disconnected projects) and being purely a public-service contractor (competing with private-sector providers); a path between pure operations and pure advocacy. National programs command large resources, and the usual complaint is that the poor get poor access. This is rarely due to a conscious government decision to exclude them, but because the basic model is designed with other customers in mind. When NGOs are able to take that model and mold it so that the poor get access, they not only improve the effectiveness of a national program but they improve equity in government services and combat exclusion.

Hence, the choice is not simply between maintaining distance from government through totally independent NGO projects, on the one hand, and losing identity through unbridled contracting, on the other. A middle course, with exciting strategic opportunities, is to explore whether collaboration with governments opens opportunities to "mass customize" national programs to the particular needs of the vulnerable.

To be effective in this work, as with advocacy, INGOs need to take a holistic approach and build up a wide array of skills, from grassroots planning to high-level influencing. INGOs will achieve more in these areas when they are more truly accountable to the people they aim to help, and when they have better (results-based) indicators of their progress than annual income figures. INGOs are potentially immensely powerful, but this power is more latent than actual for various reasons. They aren't sufficiently strategic in using their experience to influence decision-makers and publics. Their competitive instincts impede the cooperation with peers that might lead to achieving big transformations. They are averse to political controversy at home for fear of losing supporters and irritating their governments (this especially applies to US INGOs). And they focus too much on mobilizing funds in the North to finance work in the South when the transformations that would have most poverty-reducing impact are probably in the North.

For these reasons, I believe, they are largely missing a historic opportunity. There is increasing public concern about the social injustices associated with global changes, but most INGOs (with some important exceptions) stand distant from this debate. They are leaving the field clear for a medley of small civil society newcomers, whose ideas are often neither realistic nor based on poor people's concerns, to lead public debate and citizen action on these issues. We look at this phenomenon in the next chapter. INGOs might begin to look irrelevant if they don't engage in this. By using their experience, credibility, and a portion of their communications budgets to inform their home countries about development realities and the responsibilities of their own societies, and by using their field links to help Southern partners achieve a louder voice in international debate, they could galvanize a truly irrepressible movement for global economic justice.

8.

The Protest Movement and the "Dot-Causes"

The turn of the millennium has seen two dramatic new trends in civil society. Both relate to globalization and the parallel phenomenon of what some call the "rise of the network society" (Castells 1996). The first is the emergence of an increasingly popular—and sometimes disruptive—anti-globalization protest movement. The second is the birth of advocacy groups that largely inhabit Internet space and mobilize through websites rather than conventional pressure-group tactics.

This chapter explores how these trends are intertwined, and how the strengths and idiosyncrasies of the former owe much to the new mobilizing opportunities of the latter.[1] These twin trends bring together the themes of Part One and Two of this book. The new civic actors alert the widest possible audience to the injustices and inequities associated with globalization and the deficiencies of democracy, particularly in matters of global governance. But they also harvest the new opportunities globalization affords civil society and demonstrate the powerful way in which transnational networks can magnify the impact of citizen action. A new protest movement has emerged through cooperation between the new actors and many established CSOs, including unions and environmental groups. This has left behind many of the players that are most readily identified by Northern publics with questions of world poverty and justice—most of the large development NGOs and the mainstream churches.

Protest, of course, is not new. The nineteenth century saw many marches, strikes, and other forms of protest, and the birth of the labor movement (Tilly 1978; Nimtz 2002). Since World War II there has been contention in Western democracies and global social movements over civil rights, feminism, nuclear weapons, nuclear power, the Vietnam War, the environment, blood sports, animal testing, and many other issues (Cohen and Rai 2000). However, from the late 1970s to the late 1990s protests in rich countries were fewer and relatively quiet, with isolated exceptions, until the WTO meeting in Seattle in 1999 sparked off a fresh and growing wave of street activism.

Is there anything new, then, about the anti-globalization movement? No, in that it continues the tradition of left, radical, and youthful antipathy toward the capitalist-oriented status quo. But yes, in at least three respects (or perhaps one respect and two consequences). First, it is the first social movement to mobilize chiefly through the Internet. Second, it doesn't have only a global focus and global targets; it mobilizes and acts internationally and simultaneously. And third it is characterized by huge tactical diversity, ranging from colorful, carnival-like events to highly publicized scenes of violent protest.

All social movements comprise high-energy but amorphous waves of people, animated by mobilizing structures—nodes around which people cluster—that collectively create an organizing framework (McAdam et al. 1996). Within earlier social movements these structures were tangible "bricks and mortar" organizations, such as the Campaign for Nuclear Disarmament or Campaign Against the Arms Trade within the peace movement. In today's protest movement this role is largely played by "clicks without mortar" organizations such as the Wombles, Globalise Resistance, and Global Action.

Just as stock markets were turned upside-down by the "dot-com" phenomenon (until the bubble burst), the arena of civil society advocacy is now being transformed by the arrival of "dot-causes." This chapter argues that the increasing confidence and impact of the current protest movement, but also its weaknesses, owe much to its use of dot-causes for mass mobilization. This explains why it is so quick moving; how it has rapidly flowered into a new, global culture and language among youth; why it needs little assistance from conventional media to flourish; but also why it is hard to define exactly what the movement *is*; why it lacks clear leaders and spokespeople; and why it is increasingly riddled with splits and tensions over goals and tactics. To understand these features it helps to look first at the dot-cause phenomenon.

DOT-CAUSES

Though websites were used earlier to disseminate information, the Free Burma Coalition, launched in 1995, broke new ground by being the first international civil society campaign mediated entirely through the Internet. It was the first dot-cause (certainly the first working internationally) and claims to be the "largest human rights campaign in cyberspace." It is an on-line community of Burmese exiles and supporting activists in about twenty-eight countries that links with human rights, environment, and women's groups, unions, academics, politicians, students, and religious groups. Through consumer boycotts, shareholder campaigns, and other tactics, it has succeeded in persuading over fifty companies to exit Burma, including Pepsi and Texaco.

Other cyber campaigns quickly followed suit, including those targeting Shell and McDonald's (O'Neill 1999). The best-known dot-cause is the International Campaign to Ban Landmines (ICBL), which won the Nobel Prize in 1997. Illustrating how "virtual" it was, there was a delay in receiving the prize money because, until then, it didn't even have a bank account (Mekata 2000). Similarly, the French-based ATTAC (see Chapter 5) had grown to a network of over forty national-level chapters before it held its first international meeting, almost four years after its birth (George 2002).

Some dot-causes are offshoots of existing CSOs or networks. For example, ICBL is a largely Internet-mediated umbrella of initially fifty (rising to several hundred) groups concerned with armaments and with humanitarian and human rights issues (Mekata 2000). These groups organized at the local and national levels, while ICBL handled international coordination and the development of common strategy. This enabled the whole to become much more than the sum of the parts. The successful campaign to oppose the Multilateral Agreement on Investment (proposed by the OECD) was, similarly, an Internet-mediated coordination of up to six hundred NGOs and unions in over seventy countries (Kobrin 1998).

In such situations the Internet becomes a communications tool, extending the reach of the CSOs within the network. Dot-causes can, however, be stand alone—neither encumbered nor legitimized by established organizations—and hence have little or no mechanisms of accountability. Their chief weaknesses stem from their unique strength: They operate through the cheap, global, egalitarian, and rapid medium of the Internet. This presents difficulties, however, in decision-making, leadership, and quality control.

Dot-causes represent completely novel mass communications. Until recently, getting a message to millions was expensive. Now, alternative political websites offer a new conduit at very low cost—and the medium is more accessible, more fun, easier to handle, and more convincing to a growing slice of the population, particularly the youth, than traditional media. Hence, for the annual May Day protests in London, demonstrators and onlookers get information and propaganda from a wide array of often bizarrely named websites promoting the events (including Mayday Monopoly, Globalise Resistance, Guerrilla Gardening, Reclaim the Streets, and Primal Seeds). In 2001 the Wombles website urged supporters to come to planning sessions for developing strategies but were admonished not to talk with journalists. This prompted one *Guardian* journalist to remark how odd it is for a movement dependent on communications to eschew coverage in a major daily (May 1, 2001). The point is that for the first time in modern political history, groups seeking to change public opinion feel they don't *need* newspapers and other old means of communications to mobilize support; they are betting on new communications and don't *trust* old media, which all depend, directly or indirectly, on capitalism. For many, the Internet has democratized communications.

There can be debate about whether dot-causes are real or virtual organizations, but what is certain is that they represent an explosion of energy in citizen organization, their numbers are rocketing, and they are transforming citizen action and social movements.

While social movements have always been amorphous, fluid and "grainy" webs of people with loosely shared concerns or values, within them—as mobilizing structures—are more coherent affinity groups and organizations (McAdam et al. 1996). Each such group has a distinct character, but the movement as a whole is a blend of all. In older movements these groups have tended to be local; influential ones might color the movement in that country and, so endorsed, its ideas might percolate more widely through the global movement (Cohen and Rai 2000). The Leeds feminists were influential in the UK women's movement but also abroad; the San Francisco homosexual community inspired the gay rights movement globally; and Haight-Ashbury peaceniks gave much to antiwar protest throughout America and beyond. These all depended on the happy coincidence of a critical mass of like-minded activists being able to come together because of a combination of ideological and physical proximity.

Dot-causes have transformed this in two ways. First, the costs of setting up and organizing a group have been very much reduced; anyone can afford to design and run a website. Second, they have defeated distance—mobilizing groups can just as easily be global as local when the commute is in cyberspace. This permits affinity according to world view rather than locality. Hence, social movements today are fueled by very many more mobilizing groups than previously. These can be minute affinities or groups capable of organizing major events (and it isn't easy to tell which from their websites) and—barring language constraints—they can be local, national, or global. The influence of these groups comes not through being able to garner cascading approval among affinity groups in the district or country but by the number of hits on their websites.

Dot-causes are important to all social movements today. For example, Via Campesina enables peasant associations in different countries to build global solidarity. But older movements charted their philosophy and defined their character before the age of the Internet. What is different about the modern protest movement, as we now discuss, is that its whole nature is shaped by the pivotal roles played by dot-causes within it.

THE BIRTH OF THE ANTI-GLOBALIZATION MOVEMENT

Today's protest movement was born in November 1999 in Seattle during the ministerial meeting of the WTO, when approximately fifty thousand people took to the streets. There had been many demonstrations previously about aspects of globalization and against the institutions widely seen as managing it (WTO, IMF, and World Bank). But as the Indian environmental activist Vandana Shiva put it, "A new threshold was crossed in Seattle—a watershed towards the creation of a global citizen-based and citizen-driven democratic order" (*The Guardian*, December 8, 1999). The earlier demonstrations had often been as strong numerically. Indeed about eighty thousand people took part in street protests during the IMF and World Bank annual meetings in Berlin in 1988. But three features, or opportunities, distinguished the Seattle protest and the movement it spawned.

First, it came at a politically opportune moment. Normally the G7 governments agree on their line before a major international meeting; the meetings meander around topics of concern to other countries, particularly the South, before concluding pretty much what the G7 had determined in advance. The Southern countries grumble that they have yet again been shortchanged, but feel that they have at least had a hearing and can usually boast to their domestic constituencies of a few minor concessions. In Seattle, however, the two most powerful trading blocks (the United States and the European Union) entered the talks with widely differing views and trenchantly uncompromising negotiators. A sense of emergency quickly arose. The G7 spent most of the time behind locked doors—occasionally with a few other major governments by invitation—trying to resolve their differences. Most governments felt doubly angry. Their concerns hardly got a hearing, and they themselves were humiliatingly excluded from most of the sessions. The US-EU tension, coupled with the North-South tensions, led to the talks collapsing. The message of the protestors—that this was a disgustingly flawed process—suddenly seemed fitting.

Second, this was the first occasion that a major protest was orchestrated largely through the Internet. This not only allowed instantaneous communication to wide audiences of information that would otherwise be politically "filtered" by vested interests, but it demystified previously opaque processes of intergovernmental negotiations, making them globally accessible. Citizens now feel better informed and empowered to intervene in these processes. This, and the widespread—but exaggerated—view that the protests *caused* the collapse of the WTO talks has engendered a new spirit of confidence in the power of protest. Whereas previously demonstrations were largely one-time-only events (the Berlin protests of 1988, similar events at Madrid in 1994), from Seattle onward protest organizers have always had a forward calendar clearly in mind. And the Internet has allowed civic action to be both local and global simultaneously. Although about 95 percent of the participants in the Seattle protests were from North America, people throughout much of the world were able to follow the events through numerous websites and *felt* involved. They logged on, even if they couldn't march on.

Third, though much of the media attention focused on the violent anarchists and the bizarrely dressed promoters of fringe causes, the bulk of the demonstrators came from traditional CSOs (particularly unions, as we return to below). Though fragile, this unusual coalition of activists was very powerful because it seemed, arguably for the first time, to offer "*the* voice of civil society." Since cooperation was built on a shared dislike of the WTO rather than a shared vision of an alternative, and since most message-dissemination was done by the dot-causes (which are more radical than traditional CSOs), and since the anarchists' antics dominated the media coverage, the overall impression was of a very hostile civil society message.

A combination of hypocrisy and weakness on the part of the G7 added to the opportunity. The leading economies preached free markets and the global good but in practice adopted strategies of narrow, short-term self-interest. In particular the US government sought a fully open global market for its exporters, investors, and service providers but was unwilling to forego an iota of its own protectionism. The WTO appeared to developing countries and CSOs as a vehicle for global Americanization.

But for all its bullying, the Clinton Administration was extremely cautious about repressing the protests. It, and the Seattle police, didn't know how to react. The protestors' deep conviction that something was very wrong with the WTO process hit a chord; disgruntled third-world negotiators added credence to this case, as did the presence on the streets of trade unionists and churchgoers alongside more anarchic protestors. And the violence perpetrated by some protestors, together with police overreaction, guaranteed global mass media coverage. Globalization had become a clearly contested political issue, and the protest movement was born. But what exactly is it?

IS IT A MOVEMENT OR JUST A PROTEST "MALL"?

Social movement theory poses three questions (McAdam et al. 1996): What political opportunities do the movements capitalize on? How are they mobilized? And how do people identify with them? We now use this framework to analyze today's protest movement. The political opportunities are very distinct and powerfully motivating, as discussed in the previous section. The critical aspect of mobilization stems from the dot-causes embedded in it—also discussed earlier. The very plurality of these dot-causes, however, multiplies the ways that people identify with, and even see, the movement. The roots of any social movement lie in shared experience and a shared sense of grievance. In the case of the protest movement, the grievances are so many and so diverse (ranging from job security, corporate greed, and third-world debt to US cultural takeover and environmental destruction) that there is little common thread, other than a conviction that neoliberalism lies behind it all. This is a strength in widening the appeal but a weakness in being so ill-defined.

This is exemplified by the difficulty in knowing what to call the movement. Is it really an anti-*globalization* movement, as it is usually described in the press? Many within it see this as dismissive—being likened to latter-day Luddites, resisting, Canute-like, inevitable advances of commerce and prosperity that modern communications afford. Some within it certainly advocate *localization*, through a set of laws, policies, and incentives that favor local rather than international trade (Hines 2000). And in many countries (such as Thailand and Netherlands) nationalist movements are growing and rub alongside the New Age protestors. But most activists argue that they are *not* against globalization, that they even *support* reducing barriers to interaction across national boundaries. Indeed, isn't their own movement global? They are against the current management of globalization that widens inequalities. Hence they prefer terms such as *anti-global capitalist* or *anti-neoliberal globalization*.

Others stress that the movement is about justice and planetary sustainability. At the second of two huge gatherings of activists (the World Social Forum, held in Porto Alegre, Brazil, which was designed to inject some coherence and direction into the movement[2]) the rallying cry was "Another World Is Possible," but this is too vague for a title. There was a powerful effort to get adopted the title Global Economic Justice Movement, which sounds more specific, but *anyone* involved in development sees himself or herself as promoting economic justice. Others suggested *Peace* and Global Justice, since much activist energy now is directed toward opposing US military intentions, but this led to an angry walkout (and, ironically, a peaceful sit-in) by anarchist groups who were adamant that only violent tactics are effective. Because of the terminological confusion, we just call it the protest movement.

The other ambiguity concerns the movement's composition. Various groups float in and out of its boundaries depending on the issue at hand. Many established NGOs, such as Oxfam and Jubilee Debt Campaign, say they are not *part* of the movement although they sympathize with it. They focus on many of the same issues and are to be found at the same global events, often promoting similar arguments, but they criticize other aspects of analysis and tactics used by those "in" the movement.

Being mobilized chiefly through the Internet explains many other characteristics of the movement, as well as its rapid growth. The dot-causes, collectively, offer ideological diversity, learning, and exploration opportunities, alternatives to traditional media, inventories of citizens' actions, and ease in planning large-scale events into which individual groups can plug their actions. But mediation through the Internet creates difficulties in leadership and decision-making. The Internet is a better medium for disseminating information and opinions than for building trust, developing coherence, and resolving controversies. There is no alternative, yet, to meeting face to face for planning strategy. It is common for dot-causes to set a date and place for a day of action and then encourage all supporters to come to planning meetings for the actual events or to get together with like-minded activists and devise something to bring on the day. The outcome is more like a carnival than an organized protest.

Adherents of the movement make a virtue out of this political pluralism. Subcomandante Marcos—the most prominent, poetic, and philosophical advocate of the Zapatista cause in Mexico, and an important source of inspiration for the protest movement globally—describes it as a movement of "one big no and many small yeses."

Such inherent anarchism has three consequences. First, since there aren't conventional forums from which leadership can emerge or be validated, the movement has made a hallmark of rejecting leadership. The most prominent figureheads are its independent commentators or "interpreters" rather than its leaders. Naomi Klein, Lori Wallach, George Monbiot, Waldon Bello, Vandana Shiva, and Noreena Hertz are radical journalists and authors who are sympathetic to the movement but do not claim to speak on its behalf, still less to lead it. This distinguishes it from other social movements, many of whose leaders remain household names decades later.

Second, though the infrastructure of protest days is well planned (including negotiations with the police and local authorities, training sessions in direct action, guidelines on how to manufacture giant puppets, legal services for those arrested, baby-sitting facilities, and so forth), the component events are left to smaller groups of activists to decide on, as is the choice of target (the specific injustice). The net effect is that these events, and the movement more broadly, do not promote one *specific* cause, as have other modern social movements such as women's movements, the environmental movement, or the gay/lesbian rights movements. Its protagonists don't so much market a "brand" (a particular ideology or cause) as organize a "protest mall," a one-stop arcade for multi-focused demonstrators. All and sundry are invited to come, browse, and participate in whichever stall most attracts them.

Third, the movement is characterized by difficult tactical schisms. Many within it are strong advocates of nonviolence, eschewing damage to property and threatening behavior. Conversely, others (such as Global Action) promote the use of violent tactics (what one website quaintly described as "projectile reasoning"), claiming that Seattle would not have made its mark without the violence. Since each participating group decides its own strategy, it follows that everything goes; there are no rules. Even if the large majority opts for nonviolence, a few inevitably take the violent course; the latter get most of the media attention, determine the policing strategy adopted for the overall event, and hence characterize the movement as a whole.

The paradox is that the protest movement's main strength is also its weakness. Its multifaceted nature and diverse strategies encourage and empower a wide diversity of adherents, but these adherents connect with it in widely differing ways. The young middle class of the United States or Europe might be anxious about an approaching environmental Armageddon or feel alienated from political processes over which they have no say. Trade union members feel threatened by the drift toward flexible labor markets and the ease with which TNCs shift production from one country to another. Southern peasants feel threatened by the drive for agricultural markets to be opened to foods from rich countries (especially genetically modified foods) while the North denies them the chance to export reciprocally. Southern factory workers fear that introducing labor and environmental standards in world trade will present an excuse to bar importation of their products. Each group in the broad movement has its distinctive personal connection with the core issue, but these connections are so diverse as to be frequently contradictory.

THE PUSH FROM THE SOUTH AND THE ZAPATISTA EFFECT

The explosion of globalization activism has coincided with the emergence of more confident, well-organized popular movements in the South, such as the Zapatistas in Mexico, the Assembly of the Poor in Thailand, the Urban Poor Coalition in Indonesia, and the Karnataka peasants' movement. Though the Battle of Seattle and similar protests command the Western media, they are just the tip of the iceberg, say Jessica Woodroffe and Mark Ellis-Jones. After cataloguing protest movements in thirteen Latin American and African countries, they conclude: "In the global south, a far deeper and wide-ranging movement has been developing for years, largely ignored by the media. . . . [It] has a global reach and signals a deep unease at economic policies that keep the poor in poverty" (Woodroffe and Ellis-Jones 2000).

Probably the most important influence in the South has been the Zapatistas National Liberation Army (EZLN) in Mexico, stemming from the Chiapas uprising of 1994. EZLN aspires not to speak on behalf of the indigenous people but to allow them to speak for themselves. It declares no leader; Subcomandante Marcos says he is just the conduit through which communities express themselves. It has an inclusive and pro-democracy ethos but beyond this is highly plural (every community decides for itself; the poorest peasant is the true comandante). Its central message speaks of a new form of democracy (akin to old anarchism). It puts a great premium on skillful communications, particularly using the Internet. Its messages are not dull polemics but witty, poetic, spiritual, and designed to be inspirational. "It is often said that the Zapatistas' best weapon was the Internet, but their true secret weapon was their language" (Klein 2001b). There are now estimated to be forty-five thousand Zapatista-related websites in twenty-six countries.

The Zapatistas have had a profound influence on the protest movement worldwide. In 1996 EZLN organized the first "Encuentro for Humanity and Against Neo-Liberalism," to which three thousand activists came from all over the world. Many who attended went on to play lead roles in the protests in Seattle and elsewhere and have adopted the same mixture of direct action, collective decision-making, and decentralized organizing. Chiapas has become a sort of Mecca for anti-globalizers, and Marcos a sort of Gandhi.

EZLN has been taken seriously in Washington. A Rand Corporation study commissioned by the US military described it as "a new mode of conflict—'netwar'—in which the protagonists depend on using network forms of organization, doctrine, strategy, and technology."

This is dangerous, says the study, because what starts as "a war of the flea" quickly turns into a "war of the swarm" (Ronfeldt et al. 1998).

TRADITIONAL CIVIL SOCIETY AND THE PROTEST MOVEMENT

For many CSOs the protest era poses a dilemma. Those wanting to dialogue with policymakers feel they must distance themselves from both the carnival and carnage aspects of mass protests, yet the media attention protests generate has greatly elevated the causes they espouse. This may open up political space for them to advance their proposals, which seem well structured and moderate (the "respectable face of dissent") in contrast to the cacophony from "the swarm." Or it may push officials into a bunker mentality regarding civil society. In this stretched political spectrum, traditional CSOs are no longer the radical Davids battling the Goliaths of corporations and governments; they are not always comfortable being displaced by new people's champions, especially when the newcomers depict them as part of "the system." "The political space around big international meetings has been hijacked by those who want to commit violence," said Oxfam GB's policy director. "It is counter-productive. They are taking the spotlight off those who want positive change" (*Financial Times*, December 7, 2001). Others, however, see a symbiosis. The protests have focused the public, politicians, and the media on global issues, while the analyses of the established NGOs and trade unions give the movement credibility. The combination of well-researched evidence plus mass mobilization and citizen outrage has proved compelling. Each without the others is unlikely to succeed.

The dilemmas for traditional CSOs may be whether to endorse the demonstrations and encourage their supporters to join them. To do so provides unions, churches, and others a good way to acquire a less old-fashioned image among potential young recruits, but at the risk of implicitly endorsing a more radical message than their own. Many, for example, encouraged members to join the protests at the IMF/World Bank annual meetings in Prague in 2000, while the website of the loose coalition of groups that coordinated the protests listed among the menu of activities available: "appropriating and disposing of luxury consumer goods, sabotaging, wrecking or interfering with capitalist infrastructure, and appropriating capitalist wealth and returning it to the working people" (S26 Website 2000).

Some, such as Oxfam, have criticized the protests: "The isolationist and protectionist tendencies on display at Seattle, Washington and other public demonstrations against the international order show that short-sightedness and selfishness are not exclusive to politics, bureaucracy or business" (Oxfam International 2000). Jubilee 2000 and World Development Movement have found anarchist campaigns on third-world debt damage their own efforts (for example, at the IMF/World Bank annual meetings in Prague in 2001) because they have constricted the space for lobbying and led many supporters to feel they were "used" by the demonstrators (Pettifor 2001; WDM 2001). FOE, however, welcomes the protests—without which there wouldn't be such a wide debate about the WTO or GMOs—though it does not actually encourage its supporters to join.

The protest movement and radical dot-causes pose particular problems for trade unions, particularly in Northern countries. On the one hand, issues of labor rights, exploitation, and inequity are getting an airing as never before; on the other hand, the solutions presented are often an anathema to unions, and they perceive a danger of their own organizations—representing millions of workers—being eclipsed by more radical, high energy, but largely unrepresentative groups. They are acutely aware that the image of unions has become rather old-fashioned, particularly in the eyes of young workers, and that mobilizing support for the mass demonstrations has breathed new life into them. But the protests do not always reflect their agenda (especially when attacking the very Northern protectionism that Northern unions promote), even though they may provide the bulk of the demonstrators (two-thirds in Seattle—see Table 8.1). And it is galling for them that the headlines usually go to the small, radical groups or articulate individuals from the South rather than to their own leaders. The rift between the main unions and many vocal Southern critics of globalization led to a round-table meeting in Bangkok to try to iron out their differences (Focus on the Global South 2001).

The tactical schisms have deepened since the 9/11 terrorist attack. Many of the newer protest groups want to recast the movement as a *peace* movement, firmly opposed to Western military tactics; they advocate strategies of nonviolent resistance. The US trade unions, however, have supported President Bush's strategy and well know that they would lose members if they flirt with an "antiwar against terrorism" stand. Conversely, the diehard anarchists are appalled that this newfound peace agenda is leading the vast majority within the movement to seek to outlaw violent and destructive tactics.

PROTESTS WITHIN PROTESTS

There are other signs of tension within the protest movement, and they are becoming more significant as the movement becomes more

Table 8.1 Protestors in the "Battle of Seattle"

Main interest and nationality	Numbers	Percentage of total
Organized labor	30,000	66
Environment activists	5,000	11
Economic justice	3,000	7
Mixed students	3,000	7
Anarchists	2,000	4
Religious/spirituality	1,000	2
Human rights	500	1
Nationalist/indigenous/ethnic	500	1
Gender	200	0.4
Peace	100	0.2
Rural peasantry	50	0.1
Urban poor	50	0.1
USA Americans	35,000–45,000	
Canadians	3,000–5,000	
Other nationalities	1,000–3,000	

Source: Lichbach 2002.

influential and geographically spread. These are similar to problems of governance that are found in traditional CSOs:

- *Leadership issues:* Where there *are* leaders, they are largely self-appointed, with poorly defined accountability and unclear mandate—and their decisions are likely to be resented. In the first WSF many of the ten thousand participants were angry with the organizers' strict control meaning, for example, that only a chosen few (mostly white men in their fifties) got to speak from the main platform. Klein reports that some participants even staged a protest against the organizers (2001c).
- *North-South tensions:* Many Southern activists see events such as Seattle as highly Northern (especially US) dominated and focused on Northern priorities (protection of US environment, jobs,

markets; US citizens wanting to clear their conscience about child labor). They are angry that issues of concern to the South, such as Northern agricultural subsidies and dumping policies, are ignored. Conversely, Southern organized events usually attract few Northerners. Few US groups, for example, went to the first WSF and only about ten of the fifteen hundred journalists covering it were American. Even the dot-causes within the movement are Northern dominated. The International Forum on Globalization, for example, which claims to speak against global inequalities, lists sixty-one directors and associates, with thirty-six from the United States (twenty from California alone), fifteen from other OECD countries, and just ten from the rest of the world (five Asian, four Latin American, one South African).

- *Focus and mandate:* Since decision-making tends to rest on fluid leadership and haphazard processes—such as whoever turns up to a particular planning meeting—the movement is better at organizing multi-cause protests or critiquing "the system" than at creating a vision of an alternative world order. There is agreement about what is wrong but not about what should be put in its place. And many within the movement feel the need to respond to those outside who challenge its mandate and ask on what basis protestors challenge democratically elected governments. The two WSFs were intended to address these gaps. They had a huge and international participation and went some way toward addressing the mandate issue but have had limited success in providing sharper focus.

- *Tactics and violence:* For many, the greatest dilemma faced by the movement is the use of violent tactics; how far should direct action go in destroying property or hurting people? Some advocate peaceful tactics only. Some, including the Wombles (who played a prominent role in organizing May Day protests in London in 2001), promote nonviolent direct action but also tolerance of a diversity of tactics, including space for police-fighting and property-destroying anarchists and Trotskyites. Conversely, anarchist sites (such as Global Action) roundly criticize the nonviolent activists as being irrelevant. Nothing would have been achieved at Seattle, they claim, had it not been for the violence. "If the direct action protesters had not put their bodies on the line [in Seattle] then there would have been a 15 second image of a parade on the national news headlines that Tuesday evening and that would have been it." (Cockburn and St. Clair, n.d.).

HOW SHOULD POLICYMAKERS RESPOND
TO THE PROTEST MOVEMENT?

Northern politicians are confused about how to respond to the protests. British Prime Minister Tony Blair was outraged by the Genoa Summit protests: "These people can come and they can riot and protest on the streets and throw petrol bombs at the police and then we, the democratic leaders, should conclude from that that we should never meet again. I think the world has gone mad." But then French Prime Minister Lionel Jospin, speaking about the same event, said, "While denouncing the violence to which a minority resorts . . . France rejoices in the worldwide emergence of a citizens' movement, in as much as it expresses the wish of the majority of mankind better to share the potential fruits of globalization" (*The Economist*, August 4, 2001).

With the growing fear of violence, an apparent strategy of policymakers is to *avoid*, rather than curb, the demonstrations, such as by locating the 2001 WTO ministerial meeting in Doha, Qatar—where democratic traditions are weak. Protestors saw this as a ploy to neutralize them, and certainly the meetings were very peaceful. However, the whole negotiation process was closely monitored in "real time" by activists and publicly disseminated through websites (including the World Development Movement and IndyNews). This coverage inspired national demonstrations in more than one hundred cities and thirty countries with the message to policymakers that "you can run but you can't hide" and mobilized more people overall than Seattle did (George 2002).

Through describing the inequities, environmental costs, and elite-serving nature of global governance at present, and by putting Northern governments on the defensive, the protest movement and the more effective dot-causes have done much to create the public perception that there is a profound democratic deficit at the heart of how global decisions are reached. The three critical questions for policymakers are these:

- *How to contain the violence, disruption, and negative press?* A reliance on ever-stronger police and military presence adds to the media spectacle and is therefore what the violent demonstrators really want; it also risks loss of life and is expensive. Conversely, holding key international meetings in locations that are hard for citizens to reach contributes to the sense of exclusion and a widening gulf between decision-makers and the public (which is what the terrorist groups would like). The ideal is to revert to

easy-access locations but under a compact reached with protestors to cooperate with the police to ensure no violence or property
damage and to facilitate the arrest of violators, while in exchange
giving some air time in the meetings to social concerns and even
to critics. This necessitates responsibility on the part of the protest organizers but also calls for better discipline on the part of
policymakers.

- *How to get their message across about globalization?* The movement is evidently more successful than governments and IGOs in
  influencing public opinion, particularly youth, concerning globalization. They must clearly make more intensive efforts to reach
  out, both to inform people about the central issues *and* to listen
  to their concerns.

- *How to engage civil society in global decisions?* Though
  policymakers in most countries now regularly talk with CSOs,
  this is usually on quite specific policy issues and limited to established CSOs. They must now recognize the mounting popular
  clamor for global social justice and for globalization to be better
  managed. To achieve this—even just to better understand the tension—policymakers need to engage at a senior and serious level
  with CSO leaders, especially those pivotal in shaping public opinion (excluding those who advocate violent or very disruptive tactics). We return to these issues in Chapter 10.

CONCLUSIONS—
WHERE WILL THE MOVEMENT GO FROM HERE?

The events of 9/11 had an immediate curbing effect on the protest
movement, removing much of its previously gained political space. Some
protest events were canceled or turned into marches for peace, and
some groups strongly critical of the US government softened their tone
or went into hibernation. There was some early speculation of the protest movement's terminal decline, but subsequent events revealed otherwise, such as the mass participation (of about forty thousand people)
in the second WSF in Porto Alegre (February 2002).

The protest movement could take one of three trajectories. Along
one path it grows as the Internet spreads and people become increasingly disenchanted with global capitalism and the democracy deficit.
On a second path, policymakers start to address some of the movement's
core concerns, such as inequality, governance of international institutions, and citizen voice, but this generates internal tension as some
activists are drawn into policy dialogue while others criticize such

"cooptation." Along a third path the movement implodes as strengths become weaknesses (lack of leadership becomes weak strategy; plurality becomes confusion; and open access becomes lack of accountability). In this scenario the movement would stay focused largely on current injustices without being able to present credible alternatives with any authority, though splinters might break off, for example, to align themselves with the radical Muslim challenge to US hegemony.

My own hope lies along the second path, and I hope that those who would reposition it as a *global economic justice movement* hold sway. Although I am generally an incurable optimist, I am increasingly depressed by the widening inequalities within and between nations. Though globalization isn't to blame for all of this—as we discussed in Part One—the debate has highlighted how shamefully little governments at the helm of global change appear to address issues of equity and inclusion. The one bright light in this gloom is the crescendo of voices demanding change—particularly the protest movement, but also groups like Oxfam, Jubilee, Public Citizen, Friends of the Earth, and the Global Unions network. The powerful governments now feel obliged to give answers, and it is not parliaments and conventional democratic processes that have forced this but people power. It's just a pity that the questions aren't more coherent.

My hope is that the movement's more thoughtful and persuasive activists will coalesce behind some tangible and plausible demands. Though many will resist this as reformist, any specific changes won would not only be good for the poor, but would greatly increase the movement's credibility and power. There are many ideas in Chapter 10 for overhauling global governance that a popular coalition could champion, and Chapter 11 suggests many vital policy reforms. At present I have to admit this route is not likely. The mass mobilizers in the movement are mostly found at the anti-systemic, rather than constructive engagement, end of the spectrum. This could change if the more traditional CSOs—NGOs, trade unions, and others—engage more strategically with the movement.

If they do so, they could help harness its enormous public energy for practical changes that would have enduring consequences for globalization and world development. But they would also court powerful enemies. Already CSOs experience a mounting wave of criticism from establishment sources (as we discussed in Chapter 4), but this would grow. CSOs need, therefore, to analyze these criticisms carefully and to consider how best to respond to them. This is the subject of the next chapter.

9

Pressure Groups Under Pressure

The Backlash Against Civil Society

Together, we are a superpower.
—Jody Williams,
coordinator of ICBL

As civil society has become more powerful in influencing policy, it has created enemies and resentment—as if confirming the law of physics that promises each action is met by an equal and opposite reaction. It has therefore become more important that CSOs look seriously at the questions their detractors raise—those touched on in Chapter 4—and provide convincing responses. While CSOs have rightly challenged the deficient governance of IGOs, TNCs, and governments, many challenges they now face concern their own governance—questions of representivity, accountability, legitimacy, and integrity. But Northern CSOs are also experiencing a barrage of challenges from the South, which also need to be addressed. All grist for this chapter.

These issues all impinged on me while working at the World Bank, where the nature of my job required me to understand policy conflicts from the perspective of diverse stakeholders—Northern and Southern NGOs, Northern and Southern governments, World Bank management, and so on. In 1992, when I became its advisor on working with civil society, I found neither senior management nor the executive directors (EDs—the permanent representatives of member governments who comprise its board) had much interest. Over the years, the Bank put more emphasis on poverty, some of its policies and projects became highly controversial, and NGOs got more attention. This accelerated after Jim Wolfensohn was appointed president; he saw that the Bank's long-term future rested on answering the critics, and he had much sympathy with many of their arguments.

The ensuing years saw a surge in dialogue on policy issues at the global level, intense country-level discussions on the country program, and much more operational collaboration, particularly to advance participatory approaches. To make this possible we encouraged greater

Bank transparency, regular consulting with civil society on upcoming policies and country-level strategic plans (assistance strategies), and the hiring of staff from civil society backgrounds in the majority of the Bank's overseas offices. The relationship seemed to be improving; things seemed to be going swimmingly; critics seemed be focusing more on the IMF, on laggards in the provision of debt relief for poor countries, and on the new WTO. Then, in 1997, a backlash hit.

A group of EDs, mostly from developing countries, started to complain that management had gone too far, had opened the doors so wide to NGOs that the Bank's integrity had been compromised. The Bank, they asserted, is—and should remain—an institution *of* governments and *for* governments. We were jeopardizing this by giving too much information to NGOs, by negotiating draft policies with civil society before taking them to the board, and by pressing governments to involve NGOs in major roles in an increasing number of projects.

There were ready answers to these points. First, it would be hypocritical for the World Bank to urge better governance in the South if it did not follow the same practices, including transparency, itself. It is a publicly funded institution and needs to be accountable to the world's taxpayers. Second, the Bank's articles require it to reach independent judgment on all operational matters; this entails drawing on best expertise outside as well as inside the organization. In discussing draft policies with civil society before making recommendations to the board, management was not *negotiating* with civil society but rather consulting specialists. And third, when the Bank urges NGO involvement in projects, this is because its staff believe the project is more likely to succeed with such partnerships and may be wary about the capacity of government units alone to achieve the stated social objectives, not because of a *fashion* for working with NGOs.

After a year of difficult discussions, including tricky debate within management and at the board level, a strategy paper on Bank-NGO relations was eventually approved (World Bank 1998). This clarified the rationale and terms for engagement. It didn't *stop* any practices, but an echo of caution reverberated for some time. A mistake we had clearly made was not sufficiently engaging this group of EDs—who come from finance ministry backgrounds—in our NGO discussions. After this we sought every opportunity to introduce the board to NGOs, especially from developing countries.

Some governments remained very resistant to involving NGOs. I once discussed with an ED a program we had been developing to consult civil society (in country) about our Country Assistance Strategies. He retorted that in his country the World Bank accounted for just 1 percent of the investment budget. It had a parliament and mature democracy, so there was no reason why this 1 percent—that just happened to be financed by World Bank loans, rather than domestic borrowing, taxes, or other routes—should be treated any differently. If any consulting with civil society was warranted, the *government* would do it, and it didn't need any help from the Bank, thank you very much!

This revealed an inherent tension within multilateral agencies. Any decision has to balance the concerns of all members. Industrial countries embrace deliberative as well as delegative democracy and so often *encourage* the Bank to engage CSOs in its decisions—not to undermine parliaments but to strengthen democracy. Many third-world governments haven't made this leap. They resent efforts of the World Bank or anyone else to impose new ways of working on them. They also resent NGOs, whom they see as competing with them for power and resources. Governments for whom the World Bank is a marginal source of finance can easily resist; poor countries who take interest-free loans and who have few other sources of external funding cannot. So, paradoxically, the donors (for it isn't just the World Bank) are more successful in encouraging civil society participation in decision-making in poorer countries—many of which have only recently become democracies—than in better-off ones. It is important to recognize the dilemma. Donors may unwittingly be weakening new, fragile parliaments by elevating the role of CSOs (or business leaders, for that matter) in national debate.

This explains why civil society has become controversial in organizations like the World Bank, and Southern governments have allies in the North among those who dislike CSOs themselves. For example, Larry Summers, former US Treasury secretary, told a World Bank top management meeting that he is "deeply troubled by the distance the Bank has gone in democratic countries towards engagement with groups other than governments in designing projects." He added that many borrowers have complained that it is inappropriate for the Bank to anoint non-elected, self-styled representatives of civil society to interfere in Bank programs. Ouch!

The World Bank is not alone in experiencing first a surge in relations with NGOs and then a backlash. The United Nations tells a similar story. It has a long, mostly positive history of NGO-engagement (Willetts 1996), starting with the critical role NGOs played in its birth. But a whole new era was heralded by the UN Earth Summit in Rio in 1992. After this, NGO participation and influence in international forums rose exponentially as did resentment among some governments about this invasion. "In a global world without global government, NGOs have stepped in to fill the gap. But there is now a backlash against their unaccountable power. Have they become too big for their boots?" (Bond 2000).

The NGO lobby at the United Nations in New York and Geneva has attracted increasing scrutiny. While once NGOs lined up outside meeting halls for the chance to beard a delegate, they are now likely to be inside. The newest UN agency (UNAIDS) even has NGOs on its board alongside governments and official agencies, though it proves very difficult to select the NGOs (Altman 1999). One analysis concluded that an NGO's influence in the United Nations is determined not by its representivity and accountability to a base constituency but by the size of its office, its public profile, and its command of the technical issues with which the UN agency in question deals (Steele 2000). This analysis suggests that the influence of NGOs in the United Nations has grown so much that they are now involved in attending plenary meetings, working groups, and negotiations on texts. NGOs have even addressed UN Security Council members on three occasions (on humanitarian issues, AIDS, and women in conflict). Controversy has escalated in parallel. Some UN delegates (in the Economic and Social Committee) have complained about NGOs' aggressive campaign tactics and called for tighter restrictions on their access (United Nations 2001).

The UN's Senior Management Group met to discuss United Nations–civil society relations in January 2001 because "some member states resist the increased activity and presence of NGOs at the UN" and question the legitimacy of organizations, the degree to which they are representative, their sources of funding, their "hidden agendas," their effectiveness and their sustainability. The meeting, however, stressed the importance of those relations—not least for informing the world's public about the United Nation's work—and concluded that the deteriorating civil society–government–UN relations could undermine the very legitimacy of the United Nations itself. The group recognized, however, that it was becoming increasingly difficult for the UN to be able to verify the bona fides of NGOs seeking access.

As the rumblings of discontent grew, international agencies started to ask what evidence there was for the assumed benefits of working with NGOs in projects. The World Bank's evaluations department did a study (which was fairly positive, though concluding "case not proven" in many areas), while a UNICEF-commissioned report claimed that NGO health services in Mozambique were ten times the cost of those provided by the government (Bond 2000). Ironically, the increased scrutiny of NGO performance and the rise in excoriating coverage by right-wing journalists owe much to the ascendancy of CSO voices in *policy* influence, yet most operational NGOs eschew advocacy in order to avoid biting the hand that feeds them.

This chapter's opening quotation illustrates the controversy: civil society as superpower. Superpowers that are not democratic, that lack clear and independently supervised accountability, that are not fully transparent, and that are unpredictable can be very dangerous. I doubt this applies to many CSO networks, but that is how many establishment figures see them and why they resent their influence. Hence, *Financial Times* journalist Martin Wolf wrote: "The claims of NGOs to represent civil society as a whole and, as such, to possess legitimacy rivaling—perhaps even exceeding—that of elected governments is outrageous" (September 1, 1999).

These remarks confirm the ascendancy of civil society but infer that poor governance and a presumed quest to usurp power are its Achilles' heel. In this context three words come up over and over again: *representivity, accountability,* and *legitimacy.* Let us take each in turn.

REPRESENTIVITY

For whom do CSOs speak, and how can they prove it? Trade unions have mass memberships, and people join because they want a union to represent them, so unions have good answers to these questions. Many other CSOs also have mass memberships (such as environmental organizations or churches), but it is less clear that members join them because they want to be represented. The Royal Society for the Protection of Birds in the UK, for example, has more members than all UK political parties combined, but most join because they are keen birdwatchers, want access to RSPB reserves, want to be put in touch with other birders, and enjoy the information RSPB gives them. When RSPB pronounces on conservation issues, it does so with great authority, but this stems from its long experience managing sensitive habitats, not its membership. The latter might pose a threat if the officials don't listen to them; the CSOs can always mobilize mass letter writing, protests, or—in the case of unions—strikes.

Likewise, the strength of the suffragettes one hundred years ago wasn't because they could prove (by membership lists or democratic procedures) that they spoke for all women. Representivity isn't simply about speaking *on behalf* of a constituency. It is also about speaking with expertise on an issue (representing the *facts*) and knowing that you have the *support* of a constituency. When it became clear that humanitarian relief NGOs had exaggerated the suffering among Rwandan refugees in 1996, their credibility for representing the situation of refugees was dented (Transparency International 2000).

For development NGOs, what aspects of representivity are important? That they may have a million members in *rich* countries says nothing about their competence to speak for the *poor*—though it does imply persuasive skills and a support base they can mobilize to support their lobbying. In reality, NGOs rarely claim to speak *on behalf of* the poor; they represent their own evidence in urging changes in policies or programs that will benefit poor people. Their confidence comes not from any delegated authority but from long experience of working with the poor, participatory approaches they use to identify problems and solutions, and their partnerships with CSOs and others in poor countries.

So those wanting to probe the representation of a CSO should look less to the number of members it can demonstrate than to the quality of experience it represents and the degree to which others in the field admire its expertise. They should ask whether the CSO's own programs have been effective, whether it has strong "local knowledge," and whether its working style exposes it to the perspectives of poor people and their delegated representatives. And CSOs should be able to respond well to such inquiries.

ACCOUNTABILITY

The accountability of NGOs and others in civil society has generated much literature over the last decade (see, for example, Edwards and Hulme 1995). This is partly due to the increased flow of public funding through NGOs and partly due to the probing of the "they've got too big for their boots" school of thought. Since this book is primarily about civil society's role globally in shaping policies, it isn't the place to discuss issues of fiduciary responsibility and program evaluation. The questions of relevance here concern the accountability of CSOs in their policy work.

Accountability has three components: for what; to whom; and how. In the current context the "for what" is for ensuring that policy messages are both realistic and serve the goals claimed (such as the interests of the poor or the environment); that information is accurate; that the path urged is sustainable, not just a short-term expedient; that claims regarding partnerships and constituencies are genuine and that partners are satisfied with any implied identification with the CSO's work; that there are no ulterior motives (such as generating publicity for the CSO itself); and that the cause is sensitive to other important factors, such as gender, the environment, and the interests of minorities.

The "to whom" is problematic. CSOs certainly should not be accountable to elected governments (as some critics of CSOs infer) anymore than companies or newspaper editors should be accountable to governments. Most CSOs engaged in social concerns, such as development NGOs, claim moral accountability to the vulnerable groups they serve, which is good rhetoric but pretty meaningless. In practice, CSOs don't have to explain to the poor the choice of their strategy or why they took a lobbying trip to Tokyo. Nor do they have to explain these things to their members. But CSO staff do nominally account to managers and boards of trustees. In practice, this may not be very onerous. Larger CSOs generally give their lobbyists a fairly free rein unless they start losing reputation or supporters. The smaller advocacy NGOs aren't hierarchies, and their boards are picked because they support what the NGO does.

Accountability tends to be quite strong, however, to institutional donors—official aid agencies and foundations. These are well placed to ask probing questions. But do they? And should they? In practice, few donors go much beyond routine accounting matters, such as how their funds were used and what proportion went to administration. And if they are more forceful, they may start imposing their own values. (He who pays the piper calls the tune!) Even if the scrutiny is both rigorous and objective, there is something unhealthy about relying on a *caveat donor* approach. Questions of civil society accountability ought to rest with the people not with an external funding agency.

Finally, the question of "how." CSOs should maximize accountability within countries relevant to their advocacy and get as close to the citizens as possible. For development NGOs, this would include using participatory research to ensure that their arguments are based on the concerns and views of the poor. And they might use "reverse evaluations," in which CSO leaders from the South evaluate and critique the advocacy programs of INGOs. *All* CSOs should open themselves to public scrutiny (including media scrutiny) through full transparency. This is far from being the case at present. NGOs are typically coy with internal evaluations and business plans, tending only to disseminate information that puts their organization in a good light.

Since meaningful accountability to the voiceless is a pipedream, and accountability to institutions isn't fully appropriate, the best strategy to encourage is self-regulation within the CSO sector. But there is little tradition of peer review. The INGO umbrella in the United States, InterAction, has devised a very detailed set of standards (2001), but virtually every line of its sixteen pages deals with accountability to US stakeholders (supporters, child sponsors, the public, the media, staff, etc.) and there is nothing concrete on accountability to partners or other stakeholders in the South. The code provides a modicum of protection for US donors but is hardly onerous for the NGOs since it relies on self-certification. Although there is a mechanism for looking into complaints, this has only been used once to date (following a complaint to InterAction by a group of whistle-blowing staff in one NGO). An investigation confirmed the validity of some of the complaints, but the findings were not made public and the NGO was not named— instead it was given a year to clean up its act.

Some CSO watchdog groups exist in rich countries and publish ethical scorecards on nonprofit organizations (for example, in the United States, the National Charities Information Bureau 1996). The Caucus of Development NGOs and other networks in the Philippines have taken the bold step of expelling members who fail to reach their governance standards and publishing such expulsions (CODE-NGO 1997; Soledad 2001). But in general, there is scant CSO self-regulation. This could be redressed through independent CSO watchdogs or perhaps academic units specializing in CSO assessments. Such bodies in the South would be well placed to make ethical assessments of how Northern NGOs portray the South in their publicity, making accountability a two-way street.

LEGITIMACY

Whenever a small CSO causes great irritation to a large bureaucracy, the cry goes up: "What's its legitimacy; what right does it have to meddle in the affairs of legitimate companies/governments/bureaucracies?" (delete where appropriate). Central to such outbursts are questions of size and rights. The answers are very simple. Any size group has a perfect right to speak out on issues that concern it because that is what freedoms of speech and association—protected by democratic governments and international law—are all about. CSOs are legitimate as long as they are honest and the interests they promote don't harm others. If the CSO is lying or pretending to be other than it really is, it is guilty of deception, but *size* has nothing to do with legitimacy when it comes to engaging in political debate. Firms, likewise, are no less legitimate because they are small—though one would be unwise to buy a life-insurance policy from a tiny company.

We need a change of mindset. Democracy is *strengthened* not weakened when the voice of "the little people" can be heard directly. This is why broadening from delegative to deliberative democracy is so powerful. Democracy no longer rests on the shoulders of a handful of elected politicians. Companies, NGOs, unions, the media, protest movements, and intellectuals can join the deliberative process directly. It is no longer necessary to be elected, or have a constituency, or be a large organization before one can speak; an individual can be as legitimate as an MP. We're all in the debating chamber now!

If the British TV wildlife presenter David Attenborough were to proclaim on a conservation issue, he would have more clout than most MPs—yet no one voted for him, and he claims no members. The issue isn't legitimacy but advocacy effectiveness. Certainly there are pressure groups that punch well above their weight, perhaps because they have special authority on the topic in question or because they have special communication power. Some manage to get mass media support on the basis of flimsy but sensationalist evidence, but this is media irresponsibility. Those who sensationalize any controversy without checking the facts are irresponsible and deserve censure (though how is beyond the scope of this book). Some protests are irresponsible, and there are important issues about the ethics of dot-causes, but in general the expansion of public debate is enhancing not undermining democracy.

A recent campaign against a British government-funded program in India illustrates these issues. A group in Andra Pradesh protested that the Department for International Development (DFID) is funding a program that would promote prairie-style farming in Andra Pradesh, throwing twenty million people off their land. A major British INGO and a prominent UK journalist took up the cause (*The Guardian*, April 2, 2002). An instant campaign tour was organized bringing Andra Pradesh activists to the UK, which whipped up public criticism. By this time DFID had heard about the protest and issued a quick explanation. It was a preposterous (perhaps willful) misunderstanding. DFID was committed to long-term support for Andra Pradesh, including helping its government in a long-range strategic planning exercise called Vision 2020. This had concluded that the mainly rural state could only reduce poverty swiftly by generating off-farm jobs, that twenty million such jobs should be created by 2020. There was never any question of *throwing* this number (or indeed anyone at all) off their land. Maybe the Andra Pradesh group just misunderstood, but was it responsible for the UK NGO and journalist to lend the story such credence without checking the facts with DFID? The UK research institutes who helped the Andra Pradesh group compile its case have admitted that their researchers' work was flawed. The UK NGO that organized the campaign tour has admitted that the heading of its press release (about throwing twenty million off the land) was "misleading." But in spite of this and DFID's widely circulated repost, *The Guardian* repeated its story (September 14, 2002) without any qualification. There may well be a case that poor farmers should have been more seriously consulted in preparing Vision 2020, but that complaint wouldn't make headlines. Isn't it time for an ethical peer-review process within both NGOs and the media?

INTEGRITY

The issues of representivity, accountability, and legitimacy boil down to one key question: What is the integrity of CSOs seeking to influence political debate? Just as important, of course, is the integrity of politicians, officials, companies, and others who also seek to influence the debate.

There is no simple way of measuring this quality. It is a distillation of the topics above plus at least one more. In an imperfect democracy some causes are adopted by CSOs while others aren't. This risks atomizing politics into a thousand fragments rather than a coherent national strategy. This is most evident in the United States, where countless interest groups relentlessly pursue their topics. A government must listen to the cacophony but maintain a holistic view, which is hard. A more independent scrutiny of activities of interest groups (including business lobbies) is needed in order to provide governments and the public an ethics check. Balancing passionate concerns with societal needs is well illustrated by the evolution of the German Greens. When in opposition, they were like an environmental pressure group, but once in a coalition government they developed much more nuance about issues such as economic growth and energy needs.

To summarize, the ethics of CSO engagement in policy debate is a legitimate issue of discussion. There is no simple way of identifying which are "good" and which are "bad" CSOs, but there are seven integrity tests that can be usefully applied:

- *Representation test:* membership, constituency, participatory decision-making
- *Merit test:* track record, demonstrated positive impact, strong local knowledge
- *Credibility test:* whether acknowledged authority, links with credible partners
- *Values test:* proven commitment to ethical values, ethical in its internal practices
- *Governance test:* clear accountability, open, democratic decision-making
- *Responsibility test:* accurate, honest, recognize the need for issues-balance
- *Partnership test:* works openly with other CSOs, empowers Southern capacity/voice

THE BACKLASH FROM BELOW

The challenge to civil society does not just come from governments and establishment figures. There are many sources of tension and challenge within civil society itself. These include North-South tensions, splits between different categories of CSOs, and splits over tactics and politics. In the rest of this chapter we quickly describe some of the more familiar sources of tension and ways in which they are—or might be—addressed.

Northern CSO concerns seen as Western imperialism

Southern elites and the CSOs they associate with often dismiss causes such as the environment, women's rights, human rights, and good governance as being thrust down their throats by interfering Northerners—like latter-day cultural imperialists. Such campaigns, they contend, are insensitive both to their country's traditions and to its stage of development. Sometimes such arguments are lame excuses for indefensible traditions (such as summary executions or genital mutilation of girls). Sometimes there is more than a grain of truth. Lectures from well-heeled Westerners about the urgency of reducing carbon dioxide emissions must particularly stick in the craw of those in developing countries who enjoy one-twentieth the per-capita consumption of fossil fuels.

Similarly, there have been North-South splits within CSOs about including social and environmental issues in trade negotiations. Most CSOs in the South (including many unions) fear that such clauses will serve as pretexts for new Northern protectionism. For example, CSOs among Thai fishing communities are furious that US green groups seek to ban the import of Thai shrimp on the grounds that the nets used in open seas are not equipped with escape flaps for sea turtles; the CSOs insist that there *are* no sea turtles where this fishing is done. Similarly, CSOs in Bangladesh and elsewhere believe that the efforts of Northern NGOs and unions to require certification that child labor has not been used in imported textiles has worsened the situation for the poor. Many children have been laid off but haven't resumed schooling because their family poverty requires them to work; they have simply found other employment, and surveys show that this is likely to be lower paid and with greater dangers (Edwards 1999).

There can never be a single "world parliament" of civil society, but it is important to build up denser networks that span different segments of civil society as well as different regions of the world. Such networks would provide forums for discerning strategies where synergies rather than squabbles can be developed. The Internet and easier travel should make this easier.

How the South is portrayed

There has long been debate about the ethics of INGO fund-raising, particularly the "poverty pornography"—the use of graphic images of starvation in order to jerk Northern citizens into parting with their money. It is unhealthy that poverty is the only image people in rich countries have of Africa, for example. A similar concern is surfacing about how NGOs use images in advocacy—the use of both sensationalism and peasant romanticism to provoke feelings of guilt and charity, and the presentation of the Northern CSOs as saviors. This helps perpetuate images of structural underdevelopment and dependency in the South. Three-fourths of Southern NGOs taking part in a special survey had such criticisms of their Northern partners (Krut 1997).

Northern pressure may undermine Southern democracy

INGO development campaigns are likely to focus exclusively on external actors. In so doing they may weaken efforts of their Southern partners to use democratic processes. Paul Nelson gives the example of how Washington NGOs' heightened interest in the World Bank's decentralized planning process caused friction with Southern partners (Nelson 2001). The latter focused primarily on their governments and had only a secondary interest in the Bank. By elevating attention on the Bank, says Nelson, INGOs have tended to reduce local autonomy, for example concerning controversial projects. These issues have been wrestled from national debate and fed into *international* democratic forums. Nelson points out that while INGOs criticize the global policymaking elite, they are themselves *part* of that elite. As lawyers, scientists, economists, and anthropologists they are part of the same education and class tradition as staff in agencies like the Bank.

The campaign against World Bank financing of the Arun III dam in Nepal illustrates these dilemmas (Fox and Brown 1998). A Nepali NGO that helped peasants increase their income through micro-scale hydro-electricity was first to voice concern. It argued that this enormous dam was inappropriate to the country's energy needs and would kill their program to distribute micro-hydro-electricity generators, and called on INGOs to help. The campaign didn't lift off until skilled international lobbyists took it up, stressing the social and environmental damage of the dam in this remote and pristine valley. This captured the attention of international media, NGOs, and parliamentarians in many countries. Paradoxically, few valley inhabitants spoke out, and those who did just criticized the decision to reroute the road leading to the dam, since it would no longer pass near their villages. They didn't mind their Arcadia being opened to the outside world, as long as they had use of the road. The campaign ultimately caused the Bank to withdraw funding; this was probably the right decision, but more due to economics and overall national development priorities than the concerns of the valley people (World Bank Inspection Panel 1998).

Recounting this story is not intended as a criticism of anyone in-volved in the campaign, but it poses an interesting question: Where does national democracy lie in such controversies? The democratically elected Nepali government insisted that only *it* had a mandate to speak for the people. It objected to MPs in other countries even discussing, let alone opposing, its domestic matters. But it just looked at the aggre-gate—Nepal's need for faster growth and more power. It knew less than the local NGOs about the valley people's needs. Had all stake-holders been consulted, a different conclusion about how to meet the country's energy needs would probably have emerged. But such con-sultations are rare, and hence affected people will use surrogates—taking their cause outside, especially if a foreign funding agency is in-volved.

Moral issues certainly arise, especially if the international campaign distorts the issues or ignores the domestic debate. Such dilemmas need to be more honestly debated than they have been hitherto. Books have been written about the accountability of governments and international organizations, and rightly so, but the debate about accountability mecha-nisms within advocacy organizations and citizens movements is in its infancy. Such tensions will occur until all countries like Nepal have unfettered and robust civil societies and their own deliberative democ-racy.

Who has the microphone?

We have already discussed issues of representation, but the question of who should present what evidence has become an increasingly vex-ing one between Northern and Southern CSOs. The former may have topnotch communications and advocacy skills yet have virtually no experience in the South. They may *use* their Southern partners purely as a source of information and legitimization. Hence there is a growing call from Southern CSOs to hand over the reins. They argue that it is time for a new independence, for Southern civil society to speak for Southern citizens (Tandon 1995).

The case is sound but carries dilemmas. First, are capital city CSOs any closer to the citizens than their Northern equivalents? In India one finds a cascade of criticism: grassroots CSOs think those in the state capital are out of touch with the poor; those in state capitals say the same about Delhi NGOs, who in turn say the same about INGOs. Second, can there be true independence without financial independence? If Northern NGOs provide most Southern NGOs' budgets, they will continue to call the shots. Even if they agree that their partners' rather than their voices should be heard in international forums, through their funding they select *which* voices get heard. Third, effecting political change in Northern-based institutions, governments, and companies is an art that is generally more developed in the North. If getting results is the premium, such skilled campaign strategists have an important role.

What does partnership mean?

Northern NGOs are fond of talking about their Southern *partners*, while those in the South talk about their Northern *donors*. True partnership requires common goals, agreed division of labor, mutual trust, and approximate power equality within the common venture. In North-South NGO relations one rarely finds all these features—certainly not when the relationship is defined by a flow of money in one direction and of accountability in the other (Ashman 2000). Clearly, Northern NGOs have a comparative advantage in accessing funds and should use this, but the relationship must be more than this if it is to be a partnership. A few Southern NGOs have such a reputation that they can choose their funders, but most depend, somewhat precariously, on one or two donors.

Within a genuine partnership INGOs would be alert to what their partners want beyond funding, such as help to campaign against global inequities. Northern citizens are not just potential donors; they are also educators (of their children), they have a voice (through local newspapers, societies, and so on), they have a vote, they can exercise consumer power (for or against certain products), as investors they can make ethical choices, and if all else fails, they can cause trouble (through demonstrations).

Northern CSOs, perversely, often have easier access to information about a Southern country than do CSOs in that country, but many aren't conscientious about getting that information and sharing it. They may also not be good at sharing the privileged access they have to influential journalists, politicians, officials, and other decision-formers, monopolizing the air time for themselves. It may be true that their partners don't yet have strong advocacy skills, in which case they should help build these skills. The message coming from Southern CSOs is clear. They aren't telling Northern NGOs to go home, but they are saying it is time to share the reins and hand over the microphone.

The radical-reformist tensions

There are many motivations for campaigning. At one end of the spectrum is the desire to win tangible reforms; at the other is a thirst to vent anger and perhaps have a dust-up with the police. Sometimes a campaign accommodates a range of motivations, and this always leads to tension (especially if coupled with a North-South split). For example, a group of seasoned World Bank critics decided in 1994 to press the US Congress to oppose the upcoming replenishment of the soft-loan arm of the Bank until the Bank completed a series of reforms. This led to a collision with a group of Southern NGOs who argued that, though the reforms were necessary, the Bank's interest-free loans to poorer countries were vital and that Northern NGOs had no right to take this stance without consulting Southern counterparts. This was a wake-up call to the US NGOs and helped increase the prominence of Southern voices in future global advocacy (Chiriboga 2002).

In the case of debt campaigning, the NGOs were differently aligned. Jubilee 2000 was created by a network of UK development NGOs in the mid-1990s and developed a high profile and effective campaigning stance. It became known worldwide after mobilizing sixty thousand people to demonstrate for debt relief at the G7 Summit in Birmingham in 1998 by forming a human chain for 10 kilometers around the Summit venue. Jubilee 2000 encouraged similar groups to be set up in other countries. The resulting global network had wide appeal, did its homework meticulously, and made realistic demands. It undoubtedly contributed to the international agreement to give debt relief to the heavily indebted poor countries (known as HIPC). However, the network became divided over which countries should get debt relief, the extent of cancellation, and whether there should be any conditions.

The original Jubilee 2000 and many other groups argued that at least initially debt relief should be sought for the *poorer* countries, that the objective should be to reduce debt burdens to sustainable levels, and that the countries getting relief should be able to demonstrate that the savings aren't squandered but go into poverty-reduction programs. In April 1998, however, a group of fifteen African groups in the network challenged this and called for total and unconditional debt relief for *all* of Africa, and shortly afterward a Latin American group issued a statement saying that no country should pay more than 3 percent of its GNP as debt service. These more radical groups came together as Jubilee South under the slogan: "Don't owe, won't pay." This had popular appeal in the South but did little to move the cause forward in international circles. Jubilee 2000 continued in the UK and mustered increasing support for the reformist demands—especially by marshalling the support of well-known pop celebrities such as Bono and Bob Geldoff. But the split critically wounded Jubilee 2000 as a global movement (Collins et al. 2001; Greiner 2003).

Box 9.1 Civilizing civil society—five challenges for ethical CSOs

Self-regulation. *People* run CSOs, as they do companies and governments; thus CSOs are not necessarily purer. Abuses are becoming more numerous and more significant as the sector grows—hence the importance of fostering peer review and objective scrutiny. Professional civil society watchdogs and academic units specializing in CSO assessment would be useful.

Transparency. Though CSOs are quick to criticize official opacity, they are often parsimonious with their own plans, evaluations, and financial information; a discipline of CSO transparency is needed, except where it might jeopardize the human rights of partners.

Southern voice. To avoid replicating the power imbalance found elsewhere, international advocacy must become increasingly guided *and articulated* by Southern civil society—not through handpicking articulate capital city-based intellectuals who think in common with their Northern partners, but through welcoming a diversity of citizens' voices. Building the capacity of Southern CSOs for international advocacy is a priority.

Civil society networks. Denser networks of CSOs are needed, regional and issue-based, to help diverse views percolate into international advocacy and to guard against the tendency of governments and international organizations to handpick CSOs for civil society consultations.

Codes of ethics. CSO networks should devise ethical codes for various aspects of their work, including advocacy. This would include guidance for strengthening, not undermining, local democratic institutions; enhancing accountability to citizens; including the voices of women and the "excluded"; maximizing the Southern voice; consulting locally before speaking globally; and resisting exaggeration designed to maximize blame-casting and press coverage.

CONCLUSIONS—THE COST OF CONFLICT

Those who resent CSO campaigns increasingly challenge the governance deficiencies of CSOs, as we have discussed. CSOs' best response to this is to measure themselves against the ethics tests described in this chapter and to encourage the evolution of independent watchdogs of CSOs. But we are also starting to see an exploitation of divides between CSOs. Some journalists, for example, have focused heavily on the union-NGO rift over labor standards. It is difficult to know how best to respond.

On the one hand, it would be wrong to suppress the diversity that characterizes civil society; on the other hand, it is in the interests of reformers and radicals alike to avoid squabbles within the sector being overblown. When Oxfam International released its report on world trade in 2002, the attacks in right-of-center newspapers were expected, but it received a more stinging and very public rebuke from Food First, a radical US group that was angry that Oxfam International called for a *reform* of trade rules—as if the only legitimate CSO position is to oppose trade. Many of Food First's criticisms were based on a draft, circulated within Oxfam International for discussion, and didn't apply to the final version. A similar though less stinging critique was issued by Focus on the Global South in Bangkok.

There is clearly a need for more systematic strategy exchange among CSOs seeking to influence global policy; this includes trans-sectoral as well as transnational networking. The objective shouldn't be to seek consensus or to avoid peer criticism but to ensure that debate within civil society is healthy, that there is genuine listening to different viewpoints, and that criticisms are substantiated before being made public. Sloppy or vindictive infighting damages the pitch for all CSOs, and intolerance of diversity weakens the sector greatly.

In concluding Part Two there is a single, powerful message. The future holds immense opportunities for CSOs to influence international policy and alter the path of global change. But these opportunities may evaporate if energy is dissipated in infighting or disparate, uncoordinated, and unsound campaigns. To realize its potential, civil society needs to invest in much bolder networking, extending well beyond traditional partners, and more honest peer review and attention to governance. With these things, civil society has the power to transform global governance and reshape the management of globalization, which are the subjects of the final part of this book.

Part Three

The Path to Ethical Globalization

10.

Civilizing Globalization

Roles for Civil Society in Global Governance

Until now we have looked at globalization's impact: how the world is changing, problems and opportunities globalization offers poor people and poor countries, and how the forces of globalization are also changing the landscape of civil society. We now explore what can and should be done differently. Can we have the good without the bad? Can civil society, acting globally, make a difference, or are the forces immutable? This chapter looks at process: How can the institutions that determine the pace and direction of globalization be changed, reinvented or supplemented so that their mandate becomes one of harnessing the power of globalization to reduce inequality and poverty? Can lessons relating to the four pillars of governance (discussed in Chapter 4) be applied to these actors to make them more accountable and responsive to citizens who are affected by their actions? This is *civilization* in a dual sense: inculcating international policymaking with enlightened and humanized values; and expanding the civic sector's role in the governance of those institutions. There is no prospect of changing how globalization is managed without changing the institutions that steer it. The final chapter looks at content: What are the most important changes in policies and practices that could contribute to this harnessing? How can civil society promote *ethical* globalization?

Increasing global interconnectedness, the growing disparities of wealth and power, and citizens' increased perception of global economic injustice all point to the need for the leading actors in global change—governments, intergovernmental organizations, and corporations—to come to grips with ethical issues. This entails instilling social and environmental standards, principles of good governance, and openness to engaging citizens in debate (embracing deliberative democracy). Before exploring the different actors, we ask a general question: What does it take to change an institution?

189

VALUES OR ORDERS?

To expect major institutions to change how they work is a tall order. Big bureaucracies usually change at a snail's pace and are set in old ways. But my years in the World Bank (and watching other major institutions) have told me that change *is* possible, given the right combination of leadership and outside pressure—which is why the role of civil society is vital. Before working in the Bank I assumed that the first step in changing what an institution does is to change what it believes—through argument and pressure. As its values change it will start doing different things. I now realize that changed actions lead to changed values, not the other way around.

Bank staff were mostly skeptical that participatory approaches would do much to improve the design of "their" projects, although some saw potential improvements in implementation, for example, by having local groups responsible for maintenance. But enticed by some seed money for participatory innovations, a number of staff started experimenting. They were soon impressed with the insights and practical ideas coming in and naturally extended participation where they could. The numbers of staff using such approaches rose gradually with the diffusion of experience and leapt after Jim Wolfensohn, the new president, announced that this was the obvious way to work, that everyone should use participation in the future, and that he wanted monthly progress reports.

Quite soon participation became more common, and staff reports were enthusiastic. True, there was much exaggeration, but over ensuing years there has been steady change. Managers now routinely scrutinize whether staff members engage communities and use qualitative surveys as well as statistical research. Today, the project truly owned by local communities will get more praise than the one with the highest economic rate of return. Staff training now routinely includes courses in participatory rural appraisal, community-led development, and working with civil society. And staff increasingly believe in it.

This illustrates a virtuous reform cycle—learning by doing. Changed leadership signals lead to different staff instructions, and thus to new activities and new experiences; progressive staff will be delighted if there are social returns and will keenly report this, thus reinforcing the management signals; they are also more likely to be rewarded or promoted, so reinforcing progressive leadership. The initial leadership signal can result from personal values of the boss or internal pioneers pressing for change, but in any organization that is sensitive to its image or that exists in the public realm, the most effective pressure probably comes from outside. Either way, what translates the idea into institutional change is a new set of orders that triggers off the learning experience. This is the virtuous reform; there is also the "virtual reform." In this cycle new orders lead not to new *activities*, but new ways of *reporting* old activities. Management may delude themselves into thinking they are making waves, but no one outside falls for it. There is, I have to say, quite a bit of this in the Bank too. In these cases the unpopular job of CSO critics is to tell the emperor whether he's wearing clothes.

In the Bank, people started doing things differently as a result of budget incentives, changed management signals, changed reward systems, and hiring new specialists. The momentum accelerated as new permanent staff (as opposed to short-term consultants) were recruited, and some rose in the hierarchy. Over time the values have changed. Of course, many resist change and some claim to have changed but haven't really, but on balance the progress has been strong. This experience offers useful lessons to those seeking institutional reform elsewhere. Pressures can come from inside or outside, but what is most effective is a concerted pincer movement, forcing changes in what the institution does and so exposing it to new learning experiences.

CIVILIZING GOVERNMENTS

CSO innovations have done much in recent years to strengthen the pillars of governance and so enhancing accountability and responsiveness, particularly in the South, including:

- *Enhancing transparency*: CSO information channels for disseminating information on government policies and programs; training and support for investigative journalism and citizens' broadcasting; requests for greater media objectivity and prominence given to poverty issues; anti-corruption campaigns (such as Transparency International or Indonesian Corruption Watch); and campaigns to promote freedom of information.
- *Enhancing accountability*: Budget analysis and campaigns to reform spending priorities (for example, India, Brazil, and South Africa); scorecards for citizens to rank the quality of public services (for example, South India and the Philippines); watchdogs monitoring government activities and ethics; and CSOs promoting the involvement of women, minorities, and other vulnerable groups in programs of decentralization.
- *Enhancing the rule of law*: Citizens' advice bureaus; legal-aid programs; informal peoples' courts (when the state refuses to move prosecutions defending the rights of the vulnerable); rights

education to ensure people know their entitlements; pressing for public planning hearings on schemes that will affect poor people.
* *Enhancing citizens' voices:* Promoting participatory planning processes; using ICT to strengthen democracy; strengthening advocacy capacity of civil society; promoting deliberative democracy; forming groups of women and vulnerable groups to convey their concerns.

This work entails strengthening the institutions needed for good governance and ensuring that poor people can use them, including training and assisting women and minority groups to put themselves forward for election and for holding public office. It also entails strengthening civil society institutions for these tasks, especially by building networks at the local, national, and international levels to link CSOs for mutual support and exchange of experience.

One important and powerful innovation is budget analysis. The pioneering work of DISHA, an NGO working mostly with tribal communities in Gujarat, India, is particularly exciting. Every year the State Government of Gujarat publishes its forty-two-volume budget, followed by eighteen days of debate in the state parliament. The sheer volume of data is daunting, and the debates are normally quite superficial. In 1993, DISHA designed a computer spreadsheet for analyzing the budget. The minute the budget was published, DISHA started inputting all the information, taking four days and nights. When completed, it provided the *only* complete budget picture; not even the chief minister could draw all the information together and cross-reference different spending lines. The analysis revealed many things: policy commitments were often not honored; the poorest sub-districts received the least support; and there were hundreds of errors totaling hundreds of million rupees (typically as the same item appeared in different sections). Since then, budget analysis has become an annual exercise, MPs of all parties have been keen to get DISHA's analysis, and the budget debate now includes real development substance. It has also helped identify ways to address loss and corruption. DISHA has also guided NGOs in India and around the world in such work. The Ford Foundation has provided funding and also financed a new global network of NGOs using budget analysis.

CSOs concerned about the management of globalization have mostly focused on the IGOs; some recognize that this leaves a major gap regarding the roles of *governments*. In fact, one NGO network, Jubilee 2000, decided midcourse it had overemphasized IGO roles in debt relief and switched focus to the G7 finance ministers as more important targets because they preside over bigger creditor agencies *and* determine IGO policies.

In any country a broad-spectrum coalition of major CSOs arguing a common position is powerful, but were such an effort globally coordinated—including North, South, and different cultures—it could transform the voice of civil society in world affairs, and so perhaps the management of globalization. Such a concerted campaign might not lead to quick changes in trade or economic policy, but it could persuade governments everywhere to agree to a global citizenship compact in which governments commit to engage citizens and their organizations in global deliberations by embodying the principles of good governance in all aspects of international relations, that is, processes that are more open, consultative, sensitive to poverty concerns, and accountable.

Global citizenship compact

Elected governments are chosen by citizens to protect and serve their interests. But in a massively interconnected world those interests are not well served universally and in the long term by political decisions taken at the national level; national interests always interfere. Affording CSOs more structured roles and strengthening accountability mechanisms to citizens would counter these nationalistic, short-term tendencies. Ultimately, the world as a whole would prosper more if all countries were to share the pluses of global change, and all peoples were to have a say. This would enhance goodwill among nations—much needed in the aftermath of 9/11. The following are possible steps that CSOs could advocate to all governments toward reaching these goals.

- *Transparency in international relations:* Governments should make public how they vote and the thrust of the cases they promote in all IGOs. At present the United States is one of the few countries where this is the practice. This is a necessary preliminary for more informed parliamentary and civil society debate on global change. Similarly, governments should publish analyses about the national stake in international trade and economic affairs, including details of how their various trade barriers affect each trading partner, and details of all public and private loans to other countries.
- *Commitment to global equity:* Governments should be pressed to commit publicly to promoting world equity. Though broadly aspirational, this would entail specific practical commitments, such as to make global impact assessments of any proposed policy change that could affect poor countries and to monitor existing trade instruments to ensure they are not misused as further hurdles for the Third World. Such steps should involve CSO specialists or witnesses and be made public. Standing parliamentary

committees could scrutinize these processes with regular, if not permanent, civil society representation.

- *Leadership, not free-riding:* Northern governments should be urged to commit themselves to moral leadership; this means that when global commitments are made, they would race to respond rather than wait to make sure all other governments are serious. Examples would be in debt relief, overall levels of overseas aid, and giving privileged trade access and more generous aid to the least developed countries.

- *Global governance:* Northern governments should be urged to desist from caballing only with governments of other rich countries (the G7 or OECD). They should build mixed forums with Southern governments. The prime minister of Belgium proposed a new G8, comprising not countries but major regional partnerships—the European Union, African Union, Mercosur, ASEAN, NAFTA, and so on (Verhofstadt 2001). Something like this would only be effective if more than a one-off brief meeting of heads of government. To give it teeth, such a forum should focus on and resolve specific turnkey issues, such as destabilizing capital mobility. To make this problem-solving format work, there should be regular meetings of ministers relevant to the issues, over a sustained period, using occasional heads of government summits to add political commitment or break logjams. For example, there should be forums of ministers responsible for the environment, finance (or macro-economic policy), migration and immigration, agriculture, trade, financing for development, transport, health, or education—depending on the topic addressed. These forums would have professional secretariats to help them consider various scenarios and would take evidence from civil society and others; they would last until they had done their task. A trade forum of this nature would not replace the WTO—it wouldn't be able to make global decisions—but it would make recommendations to the WTO, and these would have considerable authority, coming as they do from a microcosm of the WTO's membership. Such forums would also provide links to national parliaments. In time, they might become permanent forums (with rotating membership so that all countries have some access), hence might begin to address the lacuna of global government in a world where policies reach globally. In practice, eight members would be too few, and it is a mistake to assume that regional groups all have a similar structure or can speak equally on behalf of their membership.

Curbing the G1—the challenge for US civil society

The biggest nettle to grasp, to offer any hope of globalization working well for poor countries, is to curb the power and selfishness of the United States—nicknamed the G1 because this appears to be the country grouping the United States feels is best equipped to manage global affairs. It is a matter of increasing concern that the most powerful transnational actor today is a *nation*. There are growing signs that many countries, including a few rich ones, think that it is time to resist the might and unilateralism of this superpower, but real change—a gentler, more collegial America—will only come about if US citizen groups demand it.

The European Union was angry with the United States for imposing steel tariffs, but only because its direct interests were threatened. It was less vocal about the US farm bill, though this is much more serious for the South. And rich countries have been relatively meek as the Bush Administration has delivered multilateralism an unprecedented series of slaps in the face. It has pulled out of the Kyoto climate change protocol, the anti-ballistic missile treaty, and the talks to curb trade in small arms; opposed the International Criminal Court, the ban on landmines, and new provisions of the biological warfare convention; and refused to ratify the convention on bio-diversity. Bush has orchestrated the replacement of the chair of the International Panel on Climate Change (because the incumbent, like most scientists, wanted to reduce greenhouse gasses), and the replacement of Mary Robinson as UN high commissioner for human rights (after her public criticism of the condition of Afghan war detainees held by the United States). Of the twenty-two major international human rights, humanitarian, disarmament, and environmental treaties, the United States has ratified only nine, compared with an average of nineteen for other G7 countries (Glasius et al. 2002). Other than a couple of tiny countries, the only nations with a worse record than the United States are Iraq, Afghanistan, Myanmar, and Somalia. Now governments are starting to say "enough!"

Moreover, the US government appears unable to restrain US corporate greed. Insider dealing, spectacular compensation packages, and corporate crime at least make US headlines, but when the victims are in the South, they don't. The poor-country debt-relief program is threatened, for example, because US financial speculators (called "debt vultures" by UK Chancellor Gordon Brown, *The Guardian*, May 7, 2002) buy up debt scheduled for cancellation at knockdown prices and then take legal action to demand full payment. And the victims of the 1984 Union Carbide explosion in Bhopal, India—which killed over sixteen thousand people and injured four hundred thousand—have received a pittance: fourteen hundred dollars for those who lost a parent; an average of five hundred dollars for others, not even enough for their medical costs (Sambhavna Trust 1998). The New York courts, which would inevitably have awarded higher sums, had declined to hear a compensation case. Union Carbide's total compensation was one-tenth of that paid by Exxon after the Valdez oil spill, which killed no one, and one-twentieth of what Dow Chemicals eventually paid to buy up Union Carbide. No one from Union Carbide has ever faced charges relating to the accident, but in 1991 an international warrant was issued through Interpol for the arrest of Warren Anderson, Union Carbide's former chairman. This has never been served because, say US authorities, his whereabouts are unknown. Greenpeace, however, has had no trouble finding him.

Increasing resentment about US selfishness and double standards is fueling mounting anti-Americanism around the world. US civil society has a pivotal role to play in ensuring that this mood translates to positive change rather than deepening anger. US CSOs have a duty to make sure Southern citizens' concerns are heard by decision-makers and the public, and they must make clear where they stand. They can use their very considerable access to media and politicians, their communications skills, and their vast resources to promote global responsibility, not unilateralism. They can be vital people-to-people conduits, bringing issues many thousands of miles away to life at home, hosting people from the South to convey their grievances directly, and using moral leadership to ensure that those grievances are addressed. They could do their best, for example, to get across what it is like to visit a Bhopal clinic now and see (as I have) people who are blind, in permanent pain, wracked with coughing, and visited by nightly nightmares—almost twenty years after the explosion. How could a movement for just compensation be resisted then?

Unfortunately, however, many US NGOs avoid US targets for fear of being labeled political or unpatriotic. They find attacking the IGOs altogether safer ground. Hence US development NGOs are much more likely to brief Southern CSOs about the faults of the World Bank and other IGOs and how to build campaigns on these issues than they are to work with partners in challenging US policy. The main US trade union network (American Federation of Labor–Confederation of Industrial Organizations) similarly has set up Solidarity Centers throughout Asia from which they have organized an apparently indigenous Asia Labor Network on International Financial Institutions—but not a comparable network on US policy. Why are US CSOs reluctant to criticize their government? For development NGOs it could be because their sector receives so much USAID funding. For large membership organizations—such as unions and environment groups—it could be that they don't want to appear unpatriotic and so risk losing support. For small pressure groups it could be that they fear this would jeopardize their foundation funding or media profile. Whatever the reasons, this unwillingness to bring criticism home couldn't be more unfortunate; only US CSOs have sway over US opinion, and this has to be changed if unilateralism is to give way to global responsibility and global responsiveness. US CSOs have a duty to turn the mirror inward.

CIVILIZING INTERNATIONAL ORGANIZATIONS

As mentioned earlier, there have been many significant changes toward poverty and participatory approaches in the World Bank throughout the 1990s. Though these have been promoted by staff pioneers, directed by management, and authorized by the board, I have no doubt that civil society has been the main driving force—particularly a band of twenty or so NGOs, largely but not only in Washington.

This NGO pressure started in the mid 1980s by publicly shaming the World Bank for the negative social and environmental impact of many of its projects. It then expanded to excoriate both the Bank and the IMF for the structural adjustment programs urged in response to the debt and economic crises. The Bank saw the need to make some changes, at the very least to analyze more systematically the impacts of its programs in order to design mitigatory measures. This entailed getting more local input and dialoguing more constructively with NGOs (which is why the World Bank invited me to work with it). Throughout the 1990s, although they have continued to criticize the Bank for specific projects or policies, a major thrust of NGO campaigning has been on matters of process. In fact, NGOs have pressed the Bank on the same messages of governance that the Bank has taken to developing countries.

NGOs have urged *transparency,* in particular a disclosure policy that reverses the previous emphasis on presumed confidentiality and ensures that most of the Bank's project- and policy-related documents are now in the public domain. They have pressed for public information centers to be set up in many countries and have called for Bank staff to provide briefings and "informal information" on matters that concern them.

NGOs have challenged the *accountability* of the Bank, utilizing the formal conduit, by making sure their countries' executive directors get information from grassroots CSOs, not just Bank management, about the impact of Bank activities; they have also created new mechanisms of direct citizen accountability. The latter includes public hearings giving affected citizens the chance to vent their views on specific activities (having the media present ensures a serious response) and global exercises, ideally with Bank involvement, to monitor Bank activities in selective fields, such as the Structural Adjustment Participatory Review Initiative or the World Commission on Big Dams.

NGOs have helped create a *rule of law* framework governing Bank activities through successfully pressing for more explicit policies delineating what the Bank can do, must do, and cannot do, together with an independent oversight mechanism that affected parties can appeal to if these policies are violated (the Inspection Panel). Some policies add further mechanisms of due process, for example, the environment assessment policy stipulates when there must be public hearings to which local civil society must be invited.

NGOs have made the Bank more aware of and more responsive to the *voice* of citizens who may be affected by its decisions. They have promoted participation in project design and civil society consultation in country-level strategic planning, policy formulation, and even (sometimes) Bank-government dialogue. Most recently, many NGOs have engaged with governments and the Bank in preparing poverty reduction strategy papers (PRSPs are government programs for attacking poverty, ostensibly designed in consultation with civil society and other stakeholders, that the Bank and IMF now require to be in place before approval of debt relief or adjustment loans).

This is an impressive array of reforms, and most are now recognized within the Bank as improvements, though they were often resisted at the outset. There are some valid concerns, however, that deserve mention. One is that having a rigid framework of rules curtails innovation and differentiation. Development contexts vary so greatly—and depend so much on the culture and political traditions of the country—that it is too limiting to have a single global rule book. Many policies are being endlessly rewritten to allow for such local interpretation. Another concern is that the strategies used to win some of these reforms—including building alliances with right-wing, anti-aid legislators—may have jeopardized the World Bank and multilateral aid as a whole.

Robert Wade has raised a more serious concern. In his view the US government and US NGOs have become the two most powerful forces in the Bank. The latter, he says, are particularly unaccountable and achieve influence by dramatizing failures in the Bank and other IGOs and by skewing information to gain a moral high ground and to maximize blame-casting. Sometimes these stakeholders pull in opposing directions (for example, over the World Bank's response to the East Asian economic crisis), but sometimes there is an unholy alliance that results in the Bank having to adopt standards (for example, concerning the environment or resettlement) that are higher than in many rich countries. This has led, in Wade's view, to a situation where the Bank has no option but to accept policies that are unworkable, for reasons of political expediency, and then to practice inconsistency and even deception by cutting corners in implementing them. Then the NGOs seek out all and any example of noncompliance to report to the Inspection Panel. He quotes his experience as a consultant to this panel to illustrate his case and strongly argues for curbing US influence in international organizations (Wade 2001b).

These are very real concerns and deserve serious reflection by NGOs and governments alike. However, in my view the impact of NGOs on the World Bank has been overwhelmingly positive. NGOs and others in civil society could cooperate to achieve similar reforms in the governance of other IGOs, though preferably treading more delicately through the moral maze. Clearly, the priority is on organizations relating to trade and liberalization (the WTO, IMF/World Bank, certain UN organizations, EU and US regional trade agreements). Some of the most important CSO campaign objectives might be:

- *Greater transparency:* CSOs and legislators could work together to form a panel advising and pressing for greater openness of IGOs (especially WTO); the maxim should be that information is public unless there is a compelling reason for confidentiality. Proceedings of all IGOs should be public to permit public scrutiny; significant processes (including disputes settlements hearings in WTO) should permit civil society observers. Any bilateral deal making (such as pressure from one government on another to vote in a particular way) should be reported to an ethics office within the IGO and made public.
- *Leveling the playing field:* Power will never be equal within the world's family of nations, but IGOs should serve to *reduce* inequality, not increase it, as they may do now due to skewed access. Twenty African country members of the WTO, for example, have *no* representative in Geneva (where the WTO is housed); others are represented by diplomats (not trade specialists) who also cover all other Geneva agencies. Rich countries, on the other hand, usually have at least five trade specialists permanently at the WTO (which typically has over forty formal meetings per week) and have armies of trade specialists back home, who fly in as needed on specific issues. Some specialist CSOs help to correct

the imbalance by providing technical assistance and information to Southern delegates. Although many argue that the voting distribution should be made fairer (while each country has one vote in UN agencies, votes are weighted by the size of the economy in the World Bank and IMF), this may not be the critical issue. Each country nominally has equal weight in the WTO, but in practice it is dominated by the major trading powers. Moreover, in the World Bank it is very rare for decisions to be taken by vote; generally a consensus is reached. Capacity is a bigger constraint than votes for developing countries. CSOs could also press rich countries to provide free legal aid and technical specialists to Southern delegations, especially to help them in the WTO's disputes-settlement mechanism. CSOs could also encourage developing countries to help themselves by pooling their efforts, so reducing their disadvantage. If all African countries were to pull together in the WTO, for example, they could muster a very powerful combined delegation.

- *Social and environmental auditing:* All IGOs should routinely conduct rigorous assessments of the likely impacts of proposed policies and programs—such as new measures of trade liberalization—before they are set in concrete. These audits should be conducted publicly, so that CSOs and others can contribute their views. CSOs could also be technical advisors and help design the methodology for these audits.
- *Opening dialogue:* In addition to ad hoc and country-level meetings with civil society, it would be useful to have regular international forums to enable senior IGO officials to dialogue with civil society leaders, academics, and other specialists. The experience of the International Labour Organization's new Commission on the Social Dimensions of Globalization might provide a useful model.
- *Enhancing member responsibility:* Rich countries, in particular, should reflect global citizenship, not parochialism, in their IGO negotiations. They could, for example, charge their aid ministries to work with CSOs in reviewing selected IGO programs (enabling, for example, a comparison among agencies) and could encourage legislators to scrutinize or hold panels of enquiry, with CSOs, on any controversial IGO activity.

Others have suggested a more radical range of IGO reforms, including a different voting system (such as the "binding triad"—decisions based on two-thirds of the countries, two-thirds of the population, and two-thirds of the agency's budget), or new global agencies (such as a

World Financial Authority to regulate financial markets, or a World Central Bank). These would undoubtedly be useful, but also undoubtedly won't happen in the foreseeable future. There is barely the appetite to sustain the range of international organizations we have today, and certainly no appetite within the G7 to create new institutions— and without the G7 they won't happen. It would be a better use of time and resources to urge winnable reforms in existing institutions rather than tilt at windmills.

CIVILIZING CORPORATIONS

One of the most exciting recent currents in civil society is the myriad efforts to inject environmental and social responsibility into transnational corporations. NGOs and think tanks first sat down with corporate chiefs to discuss the *values of business* and convinced them that they should be in the *business of values*. Corporate citizenship was born.

Since the Nestlé boycott that started in the 1970s (claiming Nestlé marketed baby milk irresponsibly in developing countries) and campaigns against Barclays Bank and other companies with links to apartheid South Africa, there have been numerous TNC-focused campaigns. These have attacked companies for the social impact of their products (for example, pesticides and baby milk), for their support of immoral regimes (such as those trading in Burma), for environmental damage (for example, tropical hardwood traders and mining firms), for their direct or indirect abuse of labor standards and human rights (such as sweatshop conditions in Nike's suppliers or Shell's involvement in Ogoniland), for their part in the debt crisis (the large banks), for forcing the spread of GM crops (Monsanto), and for bio-piracy (such as those seeking to patent genes for basmati and jasmine rice). There has also been consumer action on wasteful packaging (McDonalds), animal cruelty (furs and Huntington Life Science), and ozone-layer depletion (aerosols and refrigerants).

According to Noreena Hertz, "Increasingly the most effective way to be political is not to register one's demands and wants at the ballot box . . . but to do so at the supermarket. . . . All over the developed, democratic world, people are shopping rather than voting. . . . Consumer activism is beginning to enter the mainstream" (Hertz 2001). Such campaigns have hurt the companies, and though some have tended to ignore CSO criticism (notably Exxon/Mobile, the world's largest oil company), most have responded by trying to improve their company's image in various ways.

It is interesting to speculate *why* most TNC chiefs take public pressure so seriously. They are supposed to be concerned solely with making profits, and there is little evidence that these campaigns have any discernable influence on turnover or profit. Though noisy, the proportion of people actually "voting with their purse" is still quite small (Zadek 2001). Hence, the financial performance of a company is in reality largely unaffected by whether the company is gaining a better or worse reputation. But companies *act* as if there is a steep profit-reputation connection. Why do TNCs care so much about NGO campaigns, and why do they spend such vast sums on corporate public relations rather than product promotion, if the company's reputation is relatively unimportant?

Clearly, image *is* critical in the eyes of TNC chiefs. One major insurance company commissions a survey of corporate bosses each year to find out what they see as their principal risks. Usually issues such as fire, crime, and war top their list. In 2001, however, chief executives listed "reputational loss" as the main risk they face (*Financial Times*, July 27, 2001). The company accountant or stock market investor might not agree, but that is how top management sees it. Harris Interactive is a management consultancy that advises corporate clients on the various factors influencing their reputation and conducts public-opinion research to establish the image of leading companies among the US public (2002). It finds that "social responsibility" and "emotional appeal" are two of the six most important factors (others include "product quality" and "financial performance") and so strongly encourages companies to engage more in NGO and community partnerships.

There are three likely explanations for the image-consciousness of CEOs. The first is that they take a long-term perspective. Image loss today will be customer loss tomorrow. In a world where product differentiation is so small, customer loyalty is hard to come by—and once lost it will never be regained. A second explanation stems from the growth in ethical investment. In the United States over $1 trillion— one-eighth of all fund investment—is in managed portfolios that use at least one social investment strategy, a thirty-fold increase since 1984 (Hertz 2001). The membership of the US Interfaith Center on Corporate Responsibility includes 275 institutional investors with combined assets of over $110 billion. US foundations have combined assets of $486 billion (not all invested ethically). Ethical investors are now big business, and corporate CEOs are getting this message.

The third explanation—I think the strongest—concerns staff and management morale. People don't like to work for an organization accused of immoral behavior. It reduces their commitment, and perhaps performance, and leads to unproductive management time going to internal damage control and devising PR responses to public criticisms.

I remember meeting the general manager of Nestlé UK in the early 1980s about Oxfam's baby-milk campaign. I found him furious about another NGO's postcard campaign directed at top Nestlé managers throughout the world, accusing them of killing babies. He relayed how postcards started flooding in just before a key meeting of all top managers at Nestlé's Swiss headquarters. Everyone was so outraged, particularly the company president, that the whole meeting was a disaster. The managers were proud of their company and were fed up with constantly having to defend themselves, even to their own staff. Apparently they even contemplated discontinuing baby milk altogether, since it only accounted for a few percent of corporate turnover. The widespread boycott had not noticeably affected the company's finances, he said, but they were clearly worried about the image threat. The postcard campaign had hit a mark (but I couldn't fathom why Nestlé didn't more strenuously conform to the international code for marketing baby milk). The issue continues till today. Nestlé is still attacked for its marketing methods, but it has recently announced its intention to appoint an independent ombudsman to oversee the implementation of the marketing code.

In the absence of transnational legislation governing TNCs, and given the disincentives for governments to curb the overseas activities of their TNCs, most pressure for global business ethics comes from civil society. There are two broad strategies (Newell 2001). First, civil regulation in which CSOs use moral suasion to press for specific reforms and greater citizen accountability. This includes a wide range of tactics from boycotts to helping companies apply codes of conduct. The common feature is that reforms are *negotiated*. Second, transnational litigation in which CSOs use laws in the country of the TNC's headquarters to hold the parent responsible for activities of its subsidiaries. This often doesn't work (as in the failed attempt to use US courts to win compensation for the Bhopal victims) but can be applied when corruption, money laundering, or environmental damage is involved. For example, litigation has been successfully used in the United States against Texaco and Shell for environmental damage in Ecuador and Nigeria respectively.

Large companies are increasingly concerned to address or protect themselves from public criticism. The best approach, many think, is to adopt ethical standards that at least sound convincing and to reposition themselves as "corporate citizens." There has been a steep growth in TNC activity in everything from community work to global philanthropy and engagement with the United Nations, and CEOs are increasingly convinced this is good for business (J. Nelson 1996). Many TNCs are drafting and publishing codes of conduct or statements of ethics. Some now have social and environment departments, often hiring former NGO campaigners as advisors. Many subject their operations to social and environmental assessments, perhaps using one of a growing array of externally devised accreditation methodologies (such as SA8000, which assesses labor standards against UN agreements; or Global Reporting Initiative, which focuses on environmental issues). Most, however, seek no external verification of these audits (Zadek 2001).

Some TNCs have drawn up partnership arrangements with major NGOs, or commission NGOs to assess their operations and provide them feedback (see Chapter 6). Others seek to carry NGO-devised certification logos on their product labels (certifying the product as being environmentally sound, free from use of child labor, or containing wood only from sustainably managed forests). Similarly, many corporations are keen to join with NGOs and perhaps UN agencies in business-civic partnership or corporate-citizenship ventures. Sometimes unexpected partnerships arise. For example, the Environment Defense Fund in the United States (a fierce environmental campaigner) has helped McDonalds develop a replacement for the non-biodegradable polystyrene burger packaging it used to use (Newell 2000). And BP's CEO, acting for the World Business Council for Sustainable Development, recently made a joint press appeal (August 30, 2002) with a spokesman from his traditional enemy, Greenpeace. They called on governments assembling for the Johannesburg Earth Summit to take decisive and globally coordinated action on climate change, pointing out that TNCs want a level and predictable playing field. (Greenpeace pointed out that the last time it had shared a platform with BP was just before its members were arrested for chaining themselves to one of BP's North Sea oil platforms.)

The logic is clear. A UK survey showed that only about one third of people trust big corporations (somewhat more than trust government ministers), while over four-fifths trust major NGOs (Zadek 2001); an association can only do them good. Some CSOs, for this reason, are skeptical about such partnerships, arguing that they depoliticize the issues and obscure power inequalities (Newell 2002). Many go further and argue that TNCs are finding it convenient now to pitch themselves as global citizens but that in reality little has changed—and therefore CSOs risk endorsing a bogus trend.

The three questions relevant to corporate campaigners are how to make consumers more ethically aware (so ensuring that campaigns really do dent profits), how best to affect a particular TNC's reputation, and how to ensure that TNCs match up to the reforms they claim. Since corporate citizenship is becoming a more powerful concept, obviously "more of the same" is the easiest answer. The use of boycotts, "naming and shaming" in media campaigns, certification and monitoring exercises, expanding ethical investment portfolios, and taking shareholder actions (especially if backed by institutional investors such as large church agencies or even pension funds) all contribute to this. These tactics acclimatize the public to see ethics as just as much a consumer issue as value for money; they also affect the reputation (positively or negatively) of particular corporations.

There are three responses to a stubborn donkey: to offer a carrot, to threaten with a stick, or to take a bus. Similarly, there are three approaches to strengthen corporate campaigning. The first is to make the carrot more enticing; CSOs can devise ways to reward the more progressive TNCs. For example, the Council on Economic Priorities in New York issues an annual Corporate Conscience award (won once by Levi-Strauss), and Oxfam has written a public endorsement in Sainsbury's annual report. The second is to sharpen the stick, perhaps by engaging celebrities in media exposés of corporate malpractice (a sort of negative advertising approach) or by more systematic efforts to secure media coverage of companies who perform poorly. The third approach is to market alternative products that guarantee ethical social and environmental standards. Sales of Fair Trade Products in Europe have been rapidly growing and now account for about $250 million (Oxfam 2002). While originally the emphasis was on products imported by NGOs or nonprofit companies, now the favored approach is to find ethically sound producers and encourage mainstream supermarkets or wholesalers to import from these; the product is sold under a fair-trade logo, licensed by the NGO network, but without having to make up-front investment for importation. These goods are retailed at only slightly higher prices than commercial competitors yet typically provide the producer twice world market prices; a higher proportion of this price reaches the actual grower or worker. Ethical trading is even bigger business in the United States.

A way of combining all approaches would be for CSOs to join forces to devise a composite fair-trade index by which the various social and environmental pluses and minuses of different companies could be compared. Having many well-known CSOs backing it, and perhaps a bevy of celebrities, would ensure strong media coverage and the mounting interest of shareholders and institutional investors. It would influence corporate ethics by playing on companies' fear of reputational risk and thirst for positive publicity. It would also identify socially better products and could heighten customer interest in ethical criteria.

CONCLUSIONS

This chapter has described how CSOs can influence the processes of global change by reforming its main actors—governments, IGOs, and TNCs. No new magic potions are offered, because the needed wisdom is all to be found in the rich experience of the last decade. The best advice is that CSOs, and indeed the global change actors, should distill these lessons and apply them as widely as possible. Three messages recur. First, the same principles of good governance that Southern governments are urged to follow form the best reform framework for these international actors. Second, an important starting point is to convince these actors that they must assess the global social and environmental "footprints" of their decisions and take responsibility for them (accountability). And third, these messages will be hollow unless CSOs are actively engaged in applying them, using both carrot and stick. For this to be possible, the institutions should offer a global citizen compact, accepting the important part civil society plays in global governance and hence in their own institutional reforms (responsiveness).

The future *will* be frustrating. Institutions tend to resist change, and CSOs are impatient for fast action. But today's trajectory makes it clear that civil society is becoming more influential and is driving change in the leadership signals within large institutions, both public and private. Changing large institutions is like shifting an oil tanker; the captain can spin the wheel, but it takes some time before the new course is evident. But the path *will* change, and this is what is happening today with the main agents of globalization.

Unfortunately, the opportunities for greed and political self-interest are also expanding and are pulling in an opposite direction. Which forces hold greater sway? Will globalization ever truly serve the good of all? Will it be ethical?

11

Making Globalization Ethical—
by Making Ethics Global

In *Democratizing Development* (1991), I described North-South relations as like a game of Monopoly in which some players hold hotels on Mayfair while others have nothing but Old Kent Road. Debts pile up as bills simply can't be paid, but there is no ending the game. Sure, the poor players pick up £200 every time they pass "Go" (their annual aid handouts), but this is dwarfed by the bills.[1] Since then the odds have become even *worse*.

Terms of trade have deteriorated. In 2001, non-oil commodity prices, in real terms, were 15 percent lower than they were in 1990, and 46 percent lower than in 1980. True, there has been some debt relief for the poorest countries, but this just amounts to canceling some debt that was unpayable and charging the write-offs to aid budgets—which themselves have shrunk in real terms. The increasing mobility of capital now means foreigners increasingly own the South's productive assets and are keen to repatriate profits. Patent rights mean the South must pay more license fees yet is not paid for use of its traditional knowledge (for example, herbal medicines and indigenous crop strains).

The game of Monopoly is still going on, but the Mayfair players have taken over even more of the board and have hiked the price of landing on their squares. They even own much of the property on the South's squares, and someone rich has copyrighted the use of the name Old Kent Road. What's more, players now only get £150 for passing "Go."

However bleak the picture, dropping out of the game is even worse. Countries who withdraw from the world economy get poorer and their social indicators decline. The G7 governments, World Bank, and others stand accused by globalization's critics of urging countries to engage in a global capitalist system that is manifestly unfair, to the harm of the poor. The first part of the charge is fair, but the second isn't. Compare any two countries that have approached world markets differently—

North and South Korea, or India and Indonesia, for example—and it is evident that the poor have fared worse under regimes that have kept aloof from global trading. Look, too, at the reduction of poverty in countries that ended their hostility to markets (notably China and Vietnam). Of course, many other factors are involved in poverty reduction, but growth is essential. This will be elusive—especially for small countries—unless they build trade with others and allow enterprise to flourish.

CSOs are right to be concerned about globalization but would head up the wrong track if they seek to reverse it. What is needed is a broad and powerful civil society coalition pressing for globalization to be managed ethically—the subject of this final chapter. Rejecting globalization is neither realistic nor helpful to the poor, but equally seeking just to knock off its rough edges underplays the damage done by current inequities.

Integration's advocates may oversell the benefits but are guilty of two greater sins. First, they should be much more vocal in condemning the unjust nature of the system (they do speak out more than their critics credit, but not enough). Second, and more seriously, they should help find ways to increase the South's bargaining power, not just provide aid to dull the pain of today's injustices.

There is an analogy in the response of liberals to eighteenth-century slavery. Some, no doubt, flinched at the beatings slaves got if they were too ill to follow orders and raised charity to provide health care. Others would counter that such programs were part of the problem—perpetuating slavery by helping it to function. Unless liberals used every chance to condemn slavery itself, and helped slaves unite and fight against it, this charge would stick, however hard they argued that the slaves would be worse off without their help. So too in today's debate; while donors shouldn't lessen efforts to help those who are ill served by today's order, they will be charged with complicity if they don't use their experience to press governments to provide a different and fairer order tomorrow.

WHAT WOULD MAKE GLOBALIZATION ETHICAL?

Part One described globalization as a powerful force that expands aggregate opportunity but that, as currently managed, offers disproportionately more to the better off. *Ethical* globalization is about having the good without the bad—about reducing inequalities of power, income, and asset distribution so as to prioritize benefits to poor people from those opportunities. There are two aspects to this: first, process, that is, reforming the institutions that drive globalization (the governance challenges of Chapter 10); and second, substance, that is, changing the policies and programs that connect these institutions with global change. We devote these final pages to this topic.

Much has been written in recent years about rights-based development (for example, DFID 2000b; Gaventa et al. 2002; UNDP 1999). The case for this goes back to the early days of the United Nations and its Universal Declaration of Human Rights, agreed to in 1948, which enshrined economic and social rights as well as civil and political rights. These were amplified in 1966 by the Covenant on Economic and Social Rights and in 1986 by the Declaration on the Right to Development. The latter is a commitment to a development process that "aims at the constant improvement of the well-being of the entire population and of all individuals on the basis of their active, free and meaningful participation in development and in the fair distribution of benefits resulting therefrom." This includes rights to employment, basic social services, life and security, social and political citizenship, and to an identity.

While these are uplifting concepts and provide an excellent development philosophy, I wonder how useful they are as operational tools, particularly for CSOs, which are fundamentally about forging practical change. To what different destination do they take us? With civil and political rights, responsibility lies clearly with the government for protecting (or denying) rights of free speech, worship, assembly, and so on. If these rights are violated, the government is to blame and can make amends through its own actions. When people in remote areas (twelve hours on foot from the nearest road, say) don't have access to basic services, or when people lose their jobs during a national economic crisis, who has violated their rights? These rights are aspirational and relative, not the absolutes circumscribed by civil and political rights. International law, and the human rights lobby that is bent on holding governments to it, have been of practical help to prisoners of conscience throughout the world, but economic and social rights can't be used in the same way.

The aspect of the rights discourse I find most operationally powerful is the right to *inclusion*. It demands identifying and dismantling barriers of discrimination and privilege to ensure that opportunities reach those currently left out of development. Four practical strategies that CSOs (and others) can pursue constitute an inclusion framework:

- *Participation:* ensuring that people have influence over decisions affecting their lives. This concerns ways in which poor people exercise their voice through new forms of deliberation and mobilization so as to influence large institutions and their policies (Gaventa et al. 2002). Participation is about active, as opposed to passive, citizenship—"making and shaping," not just "using and choosing." Institutions rarely offer structures allowing such democratizing of influence, hence the importance of CSOs working at the local level as mobilizers and conduits for this voice.

- *Empowerment:* helping people see their own potential as active agents in development. Even if the state *affords* people rights of active citizenship, most of the poor don't take advantage because they see themselves as powerless or fear reprisals. Empowerment comes through rights-awareness work and linking people in similar situations (including those in different countries). This also is usually enabled by CSOs and is most advanced in countries where there is a strong civil society sector.

- *Equity:* ensuring that laws, services, and opportunities are afforded without favoritism and that the benefits of development are broadly shared. Laws may require this but inequalities remain, perhaps because the elites are skilled at annexing the benefits or because staff in the delivery agencies don't care about the poor. Independent watchdogs and campaigning organizations are usually needed to wrestle against such in-built prejudices.

- *Security:* ensuring that the most vulnerable people get the most protection. Every society experiences shocks, and the weak are least able to sustain them. At times of crisis, governments take protective steps, but these often attend to the big actors in the national economy, leaving the weak to fend for themselves. CSOs often have good records for providing safety nets in such situations and for advocating to governments macro-strategies that pose fewer risks. Their efforts help to ensure that the poor are included in bad years as well as good.

This framework of inclusion is good for a locality or a country. But it is also applicable at the global level, with equivalent CSO roles. All policy shifts and opportunities of globalization can be ethically tested according to how much they permit or deny the participation of poor countries and citizens in the decisions and governance of global change; how much they empower the excluded to enter these processes; whether new opportunities from global changes are equitable; and whether concomitant risks are more acute for vulnerable countries and people. These constitute an agenda for global social and economic justice. We talked about reforms within the main agencies of globalization to bolster participation in Chapter 10. In this chapter it remains, then, only to describe the other elements and how reforms in these areas could improve the management of globalization. We start with equity.

EQUITY AND GLOBALIZATION

Making globalization ethical depends on making ethics global. However, in today's fragmented world governments simply look after "their square" on the Monopoly board, assuming their citizens want them to maximize national self-interest. Governments will continue to make globalization selfish unless these signals are challenged, and civil society pressure is the best avenue for this. CSOs working in global networks are best equipped to reveal current injustices and demonstrate why these aren't compatible with a world free of suffering, hatred, violence, and even terrorism. They can lead public pressure for a level global playing field for global, not just domestic, economic justice.

Some political leaders are already personally committed to such principles. British Chancellor Gordon Brown gave a powerful speech in New York in 2001 in which he appealed for global fairness:

> The issue is whether we manage globalization well or badly, fairly or unfairly. And we have a choice. Globalization can be for the people or against the people. . . . [It] can bring stability or instability, prosperity or stagnation, the inclusion of people or their exclusion. . . . Managed badly, globalization would leave whole economies and millions of people in the developing world marginalized. Managed wisely, globalization can and will lift millions out of poverty, and become the high road to a just and inclusive global economy (Brown 2001).

But when a Northern government is faced by tradeoffs between the substantial interests of a few nationals and massive interests of the South—or when other countries become free-riders, wriggling out of making sacrifices themselves—altruism all too often goes out the window. Northern farm policy is a case in point and would make an excellent subject for a broad-based and internationally coordinated campaign (see Box 11.1). I make no apology for returning to this issue and singling it out, because I believe it will emerge as the defining issue in coming years, regarding whether there is any appetite among rich countries to allow globalization to be managed more ethically.

The eradication of third-world poverty demands two things: equity of economic and political power within nations (as discussed in Chapters 3 and 4) and, even more crucially, equity among nations. The former can be influenced by Northern CSOs through their impact on aid policies and international institutions but is largely the province of domestic politics (including, of course, Southern civil society). The goal of

---

Box 11.1 Liberty and livelihood for Southern farmers

In our bizarre world farming is of pivotal importance to poor people in poor countries and marginal to Northern economies, yet Southern governments mostly neglect farming while Northern governments subsidize it to the hilt. Northern policies favor the production of nutritionally dubious food (sugar, butter, beef, and so on), encourage heavy use of farm chemicals that leech into water systems, promote a style of farming that is bad for bio-diversity and the environment, and result in surpluses that no one wants.

But these policies are far more damaging to developing countries in two ways. The impenetrable barriers erected prevent Southern farmers from exporting goods that compete with crops grown in the North, so denying them their most obvious comparative advantages (warm climate, plentiful land, and rich bio-diversity). And second, Northern surpluses are dumped onto world markets at a fraction of their production costs—thanks to *further* subsidies—again blighting opportunities for Southern farmers. The European Union is the worst offender, but the United States, Japan, and Canada are similar, and now the United States, through its farm bill, is set to increase these obstacles. Together, these distortions probably cost the South more than it receives in aid (see Appendix 2). Adding insult to injury, Northern trade negotiators, through the WTO, are pressing developing countries to dismantle *their* barriers (designed to protect their farmers from Northern dumping).

Just as CSOs mobilized public opinion to tackle the debt burden, could it do the same here? A campaign to end production and dumping subsidies and to open markets for Southern farmers would be good for both North and South and so should attract a broad coalition: development and social justice groups, environmental groups, consumer groups, scientists and NGOs concerned about nutrition, most trade unions and business groups, outdoors pursuit groups who seek improvements in the countryside, and the churches, who would welcome better stewardship of nature's bounty. Could the main development NGOs take the lead in such a campaign? After all, they are best placed to see the damage present policies inflict, working closely as they do with poor farming communities; they also have the resources needed for mobilizing public opinion.

---

global equity is generally undermined by conventional democratic politics, since, as we've discussed, they reemphasize national interests, but this goal can be advanced by civil society acting internationally to promote economic justice. There are numerous examples of CSO campaigns that demonstrate this effectiveness—campaigns for debt relief, for increasing aid and making it more poverty focused, for providing affordable drugs to tackle HIV/AIDS and tropical diseases, for reforming the World Bank and IMF, and so on. G7 statesmen will now touch on poverty and fairer opportunities in their major speeches, and this is a testament to tireless campaigning that has put the issues on their radar screen. The challenge ahead is to ensure that the statesmen have these issues in mind as they craft their *policies*, not just their speeches.

EMPOWERMENT THROUGH UNITY

Though there are undoubted benefits, the integrating world poses growing threats to poorer countries because of its imbalance. In practice, globalization entails poor countries accepting that trade means relying on Northern markets; that finance means relying on Northern banks and other institutions; that exchange means relying on Northern currencies; and that the rules of trade, economics, and politics are forged by Northern governments. Until civil society and reformers can foster a more ethical tomorrow, today's reality is the biased Monopoly game. Pressure to change the rules is important, but so too are strategies that help insulate poorer countries from this bias and give them greater bargaining power. This calls for reforming the institutions of global governance (discussed in Chapter 10), but also for developing countries strengthening their own power base through unity. How to do this is easy to see but admittedly hard to achieve.

If developing countries increased trade links with one another, they would reduce dependence on the North. They have 78 percent of world population yet just 25 percent of trade, and only one-quarter of their exports go to other developing countries—the rest goes to the North. They sell more to the United States alone than to one another. Three-fifths of EU trade, in contrast, is within the union. If the South could match this while retaining current trade with the North, it would multiply total exports by 2.5. This would ease pressures to compete with one another for those Northern markets, so driving down prices. NGOs who provide microcredit, advice, and other help to entrepreneurs could help seek out opportunities and encourage South-South trade; they could also help strengthen regional networks of entrepreneurs (such as the African Enterprise Network).

At present, only very large countries such as China and India have such sizeable domestic markets that they aren't highly dependent on foreign trade. This gives them much greater room to maneuver. China, for example, sets its exchange rate to favor its choice exports while protecting its home industry from imports. All developing countries could move in this direction by pulling together in regional trade agreements and interregional trade preferences. They may individually be small nations, but, combined, they could offer one another a big market. The following steps, encouraged by campaigns in the South as well as pressure on donors for support, would help achieve this.

The first step is to reverse the perverse bias against South-South trade. Barriers are *lower* for trade with the North because this has been a price for "privileged access" to Northern markets. The difficulty in reversing this is very real. Poor countries have scant revenues (there are few high-earning citizens who can be taxed, indirect taxes can be difficult to enforce, and state enterprises usually lose money); hence, they like import duties. Think tanks, trade unions, and others could demonstrate that, though painful, barriers on South–South trade should be lowered, barter trade should be expanded (avoiding the need for hard currency), and non-tariff barriers should be replaced by tariffs.

A more decisive step would be for developing countries to explore currency unions. Perversely, there is a growing tendency to peg currencies to the dollar or euro, which can heighten their vulnerability to financial crises (as Argentina found to its cost). Pegs to, say, *China's* currency might make greater sense. At eight Yuan to the US dollar, the Yuan is undervalued compared with a free-market level. China has gained plaudits internationally by reducing trade barriers, but its strong export performance probably owes more to its interventionist exchange rate management, to the chagrin of competitors. This provides a lesson for the South: Through such an approach Southern countries could both expand exports to the North and trade more with one another.

There are many practical avenues for cooperation. Purchasing syndicates could enable countries to negotiate better prices for imports (as happens to some extent with basic drugs); collaboration would yield economies of scale in industrialization and processing commodities; and combined knowledge systems could provide farmers better information on crop yields, long-range weather, pests, and price forecasts. Cooperation could also promote diversification (and thus less scrambling for the same few export markets) and improved technology for storing and processing commodities (easing pressures to sell immediately after harvest, when prices are lowest). Regional CSO networks can help identify such innovations and advocate harmonized policies that would be enabling for them, and they could network with Northern partners to gain international support.

Increased regional economic cooperation should be seen as a long-haul strategy, not a quick fix; hence, another vital step is investment in infrastructure. A map of Africa, in particular, reveals that road, rail, and port building was designed to serve international trade rather than trade with neighbors. Countries that are landlocked and the hinterland of large countries are left behind in a world that disproportionately emphasizes trade with rich countries. The nearest port to the Ugandan capital of Kampala is Mombassa in Kenya. The Unilever manager there told me that it costs $40 per ton to transport palm oil from the Far East to Mombassa, but $120 per ton (and twenty-one days) to get it from Mombassa to Kampala (three times what it would cost to get it to any Western European location). Most of this is due to customs and other bureaucracy, which opens doors to corruption. Further south, however, the creation of the Maputo Corridor linking Mozambique with South Africa has greatly benefited both countries. Such regional cooperation is the best prospect for Africa. The GNP of the entire region and its 642 million people is less than that of Netherlands (population sixteen million). Excluding South Africa, it has fewer miles of paved road than Poland, and one phone per 125 people. Most Africans live more than two hours from the nearest phone, and the waiting time for a new line is three and one-half years—the longest in the world (World Bank et al. 2000).

None of this is classic Washington Consensus advice, but has the latter worked? The experience of the fast-growing "tiger economies" and countries like China, Vietnam, and Mauritius shows that—contrary to neoliberal wisdom—they did not do well simply by liberalizing their markets. They started with a period of careful import substitution in which nascent industries were incubated, nurtured on domestic markets, and only when sufficiently mature weaned off protection and sent out to play in global markets. The word *careful* is pivotal. For each country where this strategy worked, six have squandered vast amounts of taxpayers' money supporting inefficient, corrupt, and old-fashioned industries. And the tigers did much more than manage industrialization; they also invested heavily in education, land reform, and other strategies promoting equity.

However, many of the tax, trade, investment, and other policies used to such good effect by the tigers in the past would be denied by WTO rules today. Governments are told instead to rely on the magic of markets by liberalizing and getting out of the way of businesses. This isn't the experience of countries that have prospered most. They fostered domestic markets and enterprise but intervened strongly in industrialization, liberalizing some markets—such as farming—while protecting others. Generally, they dismantled trade barriers as they got richer, not the other way around (Rodrik 2001d).

Policy-oriented NGOs, the global union movement, left-leaning economists, and other CSO networks have presented a convincing challenge to the Washington Consensus, whose advice to the South seems to assume that trade is the objective of development rather than the other way around. What is now important—a challenge for the global economic justice movement—is to present a pragmatic platform for harnessing trade for the purpose of poverty-eradicating development. This platform would have to give convincing answers to three questions:

- How can global markets be made "poor friendly"?
- How can poor countries cultivate economic links that help them grow out of poverty?
- How can the full productive capacity of poor people be unleashed?

SECURITY FOR THE POOR

Since the tulip crisis of the seventeenth century, the world has seen periodic financial crashes. They arise because investment opportunities appear better than they really are. All is well until a few investors lose confidence, a selling spree leads overnight to a stampede for the door, the bubble is burst, and the enterprise is ruined. What was eminently credit-worthy one day becomes a *dis*credit the next; remember, the word *credit* stems from the Latin *credo*—meaning "I believe." The world—being more interconnected—is more prone to such crises than ever before. From 1980 to 2000 there were ninety banking crises, each of whose impact, as a proportion of GDP, exceeded the costs of the banking crash during the Great Depression in the United States (*The Economist*, January 30, 1999).

These crises may hurt investors, but they also translate swiftly into social crises (as described for East Asia in Chapter 2). The international system—led by the US Treasury and IMF—seeks to "soften the impact" of such crises but focuses overwhelmingly on the least vulnerable constituency—Wall Street investors—and gives marginal attention to the social crisis. Its first goal is to stem the disease's spread to other economies, especially the vast financial systems of the North. This is an important aim, since a global meltdown would impoverish billions, but the treatment applied not only ignores the suffering of the most vulnerable, it can actually compound it (Stiglitz 2002).

The rescue packages bail out the foreign creditors (thereby creating a perverse moral hazard, says George Soros [1998]) but require austerity measures to be adopted that compound the social impact. Devaluing currencies, hiking interest rates, cutting public spending, and allowing orderly bankruptcies of companies in trouble maximize the ability of the economy as a whole to meet its (newly expanded) external obligations, but at the expense of real wages, services, retail price inflation, job loss, and other burdens that ordinary people, particularly the working and middle classes, have to bear.

In recent crises in East Asia, Latin America, and elsewhere, civil society has presented the most effective critique of such strategies. CSOs have used community-level research to demonstrate what the crisis and response measures have meant to the poor, have mobilized demonstrations against policies that seem to favor foreign investors over nationals and to abandon national sovereignty, and have presented credible alternative economic scenarios.

A new global system is clearly needed, one that has broader international buy-in and seeks to minimize the social, not just the financial, risks. What is impressive is the degree to which transnational civil society networks are working to describe what the defining elements of the new system should be. First, it must include measures for prevention as well as cure, including monitoring systems to identify early signs of impending crises. Second, there should be much greater transparency so that all investors (and citizens organizations) can make more objective assessments of risks and opportunities. Third, there should be the equivalent of a bankruptcy procedure for governments, as promoted by NGOs such as Jubilee Research (Pettifor 2002) but now supported by some governments and the IMF chief economist (*Financial Times,* April 2, 2002). Fourth, it must include new controls to curb speculative practices that magnify risks (a powerful CSO campaign on this, which has also garnered support from some governments, is described in Box 11.2). Fifth, future rescue packages should be designed to ensure creditors bear much of the burden—in other words the emphasis should be on bailing them *in*, not out. And sixth, at the onset of crisis effective and well-resourced social programs must be swiftly put in place to minimize costs borne by vulnerable groups.

The world will never be free of financial crises, and in our interconnected and computer-linked age there will always be risks of such crises spreading—so crisis-response is a necessary evil. But rescue packages need to help wounded people as well as wounded economies. In a crisis the richest are usually largely protected because they have hard currency bank accounts and investments overseas. Often the very poorest operate largely outside the money economy and so are also less affected. Those most hit tend to be the fairly poor and middle-income groups. The international community needs to be assiduous in identifying which groups might be most hit; how various policy responses will affect them; what measures would best protect the vulnerable groups; and how feasible such measures are. Emergency programs must be implemented swiftly, but this shouldn't be an excuse for not being open with information or not permitting open debate about options.

Civil society can play crucial roles with all these processes—conveying the realities of how people are suffering and coping, ensuring that

---

Box 11.2 Civil society campaign to stem currency speculation

The East Asia crisis demonstrated how savage the impact of currency volatility and speculation can be on Southern economies and poor people. Joe Stiglitz argues that capital account liberalization was the biggest factor behind this crisis (Stiglitz 2002).

Many CSOs, of which the French-based ATTAC is most prominent, advocate a Tobin tax as a good mechanism to reduce such risks by dampening capital mobility. Such a tax could also raise large resources for aid and tackling global needs (see ATTAC's website). Named after James Tobin—the Nobel Prize–winning economist who first proposed it in 1971—it comprises a very small tax (perhaps half a percent) levied on all currency exchange. This would barely affect those changing money to import goods, who might turn over their capital two or three times per year; those who hedge against real trading risks may move their options once a month, leading to a cumulative 6 percent per year tax on capital, not unduly hiking the price of this insurance; but it would be punitive for speculators who move their capital daily, if not hourly. They would face annual tax bills many times their working capital, which would greatly curb their enthusiasm.

Though implementing this tax would be a real headache, the difficulties are not insurmountable (Spahn 2002), and European finance ministers increasingly recognize that it at least deserves closer scrutiny. This would not have been possible without CSO pressure (though Tobin himself, writing shortly before his death, was uneasy about this campaign [2001]). Even if we never see a Tobin tax, the debate might galvanize support for other schemes to dampen destructive capital mobility, such as that pioneered by Chile in which a portion of all foreign borrowing must be lodged in non-interest-bearing accounts with the central bank for one year.

---

people are fully informed about their entitlements, helping the voice of the weak to be heard in the national debate, working with governments to ensure that safety nets are effective, and developing information systems to monitor the social impact of the crisis. Mahatma Gandhi once said that "a civilization can be judged by the way it treats its minorities." So too, the measure of civilized globalization would be the protection it affords to vulnerable people and countries.

SOME CONCLUDING THOUGHTS

I have tried in this final chapter to steer a balance between presenting a catalogue of policy shifts that collectively offer a comprehensive agenda for an ethical globalization, but which would be a somewhat long and tedious list, and giving a few reflections on the broad general principles underpinning such a philosophy. Whether I have achieved this balance, I don't know. You, the reader, are the best judge. What I am sure of is that there isn't a single suggestion in this book that couldn't be realized, not a single problem described that couldn't be solved if the collective will in North and South could be mobilized for the tasks. It is abundantly clear that, left to themselves, governments won't generate this political will; their horizons are too parochial and too short term. Since we don't yet have anything remotely approaching global government or global democracy, and are not likely to in the foreseeable future, civil society offers the only avenue for fostering political concern on these global issues.

In their voting, citizens, at least in rich countries, have become more politically apathetic; however, there is a small minority thirsting to shape policies and build a fairer future, more engaged than ever before in citizen action. Collectively, this is a formidable force. What was remarkable about the 1998 Summit in Birmingham, and what made the lead story in TV news broadcasts and newspapers around the world, was that sixty thousand people bothered to turn up and form a human chain around the conference center—not that fifty-nine million British people stayed at home. The actions of a committed band, if well placed, can achieve vastly more than the occasional votes of the apathetic majority.

The tasks are truly daunting. We live in an age of runaway greed, of political myopia, of dangerous political and cultural schisms that rend the world—and the wealth gap between rich and poor is growing frighteningly. Lone voices that call for economics as if people matter, that call for trade to be fair, that call for *ethical* globalization may sound quite feeble against the roar of stock-market frenzy, corporate takeovers, and chief executive pay hikes. But they are no longer lone voices. People in the millions are joining pressure groups, refocusing unions, taking part in protests, writing to their government representatives, and in a thousand ways joining their voice to the voices of countless others. Each voice is like a raindrop falling on a mountain; some soak into the ground, but others join together to form a trickle; the trickle meets a rivulet—a local society; the rivulets join together to form a stream—an NGO; the streams join together to form a torrent—a social change movement; and the torrent gradually molds the contours of the mountain.

We are seeing the effects today. In some European countries, and even—in some circumstances—the United States, governments are voicing stronger commitment to tackle global economic injustice. They are doing this because they hear their citizens telling them to change their priorities. Many of the signals from civil society are misguided or even mischievous. But collectively there is a mounting crescendo for social justice—and people are increasingly adding their voices to it. The hope for the future, the prospect for managing globalization so that it is truly ethical, is that people are discovering the truth in the wise saying of Edmund Burke, the eighteenth-century British political philosopher: "No man made a greater mistake than he who did nothing because he could only do a little."

Appendix 1

The Theory
of Comparative Advantage

Some countries are efficient producers of one set of goods, while other countries are better in other fields. It makes good sense to specialize in what one is best at, and the shrewdest investors back this specialization. What is remarkable about the theory is that *every country* becomes better off by specializing in its advantage and trading with others to balance its needs, even if producers elsewhere can beat it in the same field. This is why it is called *comparative* advantage. Another country may be able to produce every single product more efficiently, but that competitive edge will be greater for some products than others. The comparative advantage for the first country is for the product where that edge is least. To appreciate how this works it is best to go through a "thought experiment."

Assume a world comprising just two countries, A and B, in which just two products are produced and consumed, X and Y. Each country has one hundred workers. Because of raw material availability, wage rates, degrees of mechanization, and other factors, the cost of producing these products and the number that workers can produce each day will be different for A and B, as shown in Table A.1.

Country A can produce both products more quickly and cheaply, but the competitive edge is greater for product X than Y. Country B's

Table A.1 Comparative advantage—starting point

	No. of X produced per day per worker	No. of Y produced per day per worker	Unit cost of X	Unit cost of Y
Country A	10	8	$10	$15
Country B	7	7	$16	$16

comparative advantage, therefore, is in producing Y. Now let's look at two scenarios. In the first, non-trade scenario, the work force is equally divided between the two products in both countries; let's assume this reflects the domestic demand for those products (Table A.2).

Table A.2 Scenario 1—self-sufficiency

	No. of workers producing X	No. of workers producing Y	Output of X	Output of Y	Cost of X	Cost of Y	Cost of X plus Y
Country A	50	50	500	400	$5,000	$6,000	$11,000
Country B	50	50	350	350	$5,600	$5,600	$11,200
Total	100	100	850	750	$10,600	$11,600	$22,200

In the second scenario (Table A.3) there is specialization; more workers in A are deployed in producing its comparative advantage (X) and more in B are deployed producing Y. The net effect is that more is produced of both X and Y, and yet the total cost of production is less. This looks like a win-win situation, except Country A isn't meeting the need for Y, and Country B needs more X. The solution is trade.

Table A.3 Scenario 2—specialization

	No. of workers producing X	No. of workers producing Y	Output of X	Output of Y	Cost of X	Cost of Y	Cost of X plus Y
Country A	70	30	700	240	$7,000	$3,600	$10,600
Country B	25	75	175	525	$2,800	$8,400	$11,200
Total	95	105	875	765	$9,800	$12,000	$21,800

In the second scenario each country has a surplus of its specialty; it can trade this with its neighbor to meet its deficits *and* make a profit. Country A can sell X to Country B at a high markup (say 50 percent), which is still below Country B's cost of production; while Country B can still make a profit exporting Y (albeit more modest, say 10 percent), because Country A *needs* to buy it. Hence:

- Country A exports 175 of product X to B at $15 each or a total of $2,625.
- Country B exports 160 of product Y to A at $17.60 each or a total of $2,816.

Let's now look at the end result (Table A.4). How many of X and Y do the two countries end up with (numbers produced minus exports plus imports)? And how much have these products cost (production costs less export earnings plus import bills)?

Table A.4 Scenario 2—specialization plus trade

	No. of X	No. of Y	Cost of X	Cost of Y	Cost of X + Y
Country A	525	400	$4,375	$6,416	$10,791
Country B	350	365	$5,425	$5,584	$11,009

What is remarkable is that compared with Scenario 1, *both* countries have ended up meeting their needs, gaining a surplus of their comparative-advantage product, and saving money as well. Country B (the least efficient producer) has also gained a trade surplus, which it could use to import other goods from other countries (if there were any).

The real world, of course, has close to two hundred trading countries and thousands of products, but the principle works exactly the same. All countries benefit from efficiency gains when they specialize in their comparative advantages. Trade, of course, brings transport costs (which costs the environment too), but for sea freight these are very small compared with the efficiency gains from comparative advantage. And trade is usually environmentally benign or even beneficial. One of the main sources of comparative advantage is the ability to make products in more energy-efficient ways or using cheaper, less environmentally harmful energy.

This explains why governments throughout the world are keen to safeguard their country's share of trade. Even if they have few natural assets, few investors, and few skilled workers, they will have *some* comparative advantages that they can exploit to their advantage—and the whole world benefits. Well, in theory it does.

Appendix 2

The World Trade Organization

In the aftermath of World War II, governments created various international bodies to safeguard security and to promote peace and development, including the UN system, the IMF, and the World Bank. One never got launched—the International Trade Organization. The North was loath to lose control over what it could do and what industries it could protect; it preferred bilateral trade deals. There was, instead, just a broad agreement to promote trade and reduce barriers (the General Agreement on Tariffs and Trade—GATT), formed in 1948 and overseen by a modest secretariat. Over the following decades there were various rounds of GATT negotiations leading to a series of agreements covering non-tariff trade barriers, patent regimes, health-related standards, investment-related issues, agriculture, and other issues. A disputes resolution process was also agreed upon, but it rested on voluntary participation and arbitration of compensation if any fault was demonstrated. A consensus in favor of freeing up trade began to emerge.

In April 1994 trade ministers meeting in GATT's final Uruguay Round trade talks agreed to establish the World Trade Organization to bring together the various trade agreements and give them teeth through a legally binding disputes settlement process and a stronger secretariat. The WTO was formally born on January 1, 1995. As of January 2002 it had 144 member countries with 26 more negotiating admission. Its secretariat is modest compared with organizations like the World Bank (whose ten thousand plus professional staff handles tens of billions of dollars per year). The WTO has just 550 staff and an $85 million budget (about a quarter the staff and half the budget of Oxfam GB).

The individual agreements, the dispute resolution process, and the negotiations themselves are highly complex. Some of the most important, from a Southern perspective, are described below. Powerful players, in particular the United States and the European Union, not only have armies of trade lawyers, economists, and other specialists who dominate WTO meetings but also the political muscle to kill any proposal they don't like outright, and they can use the political, military, aid, and cultural holds they have over poor countries.

Many of the WTO rules and processes are better designed for wealthy nations than poor ones. A World Bank research paper estimates that it costs a typical developing country $150 million to implement just three WTO agreements (concerning customs valuations, sanitary and phytosanitary standards, and intellectual property rights), which is equivalent to more than a year's development budget for many least developed countries (Finger and Schuler 1999). Similarly, WTO approaches concerning anti-dumping, subsidies, agriculture, textiles, investment, intellectual property, and other measures serve to protect powerful groups more than to promote development.

The WTO also addresses non-tariff barriers (NTBs) that distort trade, such as quotas, licenses, import bans, and pressure to exercise "voluntary export restraint." Though NTBs have also generally come down (in both North and South), it is difficult to judge how much they still affect trade. And governments use subsidies to protect domestic industries. Subsidies that are commonplace in the North (such as those for research or regional development grants) tend to be permitted by WTO, but those more common in the South (such as direct export assistance) are prohibited.

Agriculture

With primarily rural economies, cheap labor, and plenty of sunshine, many developing countries have a clear, natural advantage in agriculture. However, protectionist policies in the North have greatly eroded this advantage. Average tariffs on agricultural products remains about 40 percent (*The Economist*, July 28, 2001), and in addition there are production subsidies, export subsidies, quota restrictions, and an array of other protectionist measures against Southern agricultural exports. These subsidies cost Northern governments $360 billion a year ($130 billion in the European Union—the worst offender) or about $1,750 a year for an average family of four in the European Union, the United States, Japan, and Canada. In the European Union subsidies account for 40 percent of farm income (63 percent in Japan).

Ending subsidies would save taxpayers but also, according to a conservative World Bank estimate, offer third-world farmers an immediate extra $20 billion a year of business that would lift over three hundred million people above the poverty line (others estimate the much higher figure of $250 billion a year—*International Herald Tribune*, March 25, 2002). Developing countries' share of world agriculture trade has fallen from 37 percent in 1970 to 30 percent in 1996 (World Bank 2001).

Against this background the WTO's *Agreement on Agriculture* appears to favor developing countries. It requires rich countries to open up markets more rapidly than the South (reducing tariffs on agricultural imports 36 percent by 2005, compared with 24 percent for developing countries). However, high tariffs and quota restrictions aren't the main problems; agricultural subsidies are. Production subsidies, price supports, and export subsidies combined amount to about $20,000 per farmer in the European Union, the United States, and Japan (*The Economist*, November 27, 1999).

At the Uruguay Round, rich countries agreed to reduce subsidies, but so far there has been little progress. During the 2001 WTO ministerial meeting, developing countries pressed for a clearer commitment and timetable, but the European Union refused. This almost scuppered prospects for a new trade round. Eventually the European Union agreed to a statement that included the term "phasing out," but in a way that lost its impact. The parties agreed to "comprehensive negotiations aimed at: substantial improvements in market access; reductions of, with a view to phasing out, all forms of export subsidies" (WTO 2001). Even if direct subsidies were truly phased out, other types of rural support subsidies might simply replace them. This is already happening in the United States, and the trend is set to accelerate with the passage in 2002 of the farm bill.

Textiles and clothing

Rich countries have a distinct advantage in most fields of manufacturing. Capital is plentiful for plant and machinery; they have abundant skilled workers for supervising the technology; and they have good infrastructure. Poor countries, however, mostly have an advantage in textiles, garments, and footwear, since they are highly labor intensive, the equipment is relatively low-tech, and they place modest demands on infrastructure. However, rich countries have their own textile and clothing industries. And both workers and industrialists want to cling on and so demand protection from their governments. In the United States, for example, textiles and garments constitute the third-largest manufacturing sector (after motor vehicles and aerospace).

In the 1960s Southern exports of textiles and clothing to OECD countries rose steeply and industrialists' protectionist pressure resulted in a series of four multi-fiber arrangements (MFAs)—essentially frameworks for a series of bilaterally negotiated quota restrictions. It remains the only manufacturing sector still governed by global trade quotas, and the consequence is very serious for poor countries (Hamilton 1990). Bangladesh, for example, expanded textiles from a very small base in the late 1970s to an export giant employing 140,000 workers in 1985. Then France, the UK, and the United States imposed MFA quota restrictions; in the case of the United States these were minutely detailed, specifying not only the number of shirts that could be exported, but the sizes and types of fabric. As a result, thousands of workers, mostly women, were laid off (World Bank 1995).

There is now pressure to end the MFA, and OECD countries have agreed to a ten-year phase-out, up till 2005. But of the 1,264 original restrictions, by June 2000—more than halfway through this period—a paltry forty-six had been removed, and some had even been *tightened*. The United States, for example, is extending quotas to new countries. In spite of the barriers, Southern exports are increasing. Companies like Gap and Nike increasingly outsource production to independent factories in China, India, Vietnam, and elsewhere.

Global demand has increased significantly (mostly in the North) and has been met through automation in high-wage countries and new production in low-wage countries. The net effect in global employment has been remarkable constancy in textiles (16.4 million in 1980, 16.8 million in 1995, and 16.4 million in 1998), and a rising employment in clothing (8.7 million in 1995, 11.2 million in 1998). Geographically, *all* the increase has been in Asia (mostly China), and all other regions have faced a decline. Asia now represents 72 percent of the textile employment and two-thirds of clothing employment (ILO 2000).

US or European textile workers understandably think that globalization has eroded their jobs due to the differential in wages (averaging $7.60 an hour in the United States, compared with $0.45 an hour in the main Asian producers). Actually, their jobs have been threatened more by automation. In the United States, for example, one million textile and clothing jobs were lost from 1973 to 1997, while the output volume stayed level. Similarly in Europe (which has seen the sharpest job losses), employment in textiles, garments, and footwear fell 50 percent from 1990 to 1998, while output fell 10 percent. Trade barriers have restricted Southern opportunities but have saved few Northern jobs. Globalization may have actually *increased* global employment, since instead of jobs in high-wage countries being lost to machinery, some production has been relocated to Asia (ILO 2000). This may not hearten workers in North Carolina; do they care if their jobs went to machines or to Asian workers? But for devising an appropriate policy response it makes all the difference.

Recognizing that they can't buck the trend toward cheap imported goods, the latest strategy of textile lobbyists is to urge the US government to give preferences to imported textiles using US yarn. The Caribbean Basin Initiative might soon permit duty-free and tariff-free access for clothing made from US yarn.

Loopholes for protection

One of the most sensitive WTO roles is policing its members' trade-related policies to see if they break WTO rules and to guard against the abuse of loopholes. When the United States or the European Union introduces strict environmental or labeling requirements, for example, is this a back-door route to protectionism? Some of the main types of loophole abuse include:

- *Anti-dumping:* Anti-dumping is an arcane provision that allows a country to introduce protection when its market is suddenly flooded by exports below the "normal value." This is highly subjective (who decides what is a normal or an unfair price?) and hence, not surprisingly, prone to abuse. OECD countries are overwhelmingly the protagonists in anti-dumping actions, and 38 percent of these actions are against developing countries. In 1999 the United States took about three hundred actions (*The Economist,* November 27, 1999). Japan, Korea, and several large developing countries are energetically seeking reform in this area, but the United States is firmly resisting any change.
- *Sanitary and phytosanitary standards:* All governments regulate to protect citizens from health hazards; sometimes this can be seen as thinly veiled import protection, but it can also simply reflect different attitudes to risk. One of the major WTO disputes between the United States and the European Union has been over the latter's right to ban imported hormone-treated beef (agreed to by a rare consensus vote in the European Parliament). The United States won the action, claiming it was illegal because the European Union had not presented watertight scientific grounds; the United States was allowed to take stiff retaliatory sanctions (worth over $125 million) until the European Union capitulates. Such measures are most often used against Southern products. A recent example was an egregious European Union decision to drastically tighten permitted levels of aflatoxin (stemming from mildew forming in damp conditions) in groundnuts and other products. Though aflatoxin can be harmful to humans, there were no scientific grounds for the change, which damaged African exports by $670 million a year (Otsuki et al. 2000). European farmers were pleased, because groundnuts compete with the animal feed they grow.
- *Environmental protection:* Developing countries fear (with good cause) that OECD countries might abuse environmental standards, while the latter fear that conservation efforts are undermined by the WTO's disputes process (whose very first use held that the US

clean-gasoline laws were in violation of WTO rules). According to Noreena Hertz, the WTO has found *for* corporate interests and *against* national governments in every environment-related dispute taken to the WTO (Hertz 2001). It is certainly the case that WTO dispute panels don't include conservation experts. The Doha WTO meeting called for a better balance, allowing strong environmental laws providing they are not used for "arbitrary or unjustifiable discrimination between countries." It also stipulated urgent negotiations to iron out any discrepancies between WTO rules and critical multilateral environmental agreements (for example, on climate change).

* *Labor standards:* The European Union and the United States (with Japanese support) have bowed to trade union pressure and seek to incorporate core labor standards (or at least a ban on child labor) into trade pacts. As with environmental standards, however, developing countries believe this is simply another protectionist ploy and want labor issues omitted from the WTO and left as a sole preserve of the ILO, which has recently established a World Commission on the Social Dimensions of Globalization.

Disputes settlement

The main muscle of the WTO is its disputes settlement mechanism, the findings of which are binding and which can authorize very expensive retaliation. Using it requires highly specialized (and very expensive) lawyers, hence until recently it has been used mostly by rich countries, though larger developing countries are now tapping it.

From the WTO's birth in 1995 until March 2002, 253 disputes were initiated. About half the actions were taken by the United States or the European Union, and 43 percent of them were taken against developing countries. The larger developing countries (often acting together) are now becoming more willing to take actions, including against each other. While they accounted for fifty-three of the first two hundred actions, they took thirty-five of the last fifty-three.

The US-EU "banana war" is a celebrated WTO dispute. The European Union has a longstanding preferential agreement with African, Caribbean, and Pacific (ACP) countries covering bananas and other products (vital to the economic survival of small farmers in these small poor countries). However, the US government, prompted by Chiquita (the major US fruit TNC that trades in bananas from Central and South American, where fruit is mostly grown on large, TNC-owned estates) filed a case with the WTO on April 11, 1996, alleging that the ACP preference violated WTO rules. Two days later Chiquita's chief executive made a payment of $500,000 to Democratic Party funds; the company also contributed generously to the Republicans, whose Senate leaders helped spearhead the act imposing retaliatory tariffs on the European Union. The WTO panel found for the US government. While it offered some changes, the European Union tried to stand firm on its ACP preferences but eventually had to abandon them. The WTO sanctions have cost the European Union $191 million (Hines 2000).

Prospects for the next trade round

Until late 2003, WTO negotiations will focus on designing the content and process for the next trade round. The United States has a modest scope in mind: the completion of unfinished business from the Uruguay Round (particularly liberalization of agriculture and services, further tariffs reductions on industrial goods, and so on). But developing countries and the European Union both resist this narrow agenda. The South won't accept agricultural liberalization unless the North first phases out production and export subsidies (which the European Union will resist); the European Union wants a more ambitious agenda, including investment policy, competition policy, and the environment (which poor countries will resist, as will the United States if they conflict with its national laws).

Acronyms and Abbreviations

ATTAC	Association for the Taxation of Financial Transactions for the Aid of Citizens
BBC	British Broadcasting Corporation
BP	British Petroleum
CBO	Community-based organization
CEO	Chief executive officer
CODE-NGO	Caucus of Development NGOs (of Philippines)
CSO	Civil society organization
DFID	Department for International Development (UK government aid ministry)
ED	Executive director (of World Bank, IMF, and so forth)
EPZ	Export processing zones
EU	European Union
EZLN	Zapatistas National Liberation Army (Chiapas, Mexico)
FAO	Food and Agricultural Organisation (of the United Nations)
FDI	Foreign direct investment
FOE, FOE-I	Friends of the Earth, FOE-International
FSC	Forestry Stewardship Council
G7, G8	The group of the seven largest economies (plus Russia=G8)
GATS	General Agreement on Trade in Services
GATT	General Agreement on Tariffs and Trade (precursor of WTO)
GDP/GNP	Gross domestic product/Gross national product
GM, GMO	Genetically modified (organism)

GUF	Global Union Federation
HIPC	Heavily Indebted Poorer Countries (an IMF/ World Bank debt relief program initiative)
HRW	Human Rights Watch
IBFAN	International Baby Foods Action Network
ICBL	International Campaign to Ban Landmines
ICFTU	International Confederation of Free Trade Unions
ICT	Information and communications technology
IGO	Intergovernmental organization
ILO	International Labour Organisation (of the United Nations)
IMF	International Monetary Fund
INGO	International NGO
IOCU	International Organization of Consumers Unions
IPR	intellectual property rights
LSE	London School of Economics and Political Science
LSS	Living standards survey
MDB	Multilateral development bank (that is, World Bank and the regional banks)
MFA	Multi-fiber arrangement
MP	Member of Parliament (legislator in parliamentary democracies)
MSF	Médecins Sans Frontières
NAFTA	North American Free Trade Area
NGO	Nongovernmental organization
NTB	Non-tariff barrier
OECD	Organization for Economic Cooperation and Development
PPA	Participatory poverty assessment
PRSP	Poverty reduction strategy papers
PSI	Public Service International
PVO	Private voluntary organization
TI	Transparency International
TNC	Transnational corporations

TRIPs	Agreement in trade-related intellectual property rights
TUC	Trades Union Congress (UK umbrella of trade unions)
UNCTAD	United Nations Conference on Trade and Development
UNDP	United Nations Development Program
UNI	Union Network International
UNICEF	United Nations Children's Fund
USAID	US Agency for International Development (US government aid agency)
WHO	World Health Organisation (of the United Nations)
WSF	World Social Forum
WTO	World Trade Organization
WWF	World-Wide Fund for Nature (also known as World Wildlife Fund in the United States)

Notes

1. Globalization—Agony or Ecstasy?

1. Throughout this book, the North refers to the major industrialized nations of the Organization for Economic Cooperation and Development (OECD), including Australia and New Zealand in the Southern hemisphere; the South refers to the developing countries, usually including the former Eastern block—or transition—countries.

2. Neoliberalism, sometimes called the Washington Consensus, is the conviction that economic growth is of paramount importance and that governments can best achieve this by shedding markets controls or interventions, privatizing state enterprises and services, practicing fiscal austerity by reducing public spending to a minimum and ensuring a business-friendly environment—especially for foreign investors.

3. The Group of Seven largest Western economies (G7)—the United States, Japan, Germany, France, the UK, Italy, and Canada. Annual Summit meetings of heads of government and, separately, Finance Ministers coordinate economic and political policy. The Russian premier is invited (as observer or participant) to most of these, and hence the term G8 is increasingly used, though Russia is far from being a major economic power.

4. CSOs comprise many types of private, non-profit organizations, formal and informal, such as societies, trade unions, religious groups, professional leagues, peasants' associations, mass movements, and nongovernmental organizations (NGOs) providing specific types of service or advocacy. See also Chapter 5.

3. How Globalization Affects Poor People

1. For completeness, the globalizers not yet mentioned are Bangladesh, Costa Rica, the Dominican Republic, Hungary, Jamaica, Jordan, Mali, Nicaragua, Paraguay, Philippines, Thailand, and Uruguay.

2. Ironically, Zambia was praised in a 2000 report from the World Bank and four African economic agencies for having "made considerable progress towards openness levels . . . in line with those of global good practice economies" (World Bank et al. 2000), but it falls to the bottom of the class in World Bank 2002b.

3. For poor countries, taxing imports is a major source of revenue; they have few other opportunities to tax their citizens. For richer countries, direct and indirect taxation is more feasible—logistically and politically.

4. How Global Changes Affect Politics

1. Member of Parliament. Some democracies are based on forums of elected MPs that *form* government administrations *and* hold them accountable. Others (e.g., the United States) separate the administration from the legislative process of elected representatives. Henceforth, for simplicity, the term *legislatures* includes parliaments, and *parliamentarians* includes legislators, and so on.

2. Issues of CSO governance are more complex than outlined here. We return to these issues in Chapter 9.

3. Since then, Greenpeace's membership fell to 194,000 in 2002 while that of the Labour Party first increased (to 430,000 in 1997) and then declined to 270,000 by October 2002.

4. Mainstream parties, of course, continue to give most attention to issues of the economy, employment, health, education, national infrastructure, crime, and so on, which are the predominant concerns of voters.

5. This Is the Age of a *Civicus*—The Rise of Civil Society

1. A *civicus* is *"a community of individuals who discuss and act upon issues that affect the world in which they live,"* according to the mission statement of the organization called CIVICUS.

2. In this book I regard NGOs as formal organizations (whether legally registered or not) formed for tangible public benefit purposes (not just to serve their members), independent of government, with defined officers and leadership, that provide services to their constituency (which in the case of an advocacy NGO may simply be the provision of information and campaigning opportunities).

6. Civil Society in the Network Era

1. Lindenberg and Dobel (1999) present a similar list for INGOs but do not include social movements.

2. This case study is based on Tasneem Mowjee, "Consumers Unite Internationally," in Clark 2003.

3. Full members must be independent of government, have no vested commercial interest, not receive income from commercial advertisements, and be nonprofit. There are also affiliates, who may be government consumer affairs bureaus.

7. Retaining Relevance

1. Statistics up to 1988 are drawn from the OECD's Development Assistance Committee, based on information provided to it by member governments; 1999 statistics for NGOs derive from surveys of NGOs in OECD countries.

2. At the time of publication, BRAC was still considering the invitation.

8. The Protest Movement and the "Dot-Causes"

1. This chapter draws on my work with Nuno Themudo of the London School of Economics. An expanded version of these arguments is presented in a jointly authored chapter in Clark 2003.

2. For a description of the WSF and its contribution to the movement, see Schönleitner 2003.

11. Making Globalization Ethical—by Making Ethics Global

1. I learned to play Monopoly in the UK. Had I learned the US version I would say Boardwalk instead of Mayfair, and Baltic Avenue instead of Old Kent Road—and it would be $200 for passing "Go."

References

Almeida, I. 1999. "Civil Society and the Establishment of the International Criminal Court." In *Civil Society Engaging Multilateral Institutions: At the Crossroads,* ed. Montreal International Forum (FIM). Canada: FIM.

Altman, D. 1999. "NGOs on Board and on the Board." In *Civil Society Engaging Multilateral Institutions: At the Crossroads.* Montreal: Forum International de Montreal.

American Textiles Manufacturers Institute. 2002.

Amnesty International. 2000. "Changing the Way We Change: Options for Reforming AI's Decision-Making Processes and Structures." Paper submitted to all Amnesty International sections and to the 2001 International Council Meeting. Also discussions with Amnesty International staff in Amnesty International UK, Canada, and the Amnesty International Secretariat.

Anderson, M. 1996. *Do No Harm: How Aid Can Support Peace or War.* Boulder, Colo.: Lynne Rienner.

Angus Reid Poll. 1998 (December). Reported in *The Economist* (January 2, 1999).

———. 2000 (April). Available on Angus Reid website.

Anheier, H., and Themudo, N. 2002. "Organizational Forms of Global Civil Society: Implications of Going Global." In Glasius et al. 2002.

Anheier, H., M. Glasius, and M. Kaldor, eds. 2001. *Global Civil Society 2001.* Oxford: Oxford University Press.

Arquilla, J., and D. Ronfeldt. 1993. "Cyberwar Is Coming!" *Comparative Strategy* 12/2 (Summer): 141–65.

Ashman, D. 2000. "Strengthening North-South Partnerships: Addressing Structural Barriers to Mutual Influence." *IDR Reports* 16/14.

ATTAC website: www.attac.org.

Barber, B. 1995. *Jihad Versus McWorld.* New York: Times Books.

Bauck, A. 2001. "Oxfam and Debt Relief Advocacy." Case study written at the Daniel J. Evans School of Public Affairs, Washington University, Seattle.

Bauman, Z. 2002. "Quality and Inequality." In *The Moral Universe*, ed. Tom Bentley and Daniel Steadman Jones. London: Demos.

Black, M. 1992. *A Cause for Our Times; Oxfam, the First Fifty Years.* Oxford: Oxfam International.

Boehle, J. 2001. "The Growth of International Inter-religious Activity." Note produced for seminar on Transnational Civil Society, London School of Economics, 2001.

Boli, J., and G. Thomas. 1997. "World Culture in the World Polity: A Century of International Non-governmental Organization." *American Sociological Review* (April).

Bond, M. 2000. "The Backlash Against NGOs." *Prospect Magazine* (April).

Brandt Commission. 1980. *North-South: a Programme for Survival*. UK: Pan.

Brown, G. 2001. Speech to the Federal Reserve Bank, New York, November 16.

Bryer, D., and J. Magrath. 1999. "New Dimensions of Global Advocacy." *Nonprofit and Voluntary Sector Quarterly* 28/4. Supplement.

Cameron, J. and R. MacKenzie. 1995. *State Sovereignty, NGOs and Multilateral Institutions* (mimeo). Council for Foreign Relations, Washington, D.C.

Carothers, T. 1999. "Civil Society: Think Again." *Foreign Policy* (Winter), 18–29.

Castells, M. 1996. *The Information Age: Economy, Society, and Culture*. Vol. 1, *The Rise of the Network Society*. Cambridge, UK: Polity Press.

———. 2001. "Information Technology and Global Capitalism." In *On the Edge: Living with Global Capitalism*, ed. W. Hutton and A. Giddens. London: Vintage.

Chiriboga, M. 2001. "Constructing a Southern Constituency for Global Advocacy: The Experience of Latin American NGOs and the World Bank." In Edwards and Gaventa 2001.

———. 2002. "Latin American NGOs and the IFIs." In Scholte and Schnabel 2002.

Christiaensen, L., L. Demery and S. Paternostro. 2001. "Reforms, Economic Growth, and Poverty Reduction in Africa: Messages from the 1990s." Washington, D.C.: World Bank.

Clark, J. 1991. *Democratizing Development: The Role of Voluntary Agencies*. London: Earthscan; West Hartford, Conn.: Kumarian Press.

Clark, J. 1992. "Participatory Poverty Assessments" (mimeo). Paper for the World Bank's Participatory Development Learning Group. Washington, D.C.

———. 1995. "The State, Popular Participation, and the Voluntary Sector." *World Development* 23/4.

———. 1999. "Ethical Globalization: The Dilemmas and Challenges of Internationalizing Civil Society." Paper given at the 1999 International NGO Conference, Birmingham University; also published as a chapter (same title) in Edwards and Gaventa 2001.

———. 2001 (June). "Trans-National Civil Society: Issues of Organization and Governance" (mimeo). London: Centre for Civil Society, London School of Economics.

———. 2002. "The World Bank and Civil Society: An Evolving Experience." In Scholte and Schnabel 2002.

Clark, J., ed. 2003 (forthcoming). *Globalizing Civic Engagement: Civil Society and Trans-National Action*. London: Earthscan.

Cockburn, A., and J. St. Clair. N.d. "So Who Did Win in Seattle? Liberals Rewrite History." Available online at several websites.

CODE-NGO (Caucus of Development NGOs). 1997. *Code of Conduct for Development NGOs—Whitelist Project: Strategy Paper 1998–2000*. Manila: CODE-NGO.

Cohen, R., and S. Rai, eds. 2000. *Global Social Movements*. London: Athlone Press; New Brunswick: Transaction Press.

Collins, J., Z. Gariyo, and T. Burdon. 2001. "Jubilee 2000: Citizen Action Across the North-South Divide." In Edwards and Gaventa 2001.

Covey, J. 1994. *Accountability and Effectiveness of NGO Policy Alliances*. Boston: Institute for Development Research.

Crafts, N., and A. Venables. 2001. "Globalization in History: A Geographic Perspective" (mimeo). London: LSE.

Curtis, M. 2001. *Trade for Life: Making Trade Work for Poor People*. London: Christian Aid.

Davis, R. 2002. "Anti-globalization Activists and Unions Can Still Work Together." *ATTAC Newsletter* 121 (March).

De Léon, J. P. 2001. *Our Word Is Our Weapon: Selected Writings by Subcomandante Marcos*. New York: Seven Stories Press.

De Soto, H. 2000. *The Mystery of Capital: Why Capitalism Triumphs in the West and Fails Everywhere Else*. Ondon: Bantam.

DFID (Department for International Development). 1998. *Strengthening DFID's Support for Civil Society*. London.

———. 2000a. *Eliminating World Poverty: Making Globalisation Work for the Poor*. White Paper on International Development. London.

———. 2000b. *Realising Human Rights for Poor People: Strategies for Achieving the International Development Targets*. London: DFID.

Desai, M., and Y. Said. 2001. "The New Anti-Capitalist Movement: Money and Global Civil Society." In Anheier et al. 2001.

Development Initiatives. 2000. "Global Development Assistance: The Role of NGOs and Other Charity Flows" (mimeo). Somerset, UK: Development Initiatives. July.

Diamond, L. 1993. "The Globalization of Democracy." In *Global Transformation and the Third World*, ed. B. Slater, B. Schutz, and S. Dorr. Boulder, Colo.: Lynne Rienner.

Dollar, D., and A. Kraay. 2001. "Growth Is Good for the Poor." Policy Research Working Paper No. 2587. Washington, D.C.: World Bank; revised version in *Journal of Economic Growth* 7/4 (2002).

Durbin, A. 2000. "Clarifying Friends of the Earth's Position Regarding A16." E-mail to the World Bank. Washington, D.C. April 27.

Easterly, W. 2001. *The Elusive Quest for Growth: Economists Adventures and Misadventures in the Tropics*. Cambridge. Mass.: MIT Press.

Edwards, M. 1996. "International Development NGOs: Legitimacy, Accountability, Regulation, and Roles." Discussion paper for the British Overseas Aid Group. London.

———. 1999. *Future Positive: International Cooperation in the Twenty-first Century.* London: Earthscan.

———. 2000. *NGO Rights and Responsibilities: A New Deal for Global Governance.* London: Foreign Policy Centre.

Edwards, M., and D. Hulme, eds. 1992. *Making a Difference: NGOs and Development in a Changing World.* London: Earthscan.

———. 1995. *NGO Performance and Accountability: Beyond the Magic Bullet.* London: Earthscan; West Hartford, Conn.: Kumarian Press.

Edwards, M., and J. Gaventa, eds. 2001. *Global Citizen Action.* Boulder, Colo.: Lynne Rienner.

EMILY's List: www.emilyslist.org.

Environics International. 2001 and 2002. See www.environics-international.com.

European Council on Refugees and Exiles. 2002. Available at the ECRE website.

Faux, J., and L. Mischel. 2001. *Inequality and the Global Economy.* In Hutton and Giddens 2001.

Fine, B. 1999. "The Developmental State is Dead—Long Live Social Capital." *Development and Change* 30/1.

Finger, M., and P. Schuler. 1999. *Implementation of Uruguay Round Commitments: The Development Challenge.* Policy Research Working Paper No. 2215. Washington, D.C.: World Bank.

Florini, A., ed. 2000. *The Third Force: The Rise of Transnational Civil Society.* Washington, D.C.: Carnegie Endowment for International Peace.

Focus on the Global South. 2001. "Bangkok International Roundtable of Unions, Social Movements, and NGOs, 11–13 March 2001." Bangkok: Focus on the Global South and Friedrich-Ebert-Stiftung.

FOE (Friends of the Earth) sources: FOE-International Handbook 1998; interviews with FOE-I and FOE-UK management and staff, 2001; FOE website.

Foster, Jodie. 1998. Speaking at the signing ceremony for the landmine treaty, Ottawa.

Foster, John. 2001. "Knowing Ourselves: A Brief History of Emerging Global Civil Society" (mimeo). Paper presented at the Fourth Civicus World Assembly, August, in Vancouver.

Fowler, A. 1997. *Striking a Balance: A Guide to Enhancing the Effectiveness of NGOs in International Development.* London: Earthscan.

Fox, J. 2000. "Assessing Binational Civil Society Coalitions: Lessons from the Mexico-US Experience" (mimeo). Paper for the University of California Santa Cruz conference on Human Rights and Globalization, December 1–2.

Fox, J., and D. Brown, eds. 1998. *The Struggle for Accountability: The World Bank, NGOs, and Grassroots Movements*. Cambridge, Mass.: MIT Press.

Gaventa, J., et al. 2002. "Making Rights Real: Exploring Citizenship Participation and Accountability." *IDS Bulletin* 33/2 (April).

George, S. 2002. Remarks at a seminar on globalization at London School of Economics. February 14.

Gereffi, G., R. Garcia-Johnson, and E. Sasser. 2001. "The NGO-Industrial Complex." *Foreign Policy* (July/August). Washington, D.C.

Giddens, A. 1997. Speech to UNRISD conference entitled "Globalization and Citizenship."

———. 1998. *The Third Way: The Renewal of Social Democracy*. UK: Polity Press.

Glasius, M., M. Kaldor, and H. Anheier, eds. 2002. *Global Civil Society 2002*. Oxford: Oxford University Press.

Greenhill, R., and A. Pettifor. 2002 (April). "USA as a Heavily Indebted Prosperous Country: How the Poor Are Financing the Rich" (mimeo). London: Jubilee Research.

Greiner, P. 2003. "Jubilee 2000: Laying the Foundations for a Social Movement." In Clark 2003.

Hamilton, C. 1990. *Textiles Trade and the Developing Countries*. Washington, D.C.: World Bank.

Harper, C. 2001. "Do the Facts Matter? NGOs, Research, and International Advocacy." In Edwards and Gaventa 2001.

Harris Interactive. 2002. "HI Reputation Quotient." www.harrisinteractive.com.

Harriss, J., and P. de Renzio. 1997. "'Missing Link' or Analytically Missing? The Concept of Social Capital, an Introductory Bibliographic Essay." *Journal of International Development* 9/7: 919–37.

Havel, V. 1997. Speech to Parliament, December 9. Translated and printed in *New York Review of Books* 45/4 (1998).

Held, D. 1998. "Democracy and Globalization." In *Re-imagining Political Community: Studies in Cosmopolitan Democracy*, ed. D. Archibugi et al. Cambridge: Polity; Palo Alto, Calif.: Stanford University Press.

———. 2000. "The Changing Contours of Political Community." In *Global Democracy: Key Debates*, ed. B. Holden. London: Routledge.

———. 2002. "Cosmopolitanism and Globalization." *Logos* 1/3.

Hertz, N. 2001. *The Silent Takeover: Global Capitalism and the Death of Democracy*. London: William Heinemann.

Hines, C. 2000. *Localization: A Global Manifesto*. London: Earthscan.

Hirst, P., and G. Thompson. 1999. *Globalization in Question: The International Economy and the Possibilities of Governance*. Cambridge: Polity.

Hoffmann, S. 2002 (July/August). "Clash of Globalizations." *Foreign Affairs* 81/4.

Holloway, R. 1997. *How Civil Is Civil Society?* (mimeo). Washington, D.C.: PACT.

Huntington, S. 1993. "The Clash of Civilizations." *Foreign Affairs* 72/3.

Hurrell, A., and N. Woods, eds. 1999. *Globalization, Inequality and World Politics.* Oxford: Oxford University Press.

Hutanuwatr, N. 1998. "Rice Mill of NASO Farmer Association." Faculty of Agriculture. Ubon Ratchathani University, Thailand.

Hutton, W., and A. Giddens. 2001. *On the Edge: Living with Global Capitalism.* London: Vintage.

ICFTU (International Confederation of Free Trade Unions). 1998. "Statement to the 1998 APEC Leaders' Meeting." Available at ICFTU website.

———. 2001 (November). "Millennium Review: Report of the Progress Group." 117/EB/E/7. Brussels.

———. 2002. Executive board paper; "Millennium Review Process"; Brussels, November 2000; also ICFTU website.

ILO (International Labour Organization). 2000. "Labour Practices in the Footwear, Leather, Textiles, and Clothing Industries." Geneva: ILO.

Inspection Panel of the World Bank. 1998. *World Bank's Inspection Panel: The First Four Years (1994–8).* Washington, D.C.: World Bank.

InterAction. 2001. "InterAction PVO [private voluntary organizations] Standards." June. Available on the InterAction website.

International Council of Voluntary Organisations (ICVA) website.

International Organization of Migration. 2000a. *World Migration Report.* Geneva.

———. 2000b. *Trends in International Migration.* Geneva.

Jordan, L., and P. van Tuijl. 2000. "Political Responsibility in Transnational NGO Advocacy." *World Development* 28/12, 2051–65.

Jubilee 2000. Information available at website.

Kaldor, M. 2000. "'Civilizing' Globalization: The Implications of the 'Battle in Seattle.'" *Millennium* (January 29), 105–14.

Kanbur, R. 2001. "Economic Policy, Distribution, and Poverty: The Nature of Disagreement" (mimeo). Ithaca, N.Y.: Cornell University.

Kapur, D., John P. Lewis, and Richard Webb, eds. 1997. *The World Bank's First Half Century.* 2 vols. Washington, D.C.: Brookings Institute.

Keck, M., and K. Sikkink. 1998. *Activists Beyond Borders: Advocacy Networks in International Politics.* Ithaca, N.Y.: Cornell University Press.

Keynes, J. M. 1936. *General Theory of Employment, Interest, and Money.* 1973 ed. London: Macmillan, for the Royal Economic Society.

Khagram, S., et al., eds. 2002. *Restructuring World Politics: The Power of Transnational Norms, Networks, Coalitions, and Movements.* Minneapolis, Minn.: University of Minnesota Press.

Khagram, S., J. Riker, and K. Sikkink. 2002. "From Santiago to Seattle: Transnational Advocacy Groups Restructuring World Politics." In Khagram et al. 2002.

Kidder, T. 2002. "Networks in Transnational Labor Organizing." In Khagram et al. 2002.

Klein, N. 1999. *No Logo: Taking Aim at the Brand Bullies*. New York: Picador USA.

———. 2001a. "Signs of the Times: Protests Aimed at Powerful Symbols of Capitalism Find Themselves in a Transformed Landscape." *The Nation*, October 22, 2001.

———. 2001b. "The Unknown Icon." *The Guardian*, March 3, 2001.

———. 2001c. "A Fete for the End of the End of History." *The Nation*, March 19, 2001.

Kobrin, S. 1998. "The MAI and the Clash of Globalizations." *Foreign Policy* 112: 97–109.

Korten, D. 1990. *Getting to the Twenty-first Century: Voluntary Development Action and the Global Agenda*. West Hartford, Conn.: Kumarian Press.

———. 1995. *When Corporations Rule the World*. West Hartford, Conn.: Kumarian Press.

Krut, R. 1997. *Globalization and Civil Society: NGO Influence in International Decision-Making*. Discussion Paper No. 83, April. Geneva: UNRISD.

Kung, H. 1998. *A Global Ethic for Global Politics and Economics*. Oxford: Oxford University Press.

Lamy, Pascal. 2000. Speech to ARCO forum. Harvard University. November 1.

Leather, A., and R. Harris. 1999. *ITS-NGO Relations: Discussion Paper for the ITS Conference*. July 9. Geneva: Public Service International.

Lichbach, M. I. 2002. "Global Order and Local Resistance: Structure, Culture, and Rationality in the Battle of Seattle" (mimeo). College Park, Md.: University of Maryland.

Lindenberg, M., and C. Bryant. 2001. *Going Global: Transforming Relief and Development NGOs*. Bloomfield, Conn.: Kumarian Press.

Lindenberg, M., and P. Dobel, eds. 1999. "The Challenges for Northern International Relief and Development NGOs." *Nonprofit and Voluntary Sector Quarterly* 28/4. Supplement.

Lockwood, M., and P. Madden. 1997. *Closer Together, Further Apart: A Discussion Paper on Globalization*. London: Christian Aid.

Mair, P., and I. van Biezen. 2001. "Party Members in Twenty European Democracies 1980–2000." *Party Politics* 7/1.

Malena, C. 1995. *Working with NGOs: A Practical Guide to Operational Collaboration Between the World Bank and NGOs*. Washington, D.C.: World Bank.

Martinez, Elizabeth (Betita). 2000. "Where Was the Color in Seattle? Looking for Reasons Why the Great Battle Was So White." *ColorLines* 3/1 in http://www.tao.ca/~colours/martinez.html.

Mathews, J. 1997. "Power Shift." *Foreign Affairs* 76/1 (January/February), 50–66.

McAdam, D., J. McCarthy, and M. Zald, eds. 1996. *Comparative Perspectives on Social Movements: Political Opportunities, Mobilizing*

Structures, and Cultural Framings. New York: Cambridge University Press.

Mekata, M. 2000. "Building Partnerships Toward a Common Goal: Experiences of the International Campaign to Ban Landmines." In Florini 2000.

Milanovic, B. 2002a. "True World Income Distribution, 1988 and 1993: First Calculation Based on Household Surveys." *The Economic Journal* 112: 51–92.

———. 2002b. "The Two Faces of Globalization: Against Globalization as We Know It" (mimeo). Washington, D.C.: World Bank Development Research Group.

Miller, V. 1994. *Policy Influence by Development NGOs: A Vehicle for Strengthening Civil Society.* Boston: Institute for Development Research.

Moseley, S., et al. 2000. Letter to Mr. Wolfensohn, signed by twenty-two major operational NGOs, Washington, D.C., April 14.

Narayan, D., R. Chambers, M. Shah, and P. Petesch. 2000. *Voices of the Poor: Crying Out for Change.* New York: Oxford University Press.

National Charities Information Bureau. 1996. *Statement of Purpose and Standards of National Philanthropy.* New York: NCIB.

National Council of Welfare. 2001. "New Poverty Lines." Canada. February. Available at www.ncwcnbes.net.

Naughton, J. 2001. "Contested Space: The Internet and Global Civil Society." In Anheier et al. 2001.

Nelson, J. 1996. *Business as Partners in Development: Creating Wealth for Countries, Companies, and Communities.* London: Prince of Wales Business Leaders' Forum.

Nelson, P. 1995. *The World Bank and Non-governmental Organizations: The Limits of Apolitical Development.* Basingstoke, UK: Macmillan.

———. 2001. "Information, Location, and Legitimacy." In Edwards and Gaventa 2001.

Nestle, M. 2002. *Food Politics: How the Food Industry Influences Nutrition and Health.* Los Angeles and Berkeley: University of California Press.

New Economics Foundation. 1997. *Towards Understanding NGO Work on Policy.* London: NEF.

Newell, P. 2000. "Environmental NGOs and Globalization: The Governance of TNCs." In Cohen and Rai 2000.

———. 2001. "Managing Multinationals: The Governance of Investment for the Environment." *Journal of International Development* 13: 907–19.

———. 2002. "From Responsibility to Citizenship? Corporate Accountability for Development." *IDS Bulletin* 33/2 (April).

Nimtz, A. 2002. "Marx and Engels: The Prototypical Transnational Actors." In Khagram et al. 2002.

O'Brien, R., A. M. Goetz, J. A. Scholte, and M. Williams. 2000. *Contesting Global Governance: Multilateral Economic Institutions and Global Social Movements.* Cambridge: Cambridge University Press.

O'Neill, K. 1999. *Internetworking for Social Change: Keeping the Spotlight on Corporate Responsibility.* United Nations Research Institute for Social Development Discussion Paper No. 111. Geneva.

Offenheiser, R., S. Holcombe, and N. Hopkins. 1999. "Grappling with Globalization, Partnership, and Learning." *Nonprofit and Voluntary Quarterly* 28/4. Supplement.

Otsuki, T., et al. 2000. "Saving Two in a Billion: A Case Study to Quantify the Trade Effect of European Food Standards on African Exports" (mimeo). Washington, D.C.: World Bank.

Oxfam International. 2000. "Towards Global Equity: Oxfam International's Strategic Plan, 2001–2004." Adopted by the board in Melbourne in November 2000.

———. 2002. *Rigged Rules and Double Standards: Trade, Globalisation, and the Fight Against Poverty.* Oxford: Oxfam International.

Participatory Research in Asia. 1997. *Study of Social Policy Mapping of NGOs in South Asia.* New Delhi: PRIA.

Pettifor, A. 2001. "Jubilee 2000 and the Multilateral Institution." Paper for Forum International de Montreal. July 10, 2000.

———. 2002. *Chapter 9/11? Resolving International Debt Crises—The Jubilee Framework for International Insolvency.* London: Jubilee Research.

Power, J. 2001. *Like Water on Stone: The Story of Amnesty International.* London: Allen Lane.

Putnam, R. 1993. "The Prosperous Community: Social Capital and Public Affairs." *The American Prospect* 13 (spring), 35–42.

———. 2000. *Bowling Alone: The Collapse and Revival of American Community.* New York: Simon and Schuster.

Putnam, R., S. Pharr, and R. Dalton. 2000. *What Is Troubling the Trilateral Democracies?* Princeton, N.J.: Princeton University Press.

Ricardo, D. 1973. *The Principles of Political Economy and Taxation.* Dent: London.

Rich, B. 1994. *Mortgaging the Earth: The World Bank, Environmental Impoverishment and the Crisis of Development.* Boston: Beacon Press.

Rifkin, J. 2001. *The Age of Access.* London: Penguin.

Robb, C. 1999. *Participatory Poverty Assessment Report.* Washington, D.C.: World Bank.

Rodrigues, M. 2000. "Searching for Common Ground: Transnational Advocacy Networks and Environmentally Sustainable Development in Amazonia" (mimeo). Prepared for the University of California, Santa Cruz conference on human rights and globalization, December 1–2.

Rodrik, D. 1997. *Has Globalization Gone Too Far?* Washington, D.C.: Institute for International Economics.

———. 1999. *The New Global Economy and Developing Countries: Making Openness Work.* Washington, D.C.: Overseas Development Council.

———. 2001a. "The Developing Countries' Hazardous Obsession with Global Integration." Revised version of "Trading in Illusions." *Foreign Policy* (March/April).

———. 2001b. "Four Simple Principles for Democratic Governance of Globalization" (mimeo). Harvard University. May.

———. 2001c. "Comments at the Conference on 'Immigration Policy and the Welfare State.'" Trieste, June 23. Harvard University.

———. 2001d. *The Global Governance of Trade as if Development Really Mattered.* New York: UNDP.

Ronfeldt, D., J. Arquilla, G. E. Fuller, and M. Fuller. 1998. *The Zapatista "Social Netwar" in Mexico.* Arlington, Va.: Rand Corporation, 1998.

Runyan, C. 1999. "Action on the Frontlines." *Worldwatch Magazine* (November/December). Washington, D.C.: WorldWatch.

S26 website. 2000. Quoted in "Anti-Capitalist Protest: Angry and Effective." *The Economist* (September 23).

Salomon, L. 1994. *Foreign Affairs* 73/4.

Salamon, L., and H. Anheier. 1998. *The Emerging Sector Revisited: A Summary.* Baltimore: Institute of Policy Studies, Johns Hopkins University.

Sambhavna Trust. 1998. *The Bhopal Gas Tragedy: 1984– ?* Bhopal, India.

Santa Ana, F., ed. 1998. *The State and the Market: Essays on a Socially Oriented Philippine Economy.* Manila: Action for Economic Reforms.

Scheve, K., and M. Slaughter. 2001. *Globalization and the Perceptions of American Workers.* Washington, D.C.: Institute for International Economics.

Scholte, J. A. 2001a. "Civil Society in Global Governance" (mimeo). Coventry, UK: Warwick University.

———. 2001b. *New Citizens Action and Global Finance,* Notes for Seminar entitled Transnational Civil Society: Issues of Governance and Organisation. London School of Economics, June 1–2.

Scholte, J. A., and A. Schnabel, eds. 2002. *Civil Society and Global Finance.* London: Routledge.

Schönleitner, G. 2003. "World Social Forum: Making Another World Possible." In Clark 2003.

Secrett, C. 1996. "Why Do Pressure Groups Matter?" Paper for the Social Market Foundation. London: Friends of the Earth. June.

Selverston-Scher, M. 2000. "Building International Civil Society: Lessons from the Amazon Coalition" (mimeo). Paper for the University of California Santa Cruz conference on Human Rights and Globalization, December 1–2.

Sen, A. 2000. *Global Doubts.* Commencement address, Harvard University, June 8.

Slaughter, M., and P. Swagel. 1997. *Does Globalization Lower Wages and Export Jobs?* Washington, D.C.: IMF.

Smith, Adam. 1776. *An Enquiry into the Nature and Causes of the Wealth of Nations.*

Smith, J., C. Chatfield, and R. Pagnucco, eds. 1997. *Transnational Social Movements and Global Politics: Solidarity Beyond the State.* Syracuse, N.Y.: Syracuse University Press.

Soledad, F. 2001. "The Philippines Council for NGO Certification." *International Journal of Not-for-Profit Law* 3/2.

Soros, G. 1998. *The Crisis of Global Capitalism: Open Society Endangered.* New York: Public Affairs.

Spahn, P. 2002 "On the Feasibility of a Currency Transaction Tax." Commissioned by the Ministry for Development Cooperation, Germany.

Steele, D. 2000. "UN Reform, Civil and Sometimes Uncivil Society." *Transnational Associations* 6, 282–90.

Stiglitz, J. 2000. *Democratic Development as the Fruits of Labor.* Speech to the Industrial Relations Research Association, Boston, January 2000.

———. 2002. *Globalization and Its Discontents.* New York: Norton.

Summers, L. 2001. *Foreign Policy* (October).

Tandon, R. 1989. *NGO-Government Relations: Source of life or the Kiss of Death?* New Delhi: Society for Participatory Research in Asia.

———. 1995. *Networks as Mechanisms of Communications and Influence.* New Delhi: Society for Participatory Research in Asia.

Tarrow, S. 2001a. "Transnational Politics: Contention and Institutions in International Politics." *Annual Review of Political Science* 4: 1–20.

———. 2001b. "Center-Periphery Alignments and Political Contention in Late-Modern Europe" (mimeo). Ithaca, N.Y.: Cornell University.

———. 2002. "Rooted Cosmopolitans: Towards a Sociology of Transnational Contention" (mimeo). Ithaca, N.Y.: Cornell University, January 5.

Tilly, C. 1978. *From Mobilization to Revolution,* New York: Random House.

———. 1995. *Popular Contention in Britain, 1758–1834.* Cambridge, Mass.: Harvard University Press.

Tobin, J. 2001. *Financial Times.* September 11.

Toynbee, P. 2001 "Who's Afraid of Global Culture?" In Hutton and Giddens 2001.

Transparency International. 2000. Chapter 19. *Sourcebook.* Berlin.

UNCTAD. 2001a. *Trade and Development Report, 2001.* Geneva.

———. 2001b *World Investment Report.* TAD/INF/PR19. Geneva.

UNDP. 1999. *Human Development Report 2000.* New York: UNDP.

———. 2001. *Human Development Report 2001.* New York: UNDP.

UN Foundation. 2002 (August 30). Press release.

United Nations. 2001. "The UN and Civil Society: What Next?" and "Note of Discussion in Senior Management Group on UN-Civil Society Relations." Papers prepared for and record of UN management meeting, January 31, Geneva.

US Government. 1999. US–Caribbean Basin Trade Enhancement Act. S1389.

Verhofstadt, G. 2001. "Open Letter to Anti-Globalization Protestors." Brussels. September 1.

Vianna, A. 2000. "The Work of Brazilian NGOs on the International Level: Discussion Paper" (mimeo). Brazil: Instituto de Estudos Socioeconômicos (INESC).

Volker, P. 2001. "The Sea of Global Finance." In Hutton and Gittens 2001.

Wade, R. 2001a. "Global Inequality: Winners and Losers." *The Economist* (April 28).

———. 2001b. "The World Bank as a Necessarily Unforthright Organization" (working draft, mimeo). London School of Economics.

Watkins, K. 1995. *The Oxfam Poverty Report*. Oxford: Oxfam International.

Willetts, P., ed. 1996. *The Conscience of the World: The Influence of NGOs at the United Nations*. Washington, D.C.: Brookings Institution Press.

Wolf, M. 1997. "Why This Hatred of the Market." *Financial Times*, May 15.

Wolfensohn, J. 1999. *A Proposal for a Comprehensive Development Framework*. Discussion draft, January 21, 1999. Washington, D.C.: World Bank.

Woodroffe, J., and M. Ellis-Jones. 2000. "States of Unrest: Resistance to IMF Policies in Poor Countries" (mimeo). London: World Development Movement.

Woods, N. 2000. *Political Economy of Globalization*. Basingstoke: Macmillan.

Woolcock, M. 1998. "Social Capital and Economic Development: Towards a Theoretical Synthesis and Policy Framework." *Theory and Society* 27/2: 151–208.

World Bank. 1992. *Governance and Development*. Washington, D.C.: World Bank.

———. 1995. *Bangladesh from Stabilisation to Growth*. Washington, D.C.: World Bank.

———. 1996. *NGOs and the Bank*. NGO Unit, Washington, D.C.: World Bank.

———. 1998. *The Bank's Relationship with NGOs*. Washington, D.C.: World Bank.

———. 2000a. *World Bank-Civil Society Relations: Fiscal 1999 Progress Report*. Draft. Washington, D.C.: World Bank. See also previous year's annual progress reports.

———. 2000b. "Assessing Globalization." Briefing Papers, Economic Policy Group and Development Economic Group. Washington, D.C.

———. 2000c. *World Development Report: Attacking Poverty*. Washington, D.C.

———. 2001. *Global Economic Prospects*. Washington, D.C.: World Bank.

————. 2002a. *Global Economic Prospects.* Washington, D.C.: World Bank.

————. 2002b. *Globalization, Growth, and Poverty.* New York: Oxford University Press.

————. 2002c. *Building Institutions for Markets: World Development Report 2002.* New York: Oxford University Press.

World Bank et al. (four African economic agencies). 2000. *Can Africa Reclaim the Twenty-first Century?* Washington, D.C.: World Bank.

World Bank Inspection Panel. 1998. "World Bank's Inspection Panel: The First Four Years (1994–8)." Washington, D.C.: World Bank.

WDM (World Development Movement). 2001. "Report Back from the G8 Summit in Genoa." On the WDM website.

WTO (World Trade Organization). 1995. *Agreement Establishing the World Trade Organization.* Doc 95–0146. Marrakech.

————. 2001 (November 14). *WTO Ministerial Declaration.* Doha.

Wuthnow, R. 1994. *Sharing the Journey: Support Groups and America's New Quest for Community.* New York: Free Press.

Zadek, S. 2001. *The Civil Corporation: The New Economy of Corporate Citizenship.* London: Earthscan.

Index

Baby-milk campaign, 68, 72, 73, 86, 201, 203

Bangladesh: CSOs in, 179; textile industry in, 227–28; US trade boycott in, 12

Banking crises, 28, 32, 216

Barshefsky, Charlene, 25

Beef industry, 82

Bello, Waldo, 158

Bilateral agreements, 22, 78, 106

Bilateralism, 16

Billionaires, world's, 56

Binding triad, 200

Bio-piracy, 36

Black Wednesday, 30

Blair, Tony, 23, 165

Boli, John, 97

Bonds, 30

Bono, 183

BRAC, 131

Brazil, 11, 27

British Petroleum (BP), 204

Brown, D., 84

Brown, Gordon, 195, 211

Bryant, C., 137

Bryer, David, 102

Burke, Edmund, 220

Bush, George W., 195; anti-Bush sentiments, 15–16; campaign funds for 2000 election, 76; on expanding overseas markets, 23; tariffs on steel imports, 16, 34

Business Partners in Development Program (World Bank), 118

Business partnerships, with NGOs, 117–20

Call centers, 32, 38

Campaign Against the Arms Trade, 152

Campaign for the Non-Proliferation Treaty, 101–2

Campaign for Nuclear Disarmament, 152

"Campaign to Preserve US Global Leadership," 42

Canada: and positive impact of WTO, 12; poverty rates in, 53–54; and WTO, 24

Capital markets, 37–38, 39

Capitalism: anti-global capitalism movement, 5–6; liberal democratic capitalism, 6

CARE, 110, 131, 132, 133–34

Caribbean Basin Initiative, 228

Catholic church, 110, 112

Caucus of Development NGOs, 176

Center of Concern (US), 22, 42

Center for Responsibility in Business, 118

Centralized organizations, 112

Charities Aid Foundation, 117

Charities, transnational, 131, 132

Child labor, 12

Chile, 11

China: domestic markets in, 213; FDI to, 27; manufactured exports from, 31; poverty reduction in, 208; public sector in, 93; trade in, 63–64; unskilled labor in, 38; wealth of, 56, 57, 58, 60, 61

Chiquita, 230–31

Chirac, Jacques, 30

Christian Aid (UK), 25

Christian Democrat trade unions, 123

Church-based groups, 42

Churchill, Winston, 70

Citizens: citizens' voices and good governance, 84; enhancing citizens' voices, 192; global citizenship compact, 193–94

Citizenship, corporate, 203–5

Civil regulation, 203

Civil society: age of, 13–15; agenda for ethical globalization, 15–17; globalization and, 3–4, 6, 55; three sectors of, 93, 94; watchdog role of, 82–83

Author's Biography

John Clark has worked with development NGOs, the World Bank, universities, and as an advisor to governments on development and civil society issues. His career has focused on poverty reduction and bridging the gap between grassroots organizations and official agencies. He is currently visiting fellow at the Centre for Civil Society, London School of Economics, and has served on a task force advising UK Prime Minister Tony Blair on Africa. From 1992 to 2000 he worked for the World Bank as manager of the NGO and Civil Society Unit and then as lead social development specialist for East Asia. Before that he worked in NGOs for eighteen years, mostly with Oxfam UK, where he led campaigns operations and managed Oxfam's advocacy with official agencies and Northern governments on aid, debt, and trade issues. He is the author of three other books, including *Democratizing Development: The Role of Voluntary Agencies* (Earthscan and Kumarian Press, 1991).

Also from Kumarian Press...

Global Issues

Confronting Globalization
Economic Integration and Popular Resistance in Mexico
Edited by Timothy A. Wise, Hilda Salazar and Laura Carlsen

Going Global: Transforming Relief and Development NGOs
Marc Lindenberg and Coralie Bryant

Inequity in the Global Village: Recycled Rhetoric and Disposable People
Jan Knippers Black

Running Out of Control: Dilemmas of Globalization
R. Alan Hedley

Sustainable Livelihoods: Building on the Wealth of the Poor
Kristin Helmore and Naresh Singh

Trapped: Modern-Day Slavery in the Brazilian Amazon
Binka Le Breton

Where Corruption Lives
Edited by Gerald E. Caiden, O.P. Dwivedi and Joseph Jabbra

Conflict Resolution, Environment, Gender Studies, Globalization, International Development, Microfinance, Political Economy

Advocacy for Social Justice: A Global Action and Reflection Guide
David Cohen, Rosa de la Vega, Gabrielle Watson for Oxfam America and the Advocacy Institute

Better Governance and Public Policy
Capacity Building and Democratic Renewal in Africa
Edited by Dele Olowu and Soumana Sako

The Humanitarian Enterprise: Dilemmas and Discoveries
Larry Minear

Pathways Out of Poverty: Innovations in Microfinance for the Poorest Families
Edited by Sam Daley-Harris

Protecting the Future: HIV Prevention, Care and Support Among Displaced and War-Affected Populations
Wendy Holmes for The International Rescue Committee

War and Intervention: Issues for Contemporary Peace Operations
Michael V. Bhatia

Visit Kumarian Press at **www.kpbooks.com** or
call **toll-free 800.289.2664** for a complete catalog.

Kumarian Press, located in Bloomfield, Connecticut, is a forward-looking, scholarly press that promotes active international engagement and an awareness of global connectedness.